On Interpretation

Revised Edition

D0886328

On Interpretation

Sociology for Interpreters of Natural and Cultural History

Revised Edition

Photo: Paul Hosefros, NYT Pictures

Edited by
Gary E. Machlis & Donald R. Field

Oregon State University Press
Corvallis, Oregon

(∞)

The paper in this book meets the guidelines for permanence and durability of the Committee on Production Guidelines for Book Longevity of the Council on Library Resources and the minimum requirements of the American National Standard for Permanence of Paper for Printed Library Materials Z39.48-1984.

Library of Congress Cataloging-in-Publication Data

On interpretation : sociology for interpreters of natural and cultural history / edited by Gary E. Machlis, Donald R. Field. -- Rev. ed.
     p. cm.
    Includes bibliographical references and index.
    ISBN 0-87071-366-3 (cloth), -365-5 (paper) (alk. paper)
    1. Tour guides (Persons) 2. Recreation areas--Interpretive programs. 3. Recreation--Social aspects. I. Machlis, Gary E. II. Field, Donald R.
G154.7.05 1992
306.4'8--dc20   92-3386
                                      CIP

To Grant Sharpe

Colleague, friend, and teacher;

a pioneer in interpretation

who led the way

to a new appreciation

and understanding

of our natural and cultural heritage

Acknowledgments

Visitor Groups and Interpretation in Parks and Other Outdoor Leisure Settings. Adapted with permission from "People and Interpretation," by Donald R. Field and Alan Wagar. *Journal of Environmental Education* 5:1 (1973): 12-17.

Alternative Strategies for Studying Recreationists. Adapted with permission from River Recreation Proceedings, U.S. Forest Service General Technical Report NC-28. St. Paul: North Central Forest Experiment Station, 1977. The advice of Dr. Thomas Heberlein, University of Wisconsin, during the preparation of an earlier draft of this article is gratefully acknowledged.

Ethnography as a Research Tool in Understanding Park Visitors. Reprinted from *Proceedings of a Workshop on Unobtrusive Techniques to Study Social Behavior in Parks.* 1984. Edited by John D. Peine. U.S. Department of the Interior, National Park Service, Atlanta, Georgia.

Solving Park Problems: Developing a Social Science Research Plan. Reprinted from *Trends,* Vol. 20, No. 3. 1983. U.S. Department of the Interior, National Park Service and National Recreation and Park Association.

Getting Connected: An Approach to Children's Interpretation. Adapted with permission from "Getting Connected: An Approach to Children's Interpretation," by Gary E. Machlis and Donald R. Field. *Trends* 7(1974):19-25.

The Social Organization of Family Camping: Implications for Interpretation. Adapted from "Families in the Parks: An Analysis of Family Organization in a Leisure Setting," by Gary E. Machlis. (unpub. Masters thesis, University of Washington, 1975).

Interpretation for the Elderly. Adapted with permission from "Interpretation for the Elderly: A Study of the Interpretive Interests of Retired National Parkgoers," by Gordon Bultena, Donald R. Field, and Renee Renninger. *Journal of Interpretation* 3:2(1978): 29-32.

A Sociological Look at the Japanese Tourist. Adapted from "Foreign Visitors and Interpretation: A Sociological Look at the Japanese Tourist," by Gary E. Machlis, Donald R. Field, and Mark E. Van Every. (Paper presented at the Northwest Association of Interpretive Naturalists, Seattle, Washington, October 14-16, 1981.)

Cruise Ship Travelers to Alaska. Adapted with permission from "Cruise Ship Travelers to Alaska: Implications for Onboard Interpretation," by Barbara A. Koth, Donald R. Field, and Roger N. Clark. *The Interpreter* 13:1 (Winter 1981): 39-46.

Little Darwins: A Profile of Visitors to the Galápagos Islands. This paper was presented at the International Conference on Science and the Management of Protected Areas at Acadia University, Wolfville, Nova Scotia, Canada, May 14-19, 1991 and at the Travel and Tourism Research Conference, Long Beach, California, June 10, 1991.

Red, White, and Black in the National Parks. Reprinted with permission from *The North American Review,* ©1973 by the University of Northern Iowa.

Some Radical Comments on Interpretation: A Little Heresy Is Good for the Soul. Adapted from "Some Radical Comments on Interpretation," by Kenneth L. Nyberg. (Paper presented at the Annual Workshop of the Association of Interpretive Naturalists, College Station, Texas, April 7, 1977).

Interpretation in an Urban Society. Adapted from "Interpretation in an Urban Society," by Gary E. Machlis. (Paper presented at the Pacific Northwest Association of Interpretive Naturalists, Seattle, Washington. October 14-16, 1981).

Thoughts on a New Interpretation. Reprinted from *The Interpreter,* the Western Interpreters Association Journal for Environmental Communicators, fall 1985, Vol. XVI, No. 4.

Interpreting War and Peace. Reprinted from *Ranger,* the journal of the Association of National Park Rangers, summer 1985, Vol. 1, No. 3.

The Devil's Work in God's Country: Politics and Interpretation in the 1990s. Reprinted from *Journal of Interpretation,* 1989, Vol. 13, No. 5.

Photographs: page i and iii Paul Hosefros, NYT Pictures; pages 1, 75, and 178 Gary Machlis; pages 11, 24, 44, 56, 65, 88, 115, 129, 195, 206, 212, 225, 235, 245, and 275 courtesy of National Park Service, Historic Photographic Collection; photo of foreign correspondents from Southeast Asia at the Grand Canyon courtesy of National Park Service; page 161 courtesy of National Park Service; page 150 Thomas Alva Edison Foundation; page 251 photo by Sam Ham.

Preface to the Revised Edition

When *On Interpretation* was first published in 1984, we noted the relative newness of the application of sociology and studies of human behavior to interpretation. We called for a partnership between social scientists and interpreters, in the belief that the results would have significant public benefits. In the intervening years, this partnership between academic discipline and profession has been strengthened. What has emerged is a better understanding of how and why people use parks, museums, and historic sites.

Yet the task is far from finished. The challenges that face interpreters in the last decade of the twentieth century suggest a critical need to reexamine the usefulness of the sociological perspective to interpretation. Several changes are fundamental.

First, communication technologies are revolutionizing the ways people interact: we are developing an electronic tradition that competes with the oral and the written. This communication revolution fuels a second fundamental change: the juxtaposition of cultures that identifies the "postmodern" world. All aspects of culture—art, food, music, politics—are increasingly a mixture of tastes, genres, styles, and meanings. The result is a bewildering and liberating cultural diversity, and a challenge to the status quo.

A third and significant change is the emergence of a global perspective to environmental issues. Scientific data are accumulating, and public awareness is growing, that the ecological health of the planet is the result of interdependent acts taken by nations, communities, and individuals. "Think globally, act locally" is slowly becoming a mainstream strategy for environmental action.

These trends challenge the way interpretation is practiced, and increase its importance and relevance to modern society. Clearly, interpreters need to better understand their clientele. Yet a "sociology of interpretation," which we argued for in the first edition, has not fully matured as a field of inquiry. The number of studies remains low relative to the diversity of settings in which interpretation takes place. Advances in theory—critical in asking the right questions and gaining useful answers—have not occurred.

For these reasons, we have prepared a revised edition of *On Interpretation*. Almost all the original chapters are included, essentially unchanged, so readers can view them in the context that they were written. Sensitivities and styles have changed (perhaps for the better), but rather than update the material to follow current usage we have remained with the original texts. We have added new chapters to reflect the trends described above—especially the cultural pluralism and global perspective that are emerging as key themes of the 1990s.

Within each of the three sections that comprise the book, the material has been reorganized in chronological order. Thus, readers can evaluate for themselves how this partnership between sociology and interpretation has progressed. The conclusion has been extensively revised to reflect an evolution in our thinking as to how a sociology for interpreters of natural and cultural history might develop.

Jo Alexander of Oregon State University Press first encouraged us to consider a second edition of *On Interpretation*; we are grateful for her enthusiastic support and efficient, thoughtful editing. As before, Joan Klingler has provided valuable assistance in preparing the manuscript. Jeannie Harvey skillfully helped in locating references, clarifying facts, and helping to complete the revision.

Gary E. Machlis
Donald R. Field
Twin Peaks Inn
Moscow, Idaho
August 1991

Contents

Section III: Essays

Introduction

At first glance, sociology and interpretation may seem strange bedfellows. Interpreters have long been intimate with the natural sciences—biology, geology, botany, ecology, and so forth. These sciences, especially biology and geology, have provided information for countless interpretive programs, from beach walks illustrating ecological principles to exhibits describing the theory of plate tectonics. Interpreters have also been intimate with the humanities—art, music, literature, philosophy, and history. Both natural science and the humanities provide the facts and, in many cases, the inspiration for interpretation.

What about the social sciences, of which sociology is only one? Social because they deal with relations between people, and science because they adhere to the scientific method, these disciplines have not often been directly applied to interpretation. Yet they offer a critical third kind of knowledge: insight into the human context of interpretive activities, facts about the interpreter and audience, and inspiration for the process of interpretation.

The Ideology of Interpretation

Interpretation is largely a service for visitors to parks, wildlife refuges, museums, zoos, aquariums and other such leisure places. Its practical objectives are straightforward: to assist the visitor, to accomplish management goals, and to promote public understanding and appreciation (Sharpe 1982). Its techniques reflect the range of communication media, from simple storytelling to complex computerized visual displays.

Interpretation's *essence*, if we may borrow from Freeman Tilden, is much more difficult to describe. What is its role in society? What is its method—how does one *do* interpretation? What is its vocation, its central purpose? To answer these questions, we turn to Tilden as a central figure in interpretation's development.

Freeman Tilden was born in 1884, worked at his father's small-town newspaper, and then served as a reporter on papers in Boston, Charleston, South Carolina, and New York City. He then began a literary career, writing fiction for magazines, theater, and radio. At the age of 59 he again changed careers and began work for the National Park Service. Tilden wrote several books on interpretation, among them *The National Parks, The Fifth Essence,* and *Interpreting Our Heritage,* first published in 1957. He died in 1980. *Interpreting Our Heritage* has remained a classic work widely acclaimed as expressing the "ideology" of interpretation.

Tilden saw interpretation as a new kind of public service, one that had "recently come into our cultural world." Sporadically practiced by great teachers, explorer-naturalists, scientists, and others, interpretation had simply been part of their role as educators. From 1915 to the 1940s, the increasing popularity of interpretive activities among park visitors and its usefulness to management agencies brought it to the foreground. Organizations from the National Park Service to local museums recognized interpretation formally and established interpretive positions, responsibilities, policies, training programs, and so forth. In sociological terms, interpretation had been institutionalized. Tilden considered this a novel development.

> We are clearly engaged in a new kind of group education based upon a systematic kind of preservation and use of national cultural resources. The scope of this activity has no counterpart in older nations or other times (1977:9).

The institutionalization of interpretation required that some agreement be reached as to its *method.* As sociologists use the term, method differs from technique; it refers to underlying principles rather than devices, skills, or practices. To Tilden, the method of interpretation was to reveal "a larger truth that lies behind any statement of fact." An interpreter could not simply recite the facts; the facts had to reveal a larger concept. Tilden elaborated in *Interpreting Our Heritage,* suggesting principles that still claim a consensus among interpreters.

If "the work of revealing" was interpretation's method, its *vocation* revealed a higher purpose. Tilden was neither ambiguous nor objective; there is a moral quality to his admonition that interpretation is for the enrichment of the human mind and spirit.

> The appeal for a renaissance of the appreciation of Beauty—in the abstract and in its particular aspects—must not be allowed to falter. It is vital to our moral growth. It is a program of education. Perhaps

it is truer to say that it is a program of re-education, for we have always known, in our innermost recesses, our dependence upon Beauty for the courage to face the problems of life. We have let ourselves forget. *It is the duty of the interpreter to jog our memories* (emphasis added; 1977:115).

The audience is critical to interpretation, and Tilden saw that appealing to the public's interest was a necessary part of the interpreter's craft. He also knew that understanding visitors and their backgrounds was essential to the interpretive method.

The visitor is unlikely to respond unless what you have to tell, or to show, touches his [sic] personal experience, thoughts, hopes, way of life, social position, or whatever else. If you cannot connect his ego (I use that word in an inoffensive sense) with the chain of revelation, he may not quit you physically, but you have lost his interest (1977:13).

Tilden realized that social conditions influenced interpretation's effectiveness, arguing that tourists are limited by time, "absorptive capacity," and money. Yet he shied away from any kind of analytical or systematic approach to understanding visitors. Uncharacteristically, he did not call for a foundation of empirical facts or for research on visitors.

A roster of the reasons why people visit parks, museums, historic houses and similar preserves, though a fascinating excursion into human psychology, need not detain us here . . . I go upon the assumption therefore that whatever their reasons for coming, the visitors are there (1977:11).

In part, Tilden's stance may have been due to the lack of factual information about park visitors. *Interpreting Our Heritage* was written a year before a federal commission was appointed by President Eisenhower to gather such data for the first time. Little was known about the public to be served, other than the personal experience gained by each interpreter.

Now, twenty-five years later, an immense amount of information is available to the interpreter. Studies that deal with visitors to parks, environmental education, interpretation, and leisure number in the hundreds. There is on the one hand a valuable information base, and on the other an increasing "need to know." How can sociology help?

What is Sociology?

The social sciences include a range of disciplines, from anthropology to psychology. Among them, sociology focuses on the interactions among members of society. The sociologist asks: How do we behave with and toward one another? How do we organize ourselves? What meanings do we attach to the things we do?

Perhaps one of the most cogent and careful descriptions of sociology comes from the work of Max Weber (1864-1920). Weber's ideas have remained central to sociological theory and practice, and he has been called the "as yet unsurpassed master of the science of social analysis." To Weber, the fundamental value or essence of sociology is its reliance on the scientific method. The sociologist should examine how people behave in the real world and not be detoured by personal biases. Facts are to be used in testing clearly stated hypotheses. Sociology deals with what *is* rather than what *ought to be* or *might be*. Such a task demands that the sociologist distance himself or herself from the subject of interest, to be a "disenchanted observer."

Yet at the same time, studying human behavior requires the sociologist to develop special skills in analyzing what is observed. Peter Berger has written:

> While Weber was undoubtedly committed to the scientific rationality of the modern West, he had a distinctive understanding of what this meant for the study of human affairs: human phenomena don't speak for themselves; they must be interpreted (1981:10).

This idea, that social action must be interpreted, is at the core of a Weberian approach to sociology. Weber notes:

> The term "sociology" is open to many different interpretations. In the context used here it shall mean that science which aims at the interpretive understanding of social behavior in order to gain an explanation of its causes, its courses and its effects (quoted in Freund 1968:93)

Hence, the sociologist is faced with not only predicting how we behave, but providing a deeper understanding as to why we behave as we do. This is partly because the importance of social behavior lies in its "meaningfulness to others." Let us take hiking for example.

Two hikers may accidentally collide on a narrow trail; it is only when they ignore each other, apologize, or argue that social behavior begins. To Weber, the meaning of such social acts may vary; the collision may not be accidental, but an act of anger, or flirtation. The sociologist must go beyond simply reporting an event and probe its meaning.

To sociologically understand our hikers' collision, we must first gather a variety of empirical facts: Who was involved? What were their backgrounds? What occurred prior to and after the incident? At the same time, the sociologist must objectively begin to probe for meanings. We might learn about other hiking encounters, looking for a pattern of behavior leading up to each collision. We might ask why the hikers did not avoid each other, or whether it is customary to collide in such situations.

By continually using empirical facts to generate understanding and then testing such understanding against more facts, the sociologist moves toward a scientific knowledge of human behavior. That is, simply, the vocation of sociology.

If the vocation of sociology is to interpret social interaction scientifically, its application has been equally broad and far-reaching. Sociologists have studied complex organizations—corporations, bureaucracies, churches, armies, factories, hospitals, and so forth. They have studied special events—pilgrimages, wars, holidays, riots—and details of everyday behavior in public parks, at school, at home, and on the job. Sociologists have examined the behavior of small groups, families, communities, nations, social classes, and civilizations. Sociology has been applied to understanding the problems of inequality, public health, racism, sexism, poverty, environmental pollution, delinquency; the list could easily go on. The intent of this book is to illustrate still another application—sociology's usefulness to interpretation.

Sociology and Interpretation

So we return to our original question concerning interpretation as it is practiced in parks, preserves, museums, and similar settings: how can sociology help? Sociology can aid interpreters' understanding of their clientele. Imagine a newly developed nature center or museum located near a major metropolitan area. Who is likely to use this new facility? What occupational, educational, ethnic, and religious backgrounds might the visitors have? Will they be rich or poor, young or old?

Sociological surveys, census reports, and community studies can provide this kind of information and help construct a descriptive profile of the local population. They might reveal a large Hispanic population (should bilingual programs be considered?) or a nearby neighborhood of elderly Polish-Americans (would a special exhibit or an ethnic food festival be attractive?). Beyond this statistical profile of the entire community, the interpretive staff may need to understand the behavior of those who attend their new programs. Why are some audiences responsive and others unruly? Would evening programs be well attended? Does the seating arrangement matter? These are uniquely sociological questions, and their answers are needed to truly meet Tilden's expectation that interpreters "connect" with visitors.

Second, sociology can help us understand the process of interpretation. The interpreters at our new nature center will soon question (or have questioned for them) the meaningfulness of their work. What role does interpretation play in a citizen's visit to the site? Can interpretive programs increase visitors' knowledge, alter their behavior, or affect their attitudes and values? Or less abstractly, can the staff's interpretive programs attract an audience, increase visitors' enjoyment, and protect cherished resources? Again, these are sociological questions, and their answers are crucial to an objective appraisal of interpretation's importance.

Sociology can also help us understand interpretation as an institution and a profession by commenting on interpretation's role in wider society, describing changes in the work force, and examining interpretation's relationship to other elements of natural and cultural resource management. The better our nature center's interpretive staff understand their organization, the better they will be able to work within it. Sociological studies that deal with management, training, evaluation, and supervision will prove useful to them.

Lastly, sociology can offer the interpreter an attractive "way of seeing," for the sociological perspective is compatible with the interpreter's craft. Both interpretation and sociology require curiosity about the world and society. Both are based on empirical facts, and both respect the scientific method. Both Freeman Tilden the interpreter and Max Weber the sociologist saw their professions as requiring something more—a willingness to interpret what was observable.

About This Book

The articles collected in this book reflect a narrow kind of sociological perspective. Our approach is Weberian; it is interpretive sociology as discussed above. While sociology can deal with individuals, small groups, formal organizations, and social institutions, we have focused on social groups—such as an organized tour for foreign visitors, or a family at a campfire program. Our rationale is provided in the first article, "Visitor Groups and Interpretation in Parks and Other Outdoor Leisure Settings."

In addition, almost all the articles reflect "applied" sociology, research conducted for a client and for a purpose in addition to the growth of scientific knowledge. The purpose may be to solve a management problem through interpretation, to provide interpretive planners with background information, or to help train interpreters in working with new kinds of visitors. Hence, the studies include a good deal of practical information and, in some cases, specific suggestions for improved interpretive programs.

The book is divided into three sections. Section I, "Toward Theory and Technique," introduces the interpreter to sociological concepts and methods applied to interpretation. Section II, "Case Studies," includes a set of studies conducted at a variety of sites where interpretation takes place. In addition to demonstrating empirically the diversity of visitors, these case studies illustrate the potential contribution sociology can make to interpretation. Section III is called "Essays." The chapters deal with a range of contemporary issues important to interpretation and will, we hope, provoke the reader to apply the sociological perspective in the future.

Section I
Toward Theory and Technique

Theories have several functions in science: they explain things that are already known, predict what is unknown, and suggest lines of further inquiry. A sociological theory may attempt to explain why a certain pattern of social structure and behavior occurred or predict under which conditions similar events might take place in the future. For sociologists, theory guides their research efforts and places them within a body of previous studies. For interpreters, knowing the most useful questions to ask about their audiences may be a critical job skill. In short, theory helps organize our curiosity.

By labeling this section "Toward Theory and Technique," we mean to suggest that sociological research dealing with interpretation has yet to arrive at a unified set of important questions and is only now developing a wide range of understood and practiced research techniques. Theories about behavior in public places and social group processes have importance for interpretation. Clearly, interpreters can benefit from learning about people, human behavior, and the environment. The behavior of visitors at interpretive centers, for example, does not arise in isolation but is guided by the culture, community, and group of which each individual is a member. A 15-year-old male may behave differently at a local historic site depending on whether he arrives with parents, church group, street gang, or girl friend.

The first article in this section, "Visitor Groups and Interpretation in Parks and Other Outdoor Leisure Settings," takes this perspective. Its argument is the organizing principle for this book: effective interpretation requires a working knowledge of clientele groups. By stressing the importance of social groups, the article points the way toward applying sociological theory to interpretation. The direction, we hope, is toward a consideration of what classic sociological theory can offer. Simmel's work on small groups and Goffman's ideas about public behavior are examples.

As theory guides the questions asked, technique guides the way questions are phrased and shapes possible answers. We do not propose new strategies for interpretive research, for there are many available and underutilized research techniques. We do suggest that interpreters can benefit from a working knowledge of research methods. The interpreter so equipped can discuss with the sociologist the objectives of a research project, the kinds of data that can be generated, the reliability of the data, and the limitations inherent in any study. The interpreter can independently critique the usefulness of research reports, journal articles, and statistical summaries. And in many cases, interpreters with a basic understanding of research techniques can collect valuable sociological data themselves.

The second article, "Alternative Strategies for Studying Recreationists," provides an overview of social science techniques, from observation to surveys to experiments. As the author points out, the choice of research techniques must reflect the purposes for which the information is collected. Interpreters who often plan, supervise, or conduct such studies should find the article a helpful guide. The third article, "Ethnography as a Research Tool in Understanding Park Visitors," is a description of how interpreters can learn about their clients, using a technique adapted from cultural anthropology. We have chosen to include a description of the ethnographic method because its underlying premise (the researcher must learn *from* rather than *about* the subject) is an essential element of the natural history approach. Many of the case studies in Section II rely on this strategy for gathering and interpreting visitor data.

The last article in this section, "Solving Park Problems: Developing a Social Science Research Plan," discusses the preparation of an organized approach to social science research. Most parks, recreation areas, and historic sites, and particularly their interpretive services programs, have a wide range of visitor information needs. What kinds of information are required? How should it be acquired? How should such activity be organized? As the authors note, a social science research plan can help the interpreter establish priorities for conducting research, develop a coherent base of visitor information, and evaluate the social science enterprise.

Visitor Groups and Interpretation in Parks and Other Outdoor Leisure Settings
(1973)

Donald R. Field

J. Alan Wagar

From the viewpoint of society, the objective of all resource management is to create and maintain a flow of benefits for people. Clearly, resources must be protected if they are to provide a continuing stream of benefits, but we must not lose sight of the fact that the management and stewardship of resources are for human benefit. Resource managers, however, have too seldom concerned themselves with people. Instead, they have concentrated their attention on the dynamics of the physical resources under their jurisdiction.

The limited view of resource management has worked fairly well for managers concerned primarily with material products such as wood and beef, which can be removed from their place of production and consumed elsewhere. Managers of such products seldom meet the consuming client groups. However, for parks and other recreational and esthetic resources, the final products are human experiences that are produced and enjoyed at the same location.

By adopting what we consider a mistaken view of their responsibilities, resource managers have neglected human response to resources. The physical environment is only one element affecting the quality of these experiences. Of equal and sometimes overriding importance are the visitors' values, preferences, attitudes, perceptions, and social group. These in turn depend greatly upon past associations and experiences with natural areas.

A Basis for Interpretation

An understanding of individual behavior and group influences on behavior is especially important for personnel responsible for interpretation. Interpretation includes naturalist talks, exhibits, audiovisual programs, labeled nature trails, brochures, publications, and other facilities and services which are provided to help people enjoy and understand the natural and cultural resources of the areas they visit. Effective interpretation requires a working knowledge of clientele groups for whom the messages are directed so that appropriate means can be used to arouse interest and effectively transmit information.

Interpretation can raise the quality of visitor experiences, and it is one way land management agencies can increase the flow of benefits they provide to the public. Interpretation can also increase benefits indirectly by providing an understanding of resources, perhaps leading people to support the management and more prudent use of resources.

We view interpretation primarily as the successful transmission of information to clientele groups. Facilities and methods are simply means to accomplish this end. Consequently, instead of beginning with a technique—like a visitor center, amphitheater, or other familiar interpretive format—we need first to define our objectives. Second, we must evaluate alternative procedures for reaching those objectives. Only then are we in a position to select the procedures for interpreting specific attractions or ideas for specific kinds of visitors or visitor groups. We must not simply rely on a limited set of time-honored techniques without examining their current relevance to diverse visitor publics.

Therefore, in this article we will focus on two components of interpretation: the client, and procedures for transmitting information. We will draw on current knowledge about human behavior in leisure settings to suggest alternative interpretive strategies.

Unfortunately, interpretation often falls far short of its potential for enhancing visitor experiences. Major problems diminishing its effectiveness include:

Inadequate emphasis on interpretation in resource management agencies. Do resource managers overlook the benefits of interpretation and thus allocate insufficient human and physical resources to interpretive programs? Do we recruit, train, and encourage top-flight personnel for interpretive positions?

Misallocation of effort. Do we interpret at times and places suited to our visitors? Do we present the same information repeatedly to the large percentage of repeat visitors?

Working against usual behavioral patterns. Do we utilize intragroup communication or work against it?

Inadequate attention to visitor motivation. Do we consider how interpretation will reward our visitors or only what we think should be communicated and how it should be communicated?

Mismatching of messages to visitors. Do we recognize the diverse ages, backgrounds, and interests among our visitors or do we aim at a "standardized" visitor?

Not monitoring the effectiveness of our efforts. Do we clearly state what we hope to accomplish with interpretation? If objectives are clear, what feedback mechanisms do we use to diagnose how well our interpretive efforts are accomplishing these objectives?

Although research on visitor groups and interpretation is relatively new, results already suggest alternative strategies to current management practices. It is convenient to organize the search for viable alternatives around five principles.

1. Visitors and leisure settings are diverse, and a variety of approaches will be required.

2. Visitors anticipate a relaxed and enjoyable atmosphere.

3. Interpretive information must be rewarding to visitors.

4. Interpretive information must be readily understood.

5. Feedback (i.e., communication from visitors to the interpreter) is essential.

What follows is a discussion of interpretive options. Some are new; others are being employed successfully in a variety of places. Each is related to one of these principles of interpretation.

Although it would greatly simplify interpretive planning if all information could be directed in a standardized format to the "average" visitor (a mythical character who does not exist), visitors differ widely in age, educational attainment, interests, and goals to be achieved within a natural leisure setting. Many come only to enjoy a social outing, but nearly all visitors' experiences are influenced to some degree by sociability. The goals and objectives of recreationists are partially shaped by the frequency with which they visit a recreation site. Many of those who are familiar with a specific park seek experiences that build upon knowledge from previous visits.

While outdoor recreation areas do attract new visitors each year, a majority of the visitation which occurs consists of repeat visits by groups who attend regularly (Field 1972). Therefore, a re-examination of interpretive strategies is suggested. A seasonal as well as within-season rotation schedule might provide repeat visitors an opportunity to enjoy a greater variety of interpretive experiences. One reason for the disproportionate number of newcomers found in visitor centers might be that repeat visitors have previously viewed the displays and thus spend little additional time there. Many repeat visits are by residents of the immediate vicinity. Therefore, interpreters might consider having local residents plan and maintain one exhibit which is changed periodically. A theme might be park and community history, or park-community cultural and natural events.

If exhibits and displays were self-contained and movable they could be modified with ease. Following a modular unit idea, a visitor center could be changed periodically to update the content, adjust it for the time of year, or provide variety for repeat visitors. Modular units would likewise offer staff members an opportunity to test, evaluate, and modify a proposed design prior to embracing it as a permanent part of their interpretation. In addition, modular units could be rearranged to accommodate different traffic flow patterns as visitor numbers change during different parts of the season. Exhibits might also be made modular in a slightly different sense. Equipment for presenting slides synchronized with sound is now available in a variety of forms. This allows quick substitution of one program for another, permitting presentations to be tailored to the needs of the moment. An interpretive staff could use flexibility of exhibit content, design, and spatial arrangement as additional means for enhancing message reception.

Too often we find interpreters assigned to visitor contact areas where only a small proportion of the total visitors can be found. Rotating staff assignments to areas of visitor concentration might be required. An examination of interpretive emphasis (where and to whom and at what time) is needed. One might develop a balance sheet to assess where the visitors are and where interpreters are assigned. Sightseeing by vehicle, for example, is one of the most popular activities in parks. Interpreters who are available along major road systems have a greater contact opportunity. Interpreters on public conveyances such as buses likewise contact more visitors, Camping is a popular activity, and campgrounds are a traditional interpretive site. Yet very seldom do we find interpreters in campgrounds in the morning, midday, or afternoon. Because picnicking is the third most popular activity in parks, picnicking areas could be used much more widely for interpreting natural and cultural features.

People usually visit recreational areas as members of social groups. Patterns include family groups, friendship groups of the same age, and groups of different ages. Although most resource managers recognize that people come to parks with others, such managers often do not understand the social group's influence on the perceptions, attitudes, and behavior of individual members (Field 1971). Because so many of the visitors reached by interpretive programs arrive in social groups rather than as individuals, the social group is an important vehicle for the transmission of interpretive messages. One important aspect of group behavior is its role in shaping information for children of different ages. At the same time, group members who assume leadership roles as teachers or interpreters, rather than passive listeners, tend to gain improved understanding of the information they present.

We must also provide opportunities for the group to gather together to share information being received. For example, relief models that show the topography of an area are among the most popular exhibits in visitor centers (Washburne 1971). One reason for this popularity is that they readily accommodate groups. When gathered at a relief model, members of a family or other group can discuss information of interest among themselves and can set their own pace.

Visitors consider parks and other outdoor leisure settings to be places where informality prevails and group members are free to interact. Unfortunately, a great number of interpretive facilities are now designed to deal impersonally with individuals as individuals, without allowing any opportunity for group interaction. Thus in the press of serving increasing numbers of people, informal campfire programs have become formal lectures to large audiences seated in neat rows. Instead of a real live naturalist, many visitors meet only audiovisual programs and message repeaters.

We recognize that budgets for interpretation severely constrain the amount of face-to-face interpretation that can be offered. However, informal contacts with interpreters are in many cases the most rewarding for the visitor and should be encouraged to the greatest extent possible. In amphitheaters, for example, fixed benches might be replaced with less formal seating patterns, and the interpreter might move among the visitors while presenting his topic. By avoiding a stage as much as possible and allowing for periodic interruption and questions from visitors, he might create an atmosphere which encourages informality and participation.

As part of their informality, parks and other outdoor leisure settings are places where it is considered appropriate behavior for strangers to interact. This may be unique to leisure settings and should be encouraged (Cheek 1971a, 1972). Interpretive planners might capitalize on both this informality and the diversity among visitors by hiring interpreters of various age groups who could initiate informal interpretive happenings. For example, in the Southwest where many retirees visit parks, a few should be hired to specialize in informal interpretive contacts with others of the same age. Their discussions of opportunities for retired visitors could focus not only on park attractions but on the recreational and social opportunities available for older citizens in nearby communities. In other settings where teenagers are predominant visitors, selected teenagers might be employed to present interpretive information to their own age group. The familiarity of retired and teenage interpreters with the life style of their peers might make them especially effective at involving segments of our society often neglected in specialized presentations. In both cases, qualified people might well be available on a volunteer basis.

People tend to persist in doing the things they find enjoyable and rewarding. Yet this has often been overlooked in interpretation, especially among interpreters who have strong preconceptions about what people ought to know or ought to find enjoyable. For example, Graves (1972) protested the use of tape players, movies, and exhibit systems designed for participation. If, however, we want to enhance the quality of people's experiences and want to help them understand the attractions they visit, we had better reject notions that the only worthwhile visitors are those whose values duplicate those of the professional resource manager.

Our research has demonstrated a number of factors that contribute to visitor interest in interpretation. One of the most important is to provide for visitor participation and involvement. For example, at the Ohanepecosh Visitor Center in Mt. Rainier National Park, we installed a recording quizboard that simply presented four written multiple-choice questions and permitted each to be answered by pushing electric buttons opposite the answers selected (Wagar 1972b). When a correct answer button was pushed, a green panel reading "right answer" lighted up, the question panel just answered darkened, and another question panel lighted up. In addition, the quizboard made a rather satisfying clicking sound as relays snapped and as hidden counters registered people's answers. Although the other exhibits in the visitor center were extremely well done, the quizboard was the only exhibit that permitted participation and manipulation. Within seconds after it was installed, it became, for children, the most popular exhibit in the center.

We might further harness the "kid power" of participation which also increases the retention of information received. Ecological float trips, for example, have been initiated at Yosemite National Park. Other possibilities might include organized bike trips to interpret a particular topic. An organized game of litter removal can be more than a cheap way to clean up areas; it can be an interpretive device to instill a philosophy for "keeping America clean" (Clark et al. 1972a). Interpretive programs for children only, combined with an activity like roasting marshmallows (again employed at Yosemite National Park) and puppet shows or reading of stories based on ecological principles, are other examples.

To capitalize on the principle of visitor participation, living demonstrations should be encouraged like those which show eighteenth century life patterns at Colonial Williamsburg. In addition, opportunities for visitor groups to engage in an activity like painting, shooting a musket, or "throwing" a pot might be developed where appropriate to the social, cultural, and natural history of an area. Nothing is more convincing to the novice regarding the skill required to create some object or the significance of a period in history than watching his family or friends recreate the object or event.

A study of exhibits at five different visitor centers showed additional factors that were rewarding to visitors (Washburne 1971). Holistic presentations that included cause-and-effect relationships were found to be more interesting to people than isolated facts. As for subject matter, violence and violent events were of greater interest than all others (which seems to have been well known by writers and entertainers for thousands of years). Fortunately, leisure settings abound in examples of violence that can be interpreted in good taste. For example, life in the ocean is so hazardous that, for most organisms, millions of young must be hatched to insure that a few will survive to maturity.

Interest was far above average for exhibits with such dramatic or animated presentations as movies, changed lighting (to direct the visitors' attention from place to place), and recorded sound. By contrast, interest was below average for such inert presentations as texts and mounted photos. Viewed another way, visitors find the media normally used for entertainment more rewarding than the less dynamic media traditionally used for education (Travers 1967). As media commonly associated with entertainment, television, tape recorders, and radio have all been employed one place or another with varying degrees of success. However, their full potential has not been exploited.

Closed-circuit television offers enormous possibilities, especially now that relatively inexpensive videotape systems are available. For example, one interpreter at a central control unit might interact with visitors at a number of monitors. By talking to visitors at any monitor, he could determine their interests and levels of knowledge, answer their questions, and then show them a videotape while interacting with other visitors on other monitors. Where the construction of a theater in a visitor center would be questionable, television might offer a less costly alternative.

Portable cassette tape players also offer great flexibility. During a recent study visitors were able to choose tapes of different lengths for a nature trail (Wagar 1972a). The choice could have been extended to tapes with different emphases, different levels of difficulty, or even different languages.

Short-range radio transmitters are now being used in parking lots at a number of places to contact visitors through their own car radios. Use of transmitters at intervals along a road has also been considered as a means of presenting a sequence of information to visitors as they drive along. Costs per visitor contact appear to be quite reasonable. At the moment, however, it is not certain that available equipment will provide adequate range from a simple antenna without exceeding the power output permitted for unlicensed transmitters. New limits for power output currently seem to be under consideration by the Federal Communications Commission. At a substantially higher cost, cables can be laid under the roadway to control the transmission zone.

In addition to making interpretation rewarding, interpreters must use language readily understood by the visitor. For ready understanding, the terminology, examples, and analogies used for interpretation must be within the vocabulary and experience of the visitor. Ideally, examples should draw upon situations and experiences well known to the visitor. For example, it would be foolish to compare a smell to the aroma of new-mown hay for visitors whose olfactory environment has included mainly factory smoke.

In addition to easily grasped language and examples, understanding depends on prior knowledge. To understand how DDT can threaten brown pelicans with extinction, one must understand food chains and the mechanisms by which DDT is passed along from species to species in increasing concentrations. To understand a geyser, a person must recognize that the boiling point of water increases with pressure.

Where pamphlets or brochures are needed, as at park entrances or nature trails, they might well be written in several versions. A variety of styles could be employed, oriented to different visitor publics. Different versions or sections might assume different levels of prior knowledge or might be aimed at different age or interest groups. The National Park Service already has some materials for children, describing natural or cultural features in story form and including pictures which can be colored. This provides an excellent way to orient children to natural resources. A question-answer series that encourages parents and children to interact while discussing a park or recreational feature would also reinforce the natural parent-child relationship in family units. If planned to accommodate diverse groups of visitors, pamphlets or other material would better serve new visitors, repeat visitors, youth, retired visitors, or even visitors who do not speak English.

Perhaps no general concept or principle is more important for interpretation than feedback. In general terms, feedback is simply a set of signals indicating the extent to which an operation is going as planned and showing what corrective action would be useful. For interpretation, feedback is a flow of information from the visitors that lets the interpreter know how well he is achieving both his objectives and those of the visitors. Because different visitors will have different objectives, feedback is essential for tailoring presentations to a variety of people.

When an interpreter meets face-to-face with small visitor groups, feedback is readily available. Unless he is totally insensitive, the interpreter can tell from people's expressions, questions, and other behavior if they are interested or disinterested and if they understand his words and examples. Using this continuous flow of feedback, he can continually correct his presentation to increase its effectiveness.

Once the easy and informal exchange of face-to-face interpretation is lost, obtaining feedback becomes more difficult. Instead of direct interaction with a good cross-section of visitors, the interpreter is increasingly exposed to fellow interpreters, to visitors who are especially receptive to interpretive presentations, or to visitors who are too polite to criticize shortcomings. More than one interpreter has had his bad habits perpetuated by insincere compliments.

The use of feedback to evaluate effectiveness must be based on clearly stated objectives. Surprisingly, many interpreters and interpretive planners cannot specify exactly what it is they are trying to do. To be useful, objectives must be taken beyond vague generalities and stated in terms of behaviors the visitor could express as a result of interpretation (Mager 1962). An objective that lends itself to evaluation would be to enable the visitor to describe food chains in general and the particular food chain which permits solar energy to be utilized by the cave cricket.

Once clear objectives are defined, feedback procedures can be devised to monitor the effectiveness with which objectives are being accomplished. These procedures can range from the interpreter's informal collection of impressions during face-to-face contact, to suggestion boxes, to formal studies in which visitors are asked to indicate how enjoyable they found interpretation and are then tested on their understanding of the information presented. Such a test would pass or flunk the interpreter, not the visitor.

To avoid the many problems of attitude measurement, evaluation should be concentrated on objective information (Hendee 1972b). Not only are attitude changes difficult to measure, but attitudes are unlikely to change much due to the short exposure provided by most interpretation. It is far better to measure effectiveness in transmitting basic concepts. If people understand these, their attitudes and behavior are quite likely to shift in appropriate directions.

Ideally, feedback mechanisms should be designed directly into interpretive programming. The recording quizboard mentioned earlier is simply a device to determine how well visitors understand ideas presented to them. It lends itself especially well to determining whether a change in interpretation is increasing or decreasing comprehension by visitors. Currently, there are audiovisual exhibits that intermittently present the visitor with questions and record his answers. This equipment not only shows how well different kinds of visitors are understanding a presentation, it also permits interpretive presentations to be tested in a mock-up stage without great cost. Such testing is a valuable indicator of success or failure. If the interpretation is not understood, the fault usually is with the presentation, not the visitor. An added feature of experimental audiovisual equipment is the fact that it can be programmed so the visitors' responses determine the level at which additional information will be presented, permitting a wide range of visitors to be served by a single system. When integrated into interpretive programming, feedback procedures can permit the diagnosis of effectiveness and can indicate opportunities for improvement.

A central premise of this article is that the objective of all resource management is to create and maintain a flow of benefits for people. Resource managers, however, have often emphasized resource protection or manipulation, without clear recognition that such efforts are a means to an end for parks and similar resource areas where human experiences are emphasized. This view is not only inappropriate but can lead to a misconception of visitor objectives and a narrow view of what is considered appropriate human behavior in leisure settings. Resource managers responsible for interpretation must understand both human behavior and resources sufficiently to inform and enhance experiences for various visitor publics.

Alternative Strategies

for Studying Recreationists
(1977)

Roger N. Clark

Understanding recreational problems and the motives, preferences, values, and behavior patterns of recreationists is an important concern for recreation managers and researchers. Such understanding is essential for identifying the consequences of alternative recreation management strategies.

Because recreation researchers have a variety of social research tools available, care must be taken to ensure that the chosen study procedures are consistent with the subject matter to be studied. Accurate, unbiased information is essential for the development of effective recreation policies and management schemes, and it is the urgent business of recreation planners, managers, and policy makers to be just as concerned as are investigators that the research programs used are appropriate to the study and rigorously applied.

This article describes alternatives to the traditional cross-sectional survey and presents a framework for selecting when a specific data collection strategy may be appropriate or inappropriate. The framework allows the researchers to examine the alternatives in terms of the information they can and cannot provide. Such a framework should also prove useful to planners, managers, interpreters, and policy makers, because it gives a basis for evaluating whether the data developed in a study answer specific questions about recreational phenomena. The aim is to provide a general overview of when and why each approach may be best.

Basic Research Questions about Recreational Behavior

Two fundamental types of questions that researchers and policy makers might ask about recreation behavior are questions requiring description, and questions requiring explanation.

Description

Good description is the key to understanding and is often neglected in social science research. Three basic descriptive questions for which researchers or policy makers might seek information are:

What is happening, when, where, and how much? Answering this question involves a basic description of the event being studied. For example, the researcher may want to know how extensive visitor use is and how it varies from location to location or by time or season.

Who is involved? Describing the social, physical, and psychological characteristics of the persons involved in the event under investigation will answer this question. For example, who visits an interpretive center? The young? The old? The highly educated? Groups or individuals?

What do people prefer? Most people make a variety of choices daily in keeping with their personal values and goals. Describing the various preferences for types of recreation—for example, what visitors consider desirable developments or acceptable management procedures—is central to both understanding and providing for recreation opportunities.

Explanation

After a phenomenon has been adequately described, the next step is to explain why it occurs. Two general questions relating to the explanation of a phenomenon are:

Why is it happening? This involves an explanation of the phenomenon in terms of either participant motivation or various components of the environment. For example, can visits to a specific park be explained by the user's desire to be there or by the fact that few alternatives exist for that kind of experience? Why do people choose one area over another? Why do they violate well-posted rules?

How can behaviors be modified or changed? Answers to this question are often necessary for producing desirable results in recreation areas as well as other places. Changing (or maintaining) a certain behavior is often the desire of the resource manager who may be faced with problems of overuse, litter, vandalism, sanitation, conflicting uses, or intolerable resource damage. Information provided in answer to the earlier questions is often essential in preparing a study to answer this final question. Examples include: How can litter or vandalism be prevented, and what procedures will effectively disperse visitors along popular interpretive trails?

Research Designs and Data Collection Strategies

In preparing a study to answer one or more of the above questions, the researcher must choose from a variety of research designs and measurement strategies. A research design is the basic framework within which data are collected. The researcher must decide whether data about the same population will be collected only once (cross-sectional design) or more than once (longitudinal design). Or does the investigator hope to determine cause-and-effect relationships through some control procedure (experimental design)?

Measurement strategies are the various procedures by which data are collected. Does the researcher look for himself (observation) or are subjects asked to speak for themselves (self reports)? Any study is a combination of a research design and measurement strategy (e.g., a cross-sectional survey or a longitudinal observation study) or an experimental design using direct observation as a measurement strategy.

Research Designs

Cross-sectional. This design is characterized by one measurement of the phenomenon in question across a segment of the target population. It allows for intersubject comparisons of the characteristics or behaviors measured.

Longitudinal. This design (also known as panel or time-series studies) allows for measurement of attributes or behaviors within a target population two or more times. It allows for intrasubject as well as intersubject comparisons over time.

Experimental. This design is characterized by some sort of manipulation or control procedure by the investigator and an evaluation of its effect on the phenomenon in question. Did the manipulation result in any change in attitudes or behavior?

Measurement Strategies

Observation. Observation refers to systematic techniques for observing, recording, and evaluating behavior. Such observation follows specific procedures and is much more exhaustive and objective than casual observation done in the course of normal events by both managers and participants. There are three methods for observation: direct observation of events as they occur, observation of traces of behavior, and participant observation.

Self reports from subjects. The subjects under study can be asked to report the desired information to the investigator. Essentially, this requires the subjects to "observe" their own characteristics, behavior, or feelings about what they do or events that go on about them. The tools used in this approach are surveys (interviews or questionnaires) and diaries.

Advantages and Disadvantages of Alternative Research Designs and Measurement Strategies

From the researcher's perspective, answers to all five basic research questions are important for an understanding of a particular recreation phenomenon. Practically, however, some questions may be more important than others. Managers, for example, often are concerned with maintaining or modifying certain behaviors. Unfortunately, no single combination of a research design and measurement strategy will provide data to answer these questions. The method of study must be selected with two criteria in mind: Will it provide reliable and valid information to answer the questions directly? Will it provide the information efficiently?

Table 1 summarizes the relationships between the basic questions and alternative research designs and measurement strategies. The basic assumption is that the design and measurement strategy is acceptable only if it can provide valid and reliable data to answer the question directly. Therefore, conjecture and inferences based on data collected to answer other questions may not be appropriate for judging the utility of the method under consideration, particularly if there is a better alternative. Readers should refer to Table 1 during the following discussion about the advantages and disadvantages of alternative research approaches.

Table 1. Relationship of research designs and measurement strategies to basic questions about recreational behavior.

	Basic questions about recreational behavior				
	Description		Explanation		
	Questions (see below)				
Research designs	A	B	C	D	E
Cross-sectional	X	X	X	(X)	
Longitudinal	X	X	X	(X)	
Experimental			X	X	X
Measurement (data collection) strategies					
Observation:					
Direct observation	X	X	(X)	X[1]	X[1]
Trace observation	X	(X)	(X)	X[1]	X[1]
Participant observation	X	X	X	X	X[1]
Self reports					
Behavior recall surveys	(X)		(X)		(X)[1]
Surveys of reported characteristics		X			
Surveys of reported attitudes, beliefs			X	X	
Diary (log)	X	X	(X)	X	(X)[1]

A—What is happening? When? Where? How much?
B—Who is involved?
C—What is preferred?
D—Why is it happening?
E—How can it be maintained or modified?

[1]Appropriate within an experimental design
X=Acceptable alternative—provides data to directly answer the question
(X)=Acceptable under limited conditions

Research Approaches for Questions of Description

The Cross-Sectional Survey

The cross-sectional survey is the standard social science tool used in most recreation research. Indeed, it is the most common method used in all social science research. The pros and cons of using this method are presented first to serve as a baseline for comparing the other methods.

Three kinds of information are typically sought in a survey:

1. Respondents are asked to recall their past behavior or to predict future behavior (e.g., how many trips they've taken to a certain historic site).

2. Respondents are asked to report descriptive characteristics such as income, education, age, sex, place of residence, and similar items.

3. Respondents are asked to report individual psychological states, attitudes, preferences, and beliefs about such things as wilderness, rivers, recreation, and society. Examples would be survey items like "I believe there is a crowding problem at this park," or "I prefer solitude at my campsite," or "I think people should pick up the litter of a friend."

Each of these types of information is examined below.

Behavior recall. Behavior recall is often used in surveys to answer the questions, "What is happening?" and "What is preferred?" Because of the serious shortcoming of this approach, behavior recall is a poor substitute for other methods. Behaviors recalled on a questionnaire or interview are likely to be an inaccurate measure of actual behavior. In studies of littering, for example, more than 50 percent of people observed littering said they had not (Heberlein 1971).

Several factors probably account for the discrepancies observed. A common human frailty is our inability to objectively record our own behavior, even under the best conditions (Mead 1964), and particularly the motivations behind our behavior. People may simply not know or may forget what they did or when they did it. They may think events happened more recently than they actually did. Definitional problems also may operate: when asked how many times one has visited rivers in wilderness areas, a person may count trips to areas which really aren't wilderness. And, as in the case of not reporting littering behavior, people are reluctant to admit illegal or inappropriate behavior and therefore may deliberately mislead the investigator.

Reported characteristics. Asking subjects to report various personal or group characteristics is straightforward and is usually a part of most surveys. Requesting this information is usually secondary to asking about their behavior or attitudes. Many personal characteristics, although not reported without error, are sufficiently accurate for most purposes, especially when the high cost of determining such information by other means is considered.

Reported characteristics gathered through a questionnaire or interview describe many unobservable as well as observable variables related to individuals and groups ("Who is involved?"). Whether or not this measure of "who" is appropriate depends on how involvement in the event under study was determined. If involvement is based on self-reported behavior recall data, then relations between "who" and ""what" may be questionable. If, however, the investigator has some prior knowledge about actual involvement in an activity (direct observation, use registers, licenses, etc.), the sample can be restricted to those known to be involved in the event of interest. Such a description of "who is involved" is more likely to be accurate than one based purely on self-reported recall data. Generally, the results of broad surveys directed at an unidentified population must be viewed with caution.

Reported attitudes, preferences, and beliefs. Most surveys focus on respondents' attitudes, preferences, and beliefs. This approach is not without serious problems, as has been well documented in the social science literature (Heberlein 1973). Attitudes are conceptually complex and difficult to measure. An attitude survey often appears easy to carry out but in fact requires a great deal of skill in conceptualization, measurement, and analysis (Potter et al. 1972).

Further, it sometimes appears that attitude studies are done when people are really interested in behavior, and the implicit assumption has been made that attitudes closely approximate real behavior. But, there is little evidence of a direct effect of attitudes on behavior (Deutscher 1966, Hancock 1973, Heberlein 1973, Wicker 1969). Wicker's study showed that attitudes predicted real behavior only 10 percent of the time.

A basic question for which attitude studies are appropriate is "What do people say they prefer?" From a carefully conducted attitude survey of the appropriate population, a manager may accurately assess what people say they prefer. Stankey (1973) showed how wilderness purists prefer different wilderness management policies than nonpurists do. He argued that such preferences should be taken into account in wilderness management.

Attitude studies allow people to assess and consider hypothetical alternatives which do not exist. However, this hypothetical nature of the alternatives presents its own difficulties. We may be developing and managing recreation areas on the basis of hypothetical answers to attitude questions not representative of the real world.

Alternative Measurement Strategies

Self reports—diaries. This self-report procedure requires that participants record their own behavior, feelings, etc., as close to the time they occur as possible. As the name implies, diaries are kept over an extended time period, such as a float trip down a river. Respondents may be asked to record their motives for doing things as well as what they did. Diaries are particularly useful for gathering information about people while they are traveling to remote locations such as along rivers or when their travel prevents easy observation. The reduced time lag, compared with that of surveys, compensates to some extent for the inaccuracy of behavior recall described earlier.

The diary approach has many of the faults of other self-reporting procedures. For example, only normative behavior is likely to be recorded completely and accurately. Inconvenience also may prompt incomplete entries. Even with its faults, the diary is a procedure that must be considered when information over a period of time is wanted. With proper instructions to the respondent, many of its shortcomings can be reduced.

Diaries can be useful for determining "what is happening." Diaries have been successfully used by state fish and game departments to study fishing and hunting activities and by researchers to study wilderness travel (Lime and Lorence 1974). Diaries should include appropriate instructions on what to record, how to enter information, and when to log the entries. Diaries are best used when the investigator can specify things he wants documented, for example: "When and where did you camp?" "Who were you with?" "What did you do in the evening?" "How many other parties did you encounter?" Requesting that "everything you do" be recorded, over even a short period of time, is usually unworkable and puts an unnecessary burden on the respondent.

Diaries can yield accurate information about "who is involved" in an event. This information about "who" is similar to that provided on questionnaires and interviews, except that the information is presumably recorded as the events occur rather than recalled later.

Systematic observation of events as they occur. For this form of observation, the specific events or objects under study must be well defined and directly observable. This technique can be used by an observer who tallies specific events or notes certain objects by some prearranged coding schedule. Or it can be done by artificial surveillance such as remote cameras and other automatic recording devices. This approach can be used to study the amount and type of use an interpretive facility, area, or trail receives.

Systematic observation of actual behavior in recreational settings has several problems. First, the measure may be reactive; that is, the presence of an observer may affect the behavior under study. For example, measuring littering behaviour by placing observers along a trail is likely to reduce incidence of the behavior, because people tend to litter more when they are alone (Heberlein 1971). Therefore, even if observations of behavior are reliable, they may be invalid because of the reactive distortion caused by the measurement process itself. A second and more serious problem for the outdoor recreation researcher is that systematic observation of actual behavior may be inefficient and expensive, because some behavior is difficult to observe or seldom occurs. In remote settings it may take many hours to record a few observations because of infrequent and scattered use. A third concern regarding systematic observation is observer reliability (Burch 1974). Without specific training for the observer, pretested recording schedules and instructions, and continual reliability checks, a serious distortion of actual events can result. Indeed, the observer is both the strength and the weakness of this approach (Kerlinger 1973).

When events are well defined and directly observable, systematic observation will produce reliable, valid, and accurate results about "what is happening"—if the problem of reactivity can be overcome. A definite advantage of this procedure is that, with proper sampling, generalizations can be made about specific individual and collective behaviors.

Systematic observation of events can also describe "who was involved." Variables such as the subject's sex, race, age, etc., can easily be recorded at the time the event is observed. The only criterion is that "who" be clearly identifiable.

Systematic observations of events as they occur can sometimes provide data to answer the question, "what do people prefer?" For example, observation focusing on where people choose to camp along a certain river may reveal a preference for locations far from other sites. However, the correlation between the presence of other sites and actual preference may be spurious. Perhaps the locations were selected because of some other quality, such as availability of sunlight or nearness to a good landing. Some other procedure (such as a survey or diary) will be necessary to clearly establish the reason for the choice.

Systematic observation of behavioral traces. Observing the effects of previous behavior may be appropriate in some cases. Observation of traces is one way to reduce costs of direct observation and to obtain nonreactive measures, because the subjects under study need not be present when data are collected. Webb et al. (1966) described a wide array of such unobtrusive measures.

Accretion or buildup of environmental factors caused by human behavior is a good measure of such behavior. For example, how much litter accumulates at historic sites? Although these measures may be unreliable because of weather factors, they are generally useful and relatively inexpensive. Measures of the degradation or erosion of the environment also are useful. The rates at which trails are wearing down or firewood and foliage are disappearing are measures of the amount of use an area receives. A wide array of such traces may be regularly recorded in and around a recreation area by the creative investigator.

An important difference between traces and other measures of behavior is that traces usually indicate aggregate behavior rather than individual behavior. This limits the generalizations that may be made from the resulting data. When individual events need not be or cannot be observed directly to determine "what is happening," measuring their traces may be useful. By systematically observing the accretion or degradation of a variety of factors that occur as a result of recreational behavior, a measure of its impact can be determined. Such aggregate data may be sufficient for planning and policy purposes.

Trace observation can yield information about "who was involved," although validity and reliability must be seriously questioned. The presence of discarded fish bait containers and fishing gear wrappers suggests that fishermen were in the area; the presence of horse droppings or feed hay at campsites suggests that horse users were there. The precision with which such data can be measured, however, may limit its usefulness. And, because traces are a measure of aggregate rather than individual behavior, the investigator cannot determine from the above example if fishermen or horse users were the only people in the area, or if the fishermen came on horseback. Interpreting and generalizing such data are difficult, but for some purposes the knowledge that fishermen or horses were in the area may be enough.

Use of traces to determine "what is preferred" suffers from all the shortcomings of direct observation, plus those inherent in measurements of accretion and degradation as reflectors of previous events. This method should be used only when alternatives have been ruled out.

Participant observation. As Campbell (1970) points out, participant observation is more than a single method of data collection and may include a variety of techniques for gathering quantitative and qualitative data. This method is unobtrusive and relatively inexpensive. Some writers include systematic observation as a participant observer's role (Campbell 1970, Gold 1958). Discussion of this procedure is limited here to roles involving interaction with participants. That is the essence of participant observation, and the thing that distinguishes it from the other forms of observation.

The method is difficult to define simply, but it generally involves the investigator directly taking part in the activity he wishes to study. The observer is able to observe his own reactions to events taking place as well as reactions of others. Through this interaction with participants and continual data processing and evaluation, the investigator can reformulate the problems as the study proceeds and look for new information (Dean et al. 1969).

Major disadvantages of participant observation include the possible lack of objectivity and reliability of the observer, the possibility of becoming overwhelmed with large amounts of information, reactivity if the identity of the observer is known or suspected, and information that may be subjective and incomplete. Systematic theory testing requires more rigid procedures.

Participant observation is often useful as a prelude to surveys or more systematic counting of objects, specific events, or behavioral traces. Operating as both observer and participant, the investigator can gain insights that otherwise might not be apparent. Participant observation is an excellent and efficient tool for defining the dimensions of a program, because it can quickly generate a great deal of diverse information.

In the early stages of a study, participant observation is useful for determining "what is happening" at a broad level—the range of events, types of participants, activities, problems, etc. A major advantage of this method is that the observer is often able to gain access to events because he is involved in them and does not pose a threat to people being observed.

Participant observation gives a clear picture of "who is involved" in events that the observer sees. Finding out who was engaged in events not observed is also possible by talking with others. The participant observer often has access to information about "who is involved," because he is more readily accepted as a member of the group than a formal observer or authority. Thus, data on "who" result from what is seen and what is learned from others.

Participant observation should also be considered an important alternative in the study of "what is preferred," particularly in the early stages of an investigation. The observer learns about preferences by several methods—his own and other people's choices (for example, where to camp within a park) and informal talks with them to determine what they prefer. Initially, participant observation may help determine the range of preferences, but a more systematic process would best detemine their relative importance.

Alternative research designs

Longitudinal design. In addition to the problems with the survey measurement strategy, the cross-sectional design of many studies limits the generalizations that can be made from the data. With events measured only once, intersubject comparisons can be made across the population at that time only. With a longitudinal design (measurements of the same population two or more times), both intersubject and intrasubject comparisons are possible over time, and descriptive questions can be more readily answered. As an alternative to the cross-sectional design, longitudinal design of studies can clearly identify trends over time, if disadvantages of the measurement procedure are considered. Longitudinal designs, however, impose greater burdens on both researcher and subject because data are collected more than once (Crider et al. 1973).

Experimental design. In essence, an experimental analysis is a longitudinal design with some manipulation occurring between measurements. Data are collected by observation or a self-reporting procedure. The element of manipulation and before and after measurements make this process unique. Although few experiments are reported in the literature on recreational behavior, many experiments are actually done but without sufficient documentation to determine effectiveness. In day-to-day decisions, managers and policy makers initiate changes in recreational environments that may have some effect on people. For example, they may provide trash cans along a river, build a new road for boat launching, develop more campsites, add convenience facilities, or restrict access.

The manipulation or change is essentially the guts of an experiment. The impact of the change needs to be evaluated so that the desired results will be attained. More attention should be paid to documenting the cause-effect relationships implicit in most management actions to ensure that undesirable consequences do not occur. For example, as Clark et al. (1971a) illustrate, the process of "creeping campground development" in response to increasing use may have serious effects on the types of users attracted to certain areas.

An experimental design may be useful for providing data on "what is preferred." Direct observation, and to some extent self-reports (even if done within a longitudinal design), will provide partial answers on how people behave or their stated preferences. However, these approaches may have serious flaws. To determine exactly which factors influence choice implies some sort of experimental design. By systematically controlling or manipulating characteristics of campsites, for example, and measuring the effect, researchers and managers could identify important factors related to site preference and use.

Research Approaches for Questions of Explanation

The Cross-Sectional Survey

The cross-sectional survey may be suited to answer the question of "why things are happening," particularly when the answer may require a social-psychological explanation. A carefully conducted survey of attitudes can explain why the phenomenon occurred in terms of the social psychology of the action and the mediating decision process. To do a study of attitudes presumes that one knows a great deal about the process itself, but many attitude studies seeking to learn why something is occurring don't seem to have this understanding. Such studies are marked by a wide variety of unrelated questions, the lack of clear research hypotheses prior to data collection, and the general sterility of results. Further, when trying to explain why a behavior is occurring or how to control it, an attitude study may be inappropriate; situational or environmental factors may be largely responsible, and these are generally ignored in most surveys.

The cross-sectional survey is inappropriate for determining "how a behavior can be modified or maintained." Research on litter control by Keep America Beautiful, Inc. (1968) presents a good example. Respondents to a survey identified two classes of reasons for littering. The first class included individual attributes— laziness, indifference, carelessness, etc. But this description doesn't really tell us why littering occurs, because these data say nothing about the process linking such attitudes to littering behavior. The second class of reasons relates to situational factors—trash facilities, litterbags, etc. The problem here is that littering itself was not under study. Respondents were asked to give reasons why they think littering occurs or how it can be controlled. Whether or not facilities, laws, litterbags, and education had anything to do with the respondents' past, present, or future littering behavior cannot be ascertained from this type of study. Indeed, other research (Clark et al. 1972a, Heberlein 1971) suggests that laws, educational campaigns, and trash facilities have little impact on littering. And all these studies focused directly on the problem—littering and litter.

Alternative measurement strategies

Self report—diaries. Diary studies can provide information on "why a behavior is occurring" if respondents describe why they did what they did. For example, when boaters choose among streams in an area and locate their movement on a map, the investigator may want to know why they made their decisions. Reasons may include "this way was shorter," "too many people the other way," etc. This approach, however, has all the weaknesses described for the use of diaries to answer descriptive questions.

Participant observation. Participant observation can answer the question of "why a behavior occurs"—both from the point of view of the observer, who may engage in the event and record his own reactions to it, and from the perspective of those he observes. The observer interacts with other participants and is often able to learn "why" through conversation. Measurement of "why" with participant observation procedures is most useful in the early stages of a study; it can help the researcher ask the right questions later on. Participant observation is often necessary for a good attitude survey. It should be noted, however, that although participant observation may be necessary for an attitude study, it is not a sufficient replacement for such a study. Participant observation provides hypotheses, but only the carefully conducted attitude study, with its systematic sample and rigorous measurement, provides strong support for hypotheses dealing with social-psychological explanations of "why."

Alternative research designs

Longitudinal design. When the investigator wishes to determine if the reasons "why an event is happening" change over time, then a longitudinal design may be appropriate. This is a particularly useful approach when combined with a survey aimed at determining social-psychological reasons.

Experimental design. If the factors controlling a behavior are situational, experimental analysis can yield data about "why it is happening." For example, use of a visitor center may be related to access, visibility, proximity to other sites, etc. Experiments can isolate the relative impacts of the various factors.

Experimental analysis is the only method that allows the researcher to determine directly how a behavior can be modified or maintained. Although a simple observation of behavior and cognitive explanations of why it occurs may provide insight into possible control procedures, any testing of the effectiveness of controls implies an experiment. Research on litter control in recreation is an example of how experimental analysis can be used to determine effective control procedures (Clark 1976, Clark et al. 1972a, Heberlein 1971). A carefully conducted experiment is the key to determining the effectiveness of management actions, because the relative impacts of each approach can be clearly substantiated.

Related Issues

A variety of research designs and measurement strategies have been presented here within a simple framework for determining which may be appropriate for providing information about several questions concerning recreational behavior. The decisions that must be made about appropriate strategies are more complex than the framework implies. Several important related issues that the investigator should consider in designing a study will now be discussed.

Variety of Procedures

When used alone, none of the strategies described can produce data to answer directly the five basic questions about recreational behavior. Consequently, researchers interested in all of the questions must be able to use a variety of research designs and data collection strategies. Rarely will one of the five questions be studied alone; usually, a study will combine several. This makes it particularly important for the researcher to understand the limitations of the alternative procedures and to select the combination that best satisfies the study objectives.

Appropriate Research Strategy

The appropriate research strategy may depend on what is known about the events of interest to the researcher or manager. Studying a phenomenon about which little is known may require a different approach than if specific variables have been identified. Participant observation is particularly useful in early stages of an investigation and can be used to focus data on four of the five basic questions. More information is required to use the other strategies; systematic observation requires identification and definition of important variables; self reports require the right questions for pertinent responses; and experimental analysis requires identification of target behaviors and possible controls.

An effective overall approach is to focus initial data collection efforts on participant observation to identify variables that can be more accurately measured by systematic procedures. By considering what is known and which of the five basic questions should be studied, the researcher can determine the most appropriate research strategy.

Practical vs. Scientific Importance

An important concern, particularly to data users, is whether the information to be collected will have any practical importance. Consequently, both the researcher and practitioner must understand the implications that the data collection strategy has for potential application. Does the researcher want to study questions of most importance to the manager? If so, the choice of strategies is limited to those best suited to producing valid and reliable data that will directly answer questions of interest.

Conclusion

Attitude studies (primarily cross-sectional surveys), if done carefully, can play an important role in answering major questions about recreation and recreationists. They are particularly useful in explaining why certain events occur. They also give the most systematic information about what people say they prefer (although experiments may give a wider range of choice and tell more about what people actually prefer in certain settings). Attitude studies, however, seem to be done to the exclusion of both observational studies and experiments. Such a strong reliance on this technique limits the ability to increase our knowledge about a variety of recreational phenomena.

There are several possible explanations for the strong reliance on cross-sectional surveys. First, many investigators incorrectly feel that they have a good idea about what is actually happening when beginning a study. Hence, there is a tendency to neglect the basic descriptive questions and move directly to research that will explain the phenomena. Or investigators may think, inappropriately, that behavior-recall data from surveys will describe adequately what is happening and who is involved.

Another reason many investigators focus on attitude surveys is that they believe attitude studies really tell how behavior can be changed. There are strong reasons for disagreement with this point of view. It is experimental analysis focusing directly on behavior (or attitudes, if that is what one wants to change) that can do this. This problem, coupled with the poor relationship between attitudes and specific behavior, indicates that more time should be spent in direct observation or experimentation with the behaviors in question.

Finally, most social scientists conducting research on recreation are trained in survey methodology and often are not familiar with other alternatives. Consequently, this strategy is often used when other procedures would be more appropriate. All recreation researchers, regardless of academic background, need a thorough understanding of the alternative procedures available to them.

Regardless of the reasons, it seems clear that social science efforts in studying recreation, regardless of the setting, need to be refocused. The consequences of not doing so are great, particularly when the data have policy implications. Determining the best strategy for collecting data depends on a variety of factors discussed in this chapter. Individual researchers need a basic understanding of all the strengths and weaknesses of each strategy.

Ethnography as a Research Tool in Understanding Park Visitors

(1983)

Gary E. Machlis

Introduction

If we consider a park as a system, we quickly find it composed of several subsystems. Air, water, soil, animal life, and vegetation, for example, are major biological subsystems. Yet for the area to be a park, and not simply a natural area or open space, social subsystems are imposed upon the landscape—management and visitors, for example, are basic to the very definition of a park (Dubos 1980). If visitors are an integral part of park systems, then to truly understand the functioning of a particular park, the superintendent, resource manager, maintenance chief, interpreter, and ranger must know something about visitors.

This requirement is becoming more crucial as management responsibilities, legal requirements, budget pressures, and demand for services increase. In addition, the diversity of visitors to American parks is increasing. More Americans are visiting parks. More parks are located close to urban populations, and migration from the cities is giving suburban communities access to once-isolated parks. Demographic change within American society is altering the make-up of visitors as well, as our population ages, women join the workforce, and household arrangements fundamentally change. Foreign visitation is rising as the United States becomes a host nation for international tourism.

This chapter offers a particular perspective and method for understanding visitor behavior—that of ethnography. Ethnography is usually practiced by anthropologists, and usually in distant and nonindustrialized societies. Yet it has specific and significant value to understanding contemporary park visitors and can be useful to managers in solving park problems.

This chapter discusses the ethnographic perspective and provides some examples of ethnographic work. Then the basis of ethnographic research is outlined; how one does ethnography and what its limitations are. Finally, the application of ethnography to solving park problems is discussed.

Observation and the Ethnographic Perspective

Observation is the foundation of science, whether it be physics or sociology. In a useful book entitled *The Scientific Approach: Basic Principles of the Scientific Method*, Carlo Lastrucci notes:

> The basic method of data gathering in science is observation. Whether the scientist looks at a lump of coal, at the stars, at an animal, at a plant, or at other human beings—and whether he [sic] looks directly or through a visual accessory such as a telescope or a microscope—observation is by far the most commonly employed method of ascertaining what *is* (1967:158).

One of the great advances in science came early in this century, when Heisenberg, Einstein, and other physicists explained that even the most common and concrete phenomenon (a train speeding by, for example, or the movement of the sun) must be seen differently by different observers. No observation can provide the single, factual Truth. The perspective of the observer became an important consideration, first in physics and later in the social sciences.

In the social sciences, two fundamentally different perspectives to observation evolved. The first could be called the sociological perspective. From this perspective, human behavior is observed and described from the point of view of the observer. Let us take, for example, the relationship between visitors and park rangers. Sociological observers interpret what they see based on a set of assumptions, preconceptions, theories, knowledge of previous studies and so forth. Perhaps, having worked on law enforcement problems in parks and being trained in criminology, they focus upon conflict between visitors and rangers and how this conflict is managed by both groups. The actions observed are studied through the "filter" of the observer's training and beliefs.

The second perspective is the ethnographic perspective. It is based upon understanding behavior from the point of view of the subjects. The anthropologist James Spradley writes:

> Ethnography . . . is a systematic attempt to discover the knowledge a group of people have learned and are using to organize their behavior. This is a radical change in the way many scientists see their work. Instead of asking, "What do I see these people doing?" we

must ask, "What do these people see themselves as doing?" (Spradley and McCurdy 1972:9)

What a difference this shift in perspective makes! In the hypothetical example, it is not assured that rangers and visitors even categorize themselves or each other as such. Certainly, rangers have a variety of categories for visitors—from "chicken-eaters" to "scroats." And not all visitors perceive rangers as different from maintenance staff or concession employees. Hence, one of the most basic rewards of the ethnographic perspective is an understanding of taxonomies used by subjects.

Spradley, in his ethnographic analysis of transient, derelict men, provides us with a real example (1970). Most people classify these individuals as "bums," "vagrants," or "drunks." But as Figure 1 shows, this group of men had a much more complex set of categories to describe themselves. Each category, be it a "box car tramp" or a "professional nose diver," describes individuals with special characteristics and behaviors. Knowledge of taxonomy is the first step in ethnographic analysis: it is virtually impossible to understand a group and its behavior without such knowledge.

In addition to understanding how people categorize themselves, the ethnographic perspective attempts to understand the social meaning of behaviors. Why do visitors behave the way they do? What activities are important to them, and how are they accomplished? For example, in a study of family camping in the Pacific Northwest, a visitor described why she preferred a tent over a camper:

> We like the tent because we have more room and everything is always ready—don't have to fold things in and out all the time. Also, with a tent we can go away and leave things—taking the camper means somebody might take our spot (Machlis 1975:45).

By interviewing visitors, learning their taxonomies and describing their behavior, the ethnographic perspective can provide a unique profile of how visitors interact with the park as a system. We now examine ethnography in more detail.

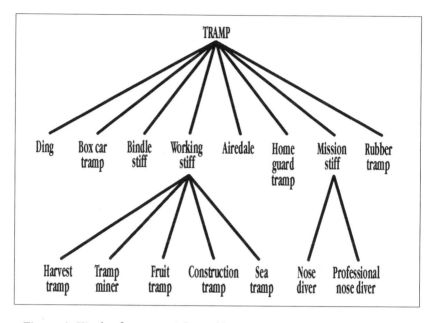

Figure 1. Kinds of tramps. Adapted by permission from Spradley 1970, p. 74. Copyright © 1970 Little, Brown & Co.

The Ethnographic Literature

Ethnographic studies have a long history in the social sciences. Classic studies include Franz Boas's *The Central Eskimo* (1888), Malinowski's *Argonauts of the Western Pacific* (1922), Evans-Pritchard's *The Nuer* (1940), Robert Redfield's *The Folk Culture of Yucatan* (1941), and Rappaport's *Pigs for the Ancestors* (1967). Applying the ethnographic perspective to industrialized societies produced William F. Whyte's *Street Corner Society* (1943), and Leibow's *Tally's Corner* (1967), as examples.

Ethnographies of contemporary people at play are rare, but some do exist. Hollingshead dealt with leisure in *Elmtown's Youth* (1949) and an edited volume by Smith, *Hosts and Guests* (1977), examined the ethnography of tourism. Ethnographic studies of taverns (Gottlieb 1957), pool halls (Polsky 1967), surfing and mountaineering (DeVall 1973), and jogging (Nash 1978) are further examples. Even rarer are studies of park visitors that employ an ethnographic perspective. Machlis (1975) used a partially ethnographic approach in studying family camping. Wedel (1981) has described tourist experiences in Yellowstone National Park, and Robertson and Wilson (1982) have begun an ethnographic analysis of visitors to Yosemite. Machlis et al., in describing the human ecology of parks, call for increased attention to ethnography:

> We suggest a "natural history" of the various visitor populations is the first step to understanding their role in parks and similar settings. Not surprisingly, the anthropologists provide useful research strategies. Participant observation, time-budget studies, ethnographic surveys, and content analysis of written materials are all appropriate research techniques and should provide the descriptive evidence needed to understand the ecological relationships that bind park ecosystems together (1981:207).

The Ethnographic Method

Unlike the laboratory experiment, or the large questionnaire survey, the ethnographic method of learning about people requires a very flexible approach. Yet there are a series of general steps necessary for ethnographic study, and these are briefly described below. More detailed discussions are available by Pelto (1970), Lofland (1976), and Spradley (1979).

Choosing a Cultural Scene

The ethnographer must carefully choose the setting for research based upon the kinds of information needed. Is he or she interested in all visitors to the park? Summer visitors? A special kind of visitor— backpackers, senior citizens, foreign tourists? The setting may be a large or small geographical locale—the Yosemite Valley, a small ruin at Wupatki, Independence Hall, or the backcountry of Olympic National Park. The official boundaries of the park may not always be useful—nearby communities like Gatlinburg, Tennessee, or Estes Park, Colorado, may be "part of the park" to visitors. Often, the choice of scene will reflect managers' need to know about a specific visitor group or place within the park.

Collecting Information

Once a particular cultural scene is selected for study, data must be collected on visitors and their behaviors. A variety of techniques is available. First is interviewing key informants. Spradley writes:

Working with informants is the hallmark of ethnographic field work. It involves an ongoing relationship. In other kinds of social research, one may never even set eyes on questionnaire respondents, and even interviews are limited in number. But the ethnographic field worker must locate helpful people, win their cooperation, and establish a close, personal relationship with them (Spradley and McCurdy 1972:41).

The choice of informants is a critical one since their view of the cultural scene will represent the wider population. Hence, an informant should be someone knowledgeable, cooperative, and representative. The number of informants usually is a function of the ethnographer's resources and time—for *Coming of Age in Samoa* (1928), for example, Margaret Mead interviewed 25 adolescent girls.

The ethnographic interview can be loosely structured, like a conversation around the campfire, or carefully organized. Table 1 provides some general questions that might be asked of park visitors; as the interviews proceed the questions become more detailed. Several methods of taking notes are acceptable—a tape recorder, journal, note cards, and so forth. The key is to respect the informant's need to be comfortable during the interview. The ethnographic interview requires good manners and curiosity; rather than "studying people," ethnography means "learning from people."

A second approach to collecting data is participant observation. Here, the researcher participates in the cultural scene as a member of the group under study. Participant observation has been used in several outdoor recreation studies (Burch 1964, Burch and Wenger

---

Table 1. Typical ethnographic questions for park visitors.

1. Could you describe your visit to this park?
2. Could you describe a typical day in the park?
3. Please tell me about your last park visit.
4. Could you use this map and trace your visit to the park?
5. What do you do when you first enter a park? Then what?
6. What different kinds of people to you meet in a park?
7. Can you describe the people you interact with while at the park?
8. Are there different kinds of parks? How are they different?

1967, Clark et al. 1971a, Field 1973). Campbell states:

> Its flexible format maximizes discovery, while its subjective character and attention to broader aspects of a problem make it well suited for descriptive and taxonomic purposes (1970:227).

Robertson and Wilson describe one incident at Yosemite:

> Wheeling our bikes across the bridge which connects Housekeeping with Lower River Campground, we ran the gauntlet of a dozen young blacks, lounging against the rail and ragging each other but not us or other white pedestrians, as a rule. Then we stopped, took some pictures, and then went back across the bridge. This time we had comments made to us, which, when we ignored them, were repeated together with vocal observations about our not having responded. We inferred that in photographing Housekeeping and them on the bridge we trespassed in a way that more matter-of-fact pedestrians did not, and thereby violated some code of *their* park (1982:10).

Participant observation requires that note taking be done unobtrusively, usually after participation. A detailed journal, including description of events and reflections on their meaning is effective if maintained carefully.

A third technique is photography. Anthropologists and sociologists often take cameras along during field work and take pictures of the visual scenes that interest them. These photographs are then used to illustrate verbal data. But can the camera do more than highlight special events? The anthropologist John Collier suggests:

> The camera's machinery lets us see without fatigue; the last exposure is just as detailed as the first. The memory of the film replaces the notebook and ensures complete notation under the most trying circumstances (1967:5).

In one study of Northwest family camping (Machlis 1975) over three hundred photographs were taken. Photographs of beach activity showed distinct spatial ordering, and pictures of family reunions were used to analyze kin networks.

In addition, the camera can aid in recording the material culture of park going. Joseph Honigmann explains the value of inventorying material culture:

The selection of objects and the nature of their grouping constitute non-verbal expressions of thought, needs, conditions, or emotions. Thus when people shape their surroundings, they introduce man-made [sic] order (1954:134).

The camera can provide reliable and reusable observations of things people take with them when they go to parks. Such a record is invaluable in constructing an ethnographic profile.

Table 2 compares the three techniques and lists major advantages and disadvantages of each. In most cases, some combination of techniques is useful—key informants familiarizing the researchers with important group activities, participant observation used to gather data on behavior, and photographs collected to document visitor activities. The techniques can also be used to check the reliability of data; participant observation of activities described by informants may reveal a bias in informants' reporting.

Writing the Ethnographic Profile

In this step, the collected data are used to prepare a written report. The report may include a careful description of the physical and social setting; maps and photographs are useful. The taxonomies used by subjects should be explained. In our example of understanding visitors and rangers, we might describe the different categories of visitors held by rangers and vice versa. A glossary of special words is often insightful.

The profile may also describe the behavior of subjects. Are there common patterns in how visitors and rangers deal with each other? A typical sequence of behaviors may be described, and special circumstances noted. The importance of certain activities or places to the participants is also described. An example is the following analysis of extended families:

> Many of the extended families observed in the National Parks were more than recreational camping. They were staging an intricate and important ritual—the family reunion. For these groups, camping in the park environ was an enjoyable medium, but not the central focus for their stay in the parks. They came to meet their relatives, to talk over recent times, to share in family fun and traditions. It is hard to over-emphasize the importance of this change in motivation (Machlis 1975:76).

The ethnographic profile then serves as a "natural history" of a particular cultural scene within the park. As ethnography describes people at a particular locale and time, revisions and updates are required if contemporary knowledge is needed about current visitors.

Limitations of the Method

Ethnography, like other research methods, has weaknesses. When an ethnographic profile is based on only a few informants, and the representativeness of these informants is not clear, the data may

Technique	Perspective	Advantages	Disadvantages	Park example
Interviewing key informants	As an outsider wanting to learn	Quick access to knowledge	Choice of informants may bias results	Interviewing group leaders of hiking clubs to learn their management preferences.
Participant observation	As a member of the group under study	Empathetic understanding of behaviors and norms	Objectivity can be lost through participation	Attending interpretive programs as a visitor to evaluate effectiveness.
Photography	As an outsider recording visual images	Enables documentation of visual information	Choice of scene is difficult	Photographing backcountry camping scenes to document use of low impact equipment.

Table 2. Comparison of three ethnographic techniques.

be misleading, if not false. An ongoing controversy surrounds Margaret Mead and her ethnographic work in Samoa. Derek Freeman, in his *Margaret Mead and Samoa: The Making and Unmaking of an Anthropological Myth,* writes:

> The explanation most consistently advanced by the Samoans themselves for the magnitude of the errors in her depiction of their culture and in particular of their sexual morality is, as Gerber has reported, "that Mead's informants must have been telling lies in order to tease her" (1983:290).

In addition, the ethnographer, in constructing a subjective picture of a cultural scene, runs the risk of seeing what he or she wants to see. Again, Freeman's critique of Margaret Mead's research is instructive, for her *Coming of Age in Samoa* has been so influential in anthropology.

> We are thus confronted in the case of Margaret Mead's Samoan researches with an instructive example of how, as evidence is sought to substantiate a cherished doctrine, the deeply held beliefs of those involved may lead them unwittingly into errors (1983:292).

Finally the ethnographic method is time consuming. Choosing and describing a cultural scene, locating and interviewing informants, participating in activities, analyzing data, and writing a profile is a labor-intensive form of research and requires the ethnographer's careful attention. In spite of these limitations, and in part because of its subjective nature, ethnography offers an important way to learn about visitors to national parks.

Application to Park Management

What application does ethnography have for park managers? What usable knowledge can it provide? First, an ethnographic understanding of visitors can correct managers' biases about visitors. At Cuyahoga Valley National Recreation Area, law enforcement rangers and young visitors had strong misconceptions about each other, and their lack of knowledge increased conflict (Machlis et al. 1981). Ethnographic profiles can provide new managerial perspectives, clear up misconceptions, alter stereotypes, and hopefully improve agency-visitor interactions. Learning park visitors' views can also be useful in policy making, and interviewing visitors regarding policy changes can provide a systematic form of public participation.

Second, ethnography can answer specific questions about visitors' motivations. Why do some visitors ask the same questions, treat the restrooms as their highest priority, or avoid a late evening campfire? The ethnographic perspective can provide managers with specific explanations. At a Northwest campground, for example, participant observation revealed that the lack of a lighted trail made attending evening programs difficult for seniors.

Ethnography can also reveal cultural norms and allow managers to improve the park's ability to meet the needs of diverse visitors. For example, a study of Japanese tourists found that souvenir shopping was important because the custom of giving gifts to travelers before their trip meant that Japanese tourists had obligations to bring gifts to many, many friends back home (Machlis et al. 1982). Since buying souvenirs was, to the Japanese, an integral part of the park experience, managers were advised to adapt their interpretive efforts to this need.

How can ethnography in parks be practiced? Certainly, park managers could attract anthropologists and their graduate students to conduct ethnographic studies of contemporary park visitors—applied anthropology is currently regaining favor in academe. Managers can also conduct ethnographic studies themselves, and this approach may have the most significant potential for solving park problems. Perhaps a staff member with an interest in anthropology could spend one day a week interviewing informants, or a seasonal worker or volunteer could be trained and assigned the task. Their new insights could be used in training, planning, and problem solving.

In this chapter, ethnography has been suggested as a valuable research tool for understanding park visitors. For superintendents, interpreters, seasonal employees, and concessionaires to adopt the ethnographic perspective is to have them learn from visitors about themselves and their jobs. The resource managers of the 1990s will need to do just that.

Solving Park Problems:
Developing a Social Science Research Plan
(1984)

Gary E. Machlis

Edwin E. Krumpe

Park managers are increasingly called upon to make difficult decisions that involve and influence a variety of people, organizations, and institutions. Parks are social creations, and it should not surprise us that much of park management is people management. A wilderness ranger may contemplate a new backcountry policy to deal with overcrowding. A state park director may face closure of a park due to budget difficulties. Urban recreation leaders may need to revise their programming as the local community changes.

Sociological information can be a distinct advantage in solving such park problems, and in some cases is a prerequisite for action. Since the 1950s, sociological studies dealing with urban, regional, and national parks have increased dramatically. Park managers have an increasing need to know about their visitors, staff, local community, and nation.

The problem is that there are so many different kinds of information that social scientists could gather for park managers. Today's manager is faced with determining what kind of information is needed to solve park problems, and how and when research studies should be conducted. A solution is for park staffs to develop a plan to guide the allocation of research money and effort. The goal of such planning is to ensure that usable knowledge is obtained. In this article, we describe the necessary parts of a social science research plan, suggest a process for developing such plans, and discuss their advantages to park managers.

What is a Social Science Research Plan?

A Social Science Research Plan (SSRP) is simply an organized, written strategy for acquiring sociological information useful to park management. The plan should demonstrate the social science needs of the park, derived from management policies, legal requirements, and park goals and objectives. It should provide a set of criteria for prioritizing information needs and evaluating research proposals. In addition, it should provide a systematic program for implementing necessary research. The SSRP serves as an advisory document to park managers.

Benefits of a Research Plan

The benefits of an SSRP are many. Accurate and useful information, available when decision makers need it, can increase efficiency and the quality of decisions. For example, constructing new visitor facilities or resolving a major resource problem may require information on visitors' desires and behaviors prior to management action. The SSRP can help ensure that the right information is available at the right time.

Another benefit is that an SSRP may improve the accountability of researchers. By prioritizing critical information needs, the plan will favor those research projects designed to produce the most needed information. Researchers working with the park (or interested in doing so) will be encouraged to align their research efforts with the needs of park management.

A third benefit of an SSRP is that it will enhance long-term planning. All planning—program, fiscal, facility, resource, or personnel—can be no better than the information on which it is based. For example, studies of recreation demand may be needed for facility planning, and a job satisfaction survey may be a necessary part of personnel planning. An SSRP helps focus research efforts on important issues.

Finally, an SSRP can be useful in soliciting research assistance from outside institutions and agencies. It is not uncommon for universities and other organizations to have particular expertise and support for certain types of research. Faculty and graduate students are often looking for worthwhile research projects. With an SSRP in hand, the park manager can provide these institutions and researchers with a list of important research topics, and identify those individuals who might be able to provide help.

Contents of a Social Science Research Plan

The plan need not be a lengthy document, yet several components are necessary. First, it should include a list of the park's social science needs. Does a particular section of the park receive heavy vandalism, with no apparent explanation? Is the number of visitors per year an important figure for budgeting, but does no accurate information exist? These information needs should be stated as clearly as possible in the plan.

Second, the plan should include some evaluation of the identified research problems. Which are most critical? Which require immediate action? For parks with numerous needs, a prioritized list should be part of the plan. A final component should be a schedule for implementing the research. It should include a short-term schedule for proposed projects (dates for starting, completion, and delivery of information to managers), as well as a long-term schedule of what research is necessary over the next five years. Recommendations for funding sources and available assistance also can be part of the document, along with a list of those involved in the plan's preparation.

Procedures for Developing an SSRP

Several steps are necessary to develop an SSRP. A basic outline is provided below.

1. Park management should conduct or commission a review of all social science research specifically relevant to the park. This would include graduate students' theses, special surveys, unsolicited research, broader studies that include data on the park, historical reports, and program evaluations. This literature review inventories the amount and type of information that is already available.

2. A planning team is assembled. Each organizational unit of the park (resources management, visitor services, administration, maintenance, and so forth) should be represented. A trained scientist, with experience in applied social science and recreation management, should be part of the team. Such expertise is often available through universities or other public service agencies. Citizens' groups and the general public might also be represented on the planning team.

3. The planning team should identify management issues and problems. Staff members might be asked: What information about people do you need to do your job? In addition, legislative mandates, court orders, management policies, and capital development plans might be reviewed. Public input such as hearing records and letters are also valuable sources.

Table 1. Examples of criteria for evaluating social science research.

Is the problem critical?

1. Is the study required by legislative mandate or court order?
2. Would information from the study be valuable in an anticipated lawsuit?
3. Is the study needed because of an identified threat to human health or safety or visitor experiences?
4. Is the study critical to the preservation of natural or cultural resources?
5. Will the information from this study lead to potentially significant savings of funds?
6. Does the study relate to a problem that is presently or could reasonably be expected to become highly controversial?
7. Is the study needed to provide information for a specific park program?

Will the results be useful?

1. Can the need for information addressed by the study be adequately met in other ways?
2. Will the study duplicate work that has been or is presently being done by someone else?
3. Will the study results help improve visitor experiences? If so how?
4 .Will the study results help improve the management of natural or cultural resources? If so, how?
5. Will the results be provided to managers in time to be used in decision making?
6. Will the study results be useful in addressing more than one management issue?
7. Does the study have significant scientific value apart from its application to park management?

Is the project possible?

1. Is there sufficient time and money to successfully complete the study?
2. Will the study have any unacceptable impacts upon natural or cultural resources of the park?
3. Will the study have any unacceptable impacts upon park visitors and/or staff?
4. Can sufficiently accurate data be collected?
5. Does the investigator have the expertise to successfully conduct the study?
6. Is the design of the study scientifically sound?
7. Does the design of the study meet all legal requirements for collecting data?

Adapted from Johnson and Aho, n.d.

4. Once identified, the issues and problems should be prioritized based on three major criteria: How critical is the problem? How useful will the research results be? How feasible is the research project?

Table 1 provides a sample checklist that the team might use in evaluating possible research projects. In a small park area with few research needs, this kind of checklist could be used to screen out inappropriate projects. In areas with many needs and numerous proposals, the list could be used to give proposed studies a numerical score and ranking. In any case, the park manager can reasonably require the social scientist to respond to the questions in Table 1 prior to beginning any study.

5. The team then prepares a draft SSRP. The draft includes the prioritized list of research needs, a schedule of proposed projects, recommendations for possible research strategies or methods of collecting data, and possible sources of funding and assistance.

6. The draft plan is reviewed by the chief administrator of the park, as well as by other selected park staff. Omissions, corrections, and suggestions for improvement are provided to the planning team. The final report is prepared and sent to the chief administrator for approval.

7. The plan is officially accepted. The highest administrative level of the park should endorse the plan. Although this may not be a commitment to carry out all of the plan's proposals, it should be a commitment to follow the recommendations whenever social science research projects are being considered.

After the plan is accepted, it is used in preparing requests for research projects and in evaluating unsolicited research proposals. Since the information needs of park management will change over time, the SSRP will need to be reviewed and revised regularly.

Conclusion

The park managers of the 1990s, faced with smaller budgets, more demand for services, and increasing responsibilities, need useful and timely information to do their jobs. Social science research can often provide such usable knowledge, but the occasional thesis project, unplanned survey, or single research study is not enough. To be useful, social science must be organized and planned in advance to meet the needs of managers. This requires park professionals to play an active role in setting research agendas, and to develop a working partnership with social scientists. A social science research plan is a necessary, beneficial, and feasible tool in solving park problems.

Case Studies

The case study has long been a traditional technique of sociology. By focusing attention on a particular person, group, or institution, the case study allows the subject to be examined in some depth and with the kind of special insight not available with other methods, such as the sample survey. Hobbs and Blank write:

> One case study by itself cannot prove much of anything. But if there are many case studies that tend to agree and that tend to provide insights to more general conditions, then sociologists are on the road to a generalization that could prove significant (1982:18).

Hence, case studies usually have broken new ground, exploring for the first time a variety of "cultural scenes." Classic sociological case studies include vagabonds (Anderson's *The Hobo*, 1923), pool hustlers (Polsky's *Hustlers, Beats and Others*, 1967), working-class men (Whyte's *Street Corner Society*, 1943), ethnic groups (Leibow's *Tally's Corner*, 1976), and communities (Warner's *Yankee City*, 1963).

The case studies in this section share several characteristics. First, each deals with a specific clientele group found in parks, forests, museums, and other interpretive settings. Individual chapters deal with children, families, senior citizens, foreign tourists, cruise ship travelers, an ethnic group, and ecotourists. These chapters are modest efforts to show examples of research on social groups of interest to the interpreter.

Second, a variety of research techniques is used in these case studies. Participant observation—where the researcher observes behavior in the field—is central to several of the studies. Bultena et al. observed senior citizens at over one hundred interpretive programs, and the study of family camping involved two and one-half months' field work. The chapters on children and foreign tourists are descriptive accounts based on data (contemporary at the time) collected for other purposes. In the case of the visitor survey on the Galápagos Islands, a survey was conducted specifically to gain insights for the tourism manager, and the observations on Hispanic recreation patterns were gleaned from the survey results of several different studies.

A third similarity is that all these case studies explore the relationship between human behavior and recreation environments. Some focus on specific facilities such as visitor centers, nature trails, and urban science museums, while others examine human use in marine environments, island ecosystems, mountain systems, and coastal shores.

Finally, all of the case studies offer evidence for the diversity of visitor groups suggested in earlier chapters. Machlis found, for example, that treating families as a unique visitor public was an oversimplification. He describes the behavioral differences among family types as significant in their impact on the use of interpretive services. While the demographics of American family life have changed dramatically since the mid 1970s, the underlying trend of diversification of family types that was described 15 years ago continues. Gramann et al. suggest that Hispanic visitors to national parks are extremely interested in interpretive services, but because they comprise a small proportion of the overall visitation to parks, they can be incorrectly identified as not involved. Whether it be children at different stages of development, Japanese visitors on a package tour, or retirees traveling the "snowbird circuit," these case studies illuminate the rich variety of social groups that form the interpreter's audience.

Getting Connected:
An Approach To Children's Interpretation
(1974)

Gary E. Machlis

Donald R. Field

"... to find the human key to the inhuman world about us; to connect the individual with the community, the known with the unknown; to relate the past to the present and both to the future."

P. L. Travers, "Only Connect" (1969)

While there are various definitions of interpretation, most agree that either the transmission of information to visitor publics or the stimulation of a desire to acquire information is a key aspect. Simple as it may sound, matching an interpretive approach and material with the appropriate audience is perhaps the most difficult challenge facing those responsible for the array of public contact programs.

All too often the audience has been taken for granted, misread, or incorrectly identified. Elsewhere several writers have indicated that the manager's conception of the visitor, who he is, and what he seeks in recreational places differs from what the visitor assumes about himself and from what the visitor actually seeks in leisure places (Clark et al. 1971b). This finding is perpetuated by the mass-oriented interpretive programs prevalent in many recreational places, which assume that all visitors are alike. But all visitors are *not* alike. Instead a diversity of visitor groups can be found in recreational places like national parks. The interpretive programs offered also must vary in intent, content, and approach (Field and Wagar 1973).

The bases for assessing differences are numerous. Visitor publics vary in terms of the frequency with which they come to parks and in their previous experience with outdoor leisure places. Perhaps the most obvious difference among visitors is their age. Yet an assessment of programs offered reveals a low number of interpretive options specifically designed for either the young or the old.

This article is directed toward one segment of the visitor public—children. Its purpose is to aid in "connecting" interpretive programs with them. Getting connected requires:

1. An understanding of the developmental phases of childhood growth and how they offer opportunities and limitations for children of various social and chronological ages.

2. Consideration of the importance that group life has on children and how social groups can affect interpretation.

3. An understanding of three basic interpretive approaches that should be central to any program dealing with children.

Any fruitful approach to children's interpretation must have a conceptual framework soundly based on the way children behave. Interpreters may ask, "Under what conditions will a particular program be exciting and effective for children?" or "How can we design an interpretive program for school-age youngsters?" The answers lie in understanding human behavior.

When examining children's interpretation, it is useful to think in terms of communications flow. To be connected with children the message must pass through the interpreter, the medium of communication being used, and the social situation in which it is being delivered—all before it reaches the child. Each of these factors can potentially encourage effective interpretation or discourage such efforts. If the message is incomplete, the interpreter inarticulate, the equipment jammed, the screen torn, or the room lighting too bright, immediately there are barriers to communication. If the social environment is inappropriate, the message may not be received. If the child is not developmentally mature enough to participate at the level of an interpretive program, getting connected is extremely difficult. Hence, understanding the behavior of youngsters in each developmental phase will help in providing interpretation that truly connects with the young visitor.

How Developmental Phases Affect Interpretation

This same sort of negative/positive potential can be of value in looking at the phases of childhood development. In each phase, certain characteristics can act as limitations on getting connected, while others can act as motivators. *Children's interpretive programs need to exploit those characteristics that act as motivators.*

Example: If five-year-olds learn primarily through the sense of touch, then interpretive exhibits that allow tactile responses will motivate these children. Exhibits labeled "don't touch" will limit their own effectiveness.

In discussing developmental phases of childhood, many cautions must be observed. These phases are purely conceptual, and no child goes to sleep one night in the latency period to awake as a preadolescent. Rather, there is a continuum of development wherein physical, emotional, and cognitive changes gradually occur. These changes happen at different chronological ages from child to child and vary from generation to generation. To further complicate matters, children may be in transition from one phase to the next, or may just be developing at a slower chronological rate.

For the preschooler, who is cognitively just beginning to make associations of cause-and-effect, interpretation of simple natural relationships can be exciting. Preschoolers have abundant energy and large active movements. Their interest span is short, so interpretive programs should be constructed in small sequential units. They are primarily self centered and work better individually. The preschooler is concerned with scales: "big and small" are important concepts.

Example: An interpretive program that involves the children physically in a "miniature ecosystem" running and climbing up small valleys and along creeks and streams. There are natural places to hide, logs to cross, and all at a scale appropriate to the children.

At about five years of age, the child enters what can be called the school-age phase. Cognitively, comparison becomes a prime mode of analyzing information. Interpreters have assumed that school-age children are interested in factual data concerning natural history: "The tree is 110 feet tall." However, the interest may be not with the data as such, but in how this particular tree measures up to the tallest tree in the area. Comparisons can make data come alive for the school-age child. The school-age child is only tentatively beginning to form relationships with adults outside the family, briefly leaving the protection of the caring person, usually the mother. Physical growth becomes more gradual.

Physical growth continues into the preadolescent phase, which begins around the age of nine. There is wide variation in development from child to child, with interests and curiosities varying even more. The preadolescent is beginning to enjoy group life and is finding parent substitutes in teachers and group leaders. The credibility of the interpreter in the eyes of the child becomes extremely critical. There is a striving to attain skills and a concern with things rather than ideas.

Example: A "living history" program where groups of children could learn about frontier baking by grinding flour, stoking the oven, and eating the final product.

This concern for things rather than ideas changes as the adolescent phase begins, at about twelve to thirteen years of age. At this stage, a desire arises for intellectual freedom and for authentic information with which to make independent decisions. The adolescent is struggling for independence, yet critically needs peer group approval. An interpretive program that allows for teenage leadership and self-discovery is apt to be more effective than one based on adult supervision and fixed rules.

Example: A program of volunteer environmental cleanup projects, bringing trash back from high mountain country; or teenagers leading younger children on interpretive walks.

The first goal in getting connected is to use the motivators inherent in each developmental phase to best advantage.

Children and Social Groups

More than any other segment of our society, children participate in interpretive experiences while in a group. A family may visit an interpretive center, a school class may take a trip to a historical site, or a group of campers may go for a nature walk around camp. Central to understanding child behavior is the social context in which interpretation takes place. One cannot effectively develop interpretive programs for children without understanding the dynamics of children's groups. Like the concept of developmental phase, social context can act as a limitation or a motivation in connecting the message. What are some of the variables affecting the social context of children's interpretive programs?

The Purpose of the Group

Before other questions are addressed, it is useful to consider the basic purpose of any children's group. The purpose may be education, recreation, entertainment, or simply delivery of an agency message. The group may be used to offer new experiences to the young or to supervise and control behavior.

Also, it is important to ask who defines the purpose of such a children's group. Little league baseball is an example of a children's group whose purpose is largely defined by adults. Children quickly learn the real purpose for their group's existence and often act accordingly.

Example: Is the campfire's purpose to present an agency message and supervise children, or to teach environmental concepts and give kids a chance to relax and enjoy themselves?

Group Size

Group size is an important factor. Active outdoor games may be motivators for large groups of early school-age children and indoor activity may be severely limiting.

Example: It is unreasonable to plan a structured, passive program for large groups of eight-year-olds. They have incredible amounts of energy, are intensely physical, and desire attention from adults. Nonconstructive chaos is almost inevitable.

Group Composition

The composition of the children's group also defines social context. Since the interpreter often has little control over group composition, interpretive programs must be flexible to adapt to changes in group composition. We need to ask if the children in a particular group are currently in different phases. Or, as is more likely, are some in a specific phase and others in transition? Will these differences affect the group and its purpose?

Other variables need to be examined also. What is the social and educational background of the children? The proportion of males to females becomes crucial in the preadolescent phase and continues to influence behavior into adulthood. Partly because of urbanization and the decline of open space in urban areas, interpreters must be aware of the environmental experience of the children. How many different environs has the group been exposed to, and in which settings are they motivated or limited? Children of the city cannot be expected to spontaneously relax and enjoy wilderness environments without previous successful experiences. Fritz Redl speaks of urban children's summer camp experiences:

> City children have heard and read about storms, animals, and nature and have used these images as props in their nightmares and daydreams. What isolated contacts they have made with nature usually were in broad daylight or in the protective custody of father or mother on that car trip. Suddenly all nature is let loose on the child from town; the result is that many children are frightened at camp much of the time (1966:441).

The effective interpreter will consider these variables in planning and conducting interpretive programs.

Example: A group of young scouts is preparing for its first campout. It is obvious to the adult leader that while most of the group enjoys group life, several "loners" are involved. The leader offers responsibility for keeping a journal of their trip to several of the loners, giving them the very needed chance each day to relax from the requirements of group life inherent in scout trips.

The second goal of getting connected is to use the social context of the group as a motivator.

Interpretive Approaches

The next step in getting connected is to examine various interpretive approaches. An interpretive approach should not be confused with a medium such as films or the written word, or with schedules of interpretive activity. Such an approach is a way of programming built upon three basic modes of human expression: action, fantasy, and instruction.

Action

Children learn by doing. They learn physical skills such as skipping and throwing by imitation and repetition. They want to be able to do things and are not truly content with being told how or shown. An impatient "Let me do it!" is a signal to the interpreter that his interpretive approach is ignoring this important mode.

Action is valuable in the development of other kinds of skills. Participation in an activity offers children practice in interacting with others, and helps them to empathize with others' emotions—an important part of what adults consider maturity. Indeed, sometimes the only way for a child to understand how another feels may be to act out the role.

Example: An interpreter is explaining to a group of school-age children that for the pioneers coming west on the Oregon Trail, winter was a hard time. The children do not react. The interpreter asks them to act out winter on the Trail, without fresh food, warm clothes, or adequate shelter. The play acting goes on for about five minutes. The interpreter then continues his story, carrying along with him the children's interest and understanding.

Fantasy

Perhaps the most powerful and far-reaching mode of interpretation is fantasy. Fantasy is an intimate, personal, and imaginative thing. To the child there is a potential for fantasy within every experience. Indeed, when modern children are confronted with a basket woven by Native Americans hundreds of years ago, we are inviting them to fantasize about a life and culture far different from their own. Interpretive displays that encourage fantasy can spark interest and involvement, even though the display itself may be quite static. Yet while the children are so involved in fantasy, it is seldom openly used by interpretation planners and programmers. And why not? C. S. Lewis notes:

> He [the child] does not despise real woods because he has read of enchanted woods: the reading makes all woods a little enchanted (1969:215).

Instruction

Instruction is by far the most accepted and expected mode of interpretation. It is the main way we teach children in our schools and whether by slide show, campfire talk, or museum exhibit, one-way communication of information is the most prevalent method of interpretation.

For youngsters the importance of information is directly related to its usefulness.

Example: To know how to identify Oregon Grape may be mildly interesting, but the information comes alive when it is made known that the berries can be used to stain decorations onto cloth.

To be valuable, instruction should concentrate on providing information that can be directly incorporated into the lives of children.

For children, these modes of expression are closely related with each offering strong motivations. The effective interpreter weaves them all together, moving from one mode to the other as the individuals and group require.

Example: A group of seven-year-olds is learning about salmon. The interpreter begins by showing the children pictures of the large fish, and asks if they have ever seen one. The children are told that salmon can often weigh nearly one-half of what they (the children) weigh. Can they imagine being such a large fish in a shallow stream? Could they show what it would be like to be a salmon swimming upstream? "What happens if there is a dam?" asks the interpreter. The children act out climbing a fish ladder, if possible on a small ladder built for such activity. The play acting goes on for several minutes. The interpreter tells the children the rest of the story about the salmon's life cycle. It is mentioned that no one understands why the salmon can return to the same stream where they began life as eggs. The children are asked: "Can you think of a reason?"

Obviously, using these conceptual tools requires a great deal of prior planning on the part of the interpreter. Given the complexity of the groups, he or she cannot be expected to utilize every possible motivator in each interpretive encounter. What is needed is a systematic planning process for children's interpretive programs.

Summary

"Getting connected" seemed appropriate for the title of this article, because many of the ideas germinated while reading P. L. Travers' article on children's literature, "Only Connect." Some important things to consider here are: the developmental phases of growth, the social context of the children's group, and modes of interpretation—action, fantasy and instruction. Books, papers, and articles that discuss these concepts can aid in getting connected. But alone, this understanding and discussion cannot create enjoyable children's programs. Getting connected ultimately requires creativity, love of children, curiosity, and an ability to look on the role of adult with bemused suspicion.

The Social Organization
of Family Camping:
Implications for Interpretation
(1975)

Gary E. Machlis

Introduction

On a summer weekend almost anywhere in our country, the campgrounds are full to overflowing; trailers and tents of every description fill the many campsites. Many of these weekend shelters are inhabited by families; as family members, they build fires, make friends, and go to evening programs. This chapter is concerned with family groups and how they organize themselves while camping. Using the techniques of participant observation, four kinds of families were examined—the *nuclear, multiple, extended,* and *partial* family. The objective was to discover patterns of social organization associated with the activity of camping as they might be manifested in each family type.

A family camping trip is an important event and requires social and economic resources heretofore sparsely treated in the literature of family life. To those families for whom camping is a primary group activity, participation may be critical to maintaining family ties—invaluable in a society that in many ways serves to separate family members from one another.

It is also important that family camping be understood by those responsible for the management of our country's parks, recreation areas, and campgrounds. Families comprise one of the largest categories of park visitors, and their impact on the physical and social environments of these areas may be significant. As families are active participants at interpretive events, describing family behavior at campgrounds may be useful to interpreters.

Methods

The study was undertaken at Mt. Rainier, Olympic, and Crater Lake national parks during the summer season of 1974. Participant observation was used to gather data on families camping overnight in developed campgrounds within the parks. More than 74 hours were spent purely as an observer; a similar amount of time was spent participating in camping activities with family groups.

While observations were taken of both individuals and groups, the unit of analysis was the social group. Observations were stratified by family type to compensate for a preponderance of nuclear families in the campgrounds. Four family types were examined: *nuclear* (parents and their children), *multiple* (several nuclear families permanently or temporarily combined), *extended* (encompassing the kin network), and *partial* (single-parent families).

In addition to observation periods, interviews were conducted with family groups. These interviews were in-depth and informal, and questions were open ended. Families were encouraged to speak freely and discuss their camping experiences and organization. The nonrandom sample was again stratified, so as to provide adequate data on single-parent and extended families. Photography was used to record special behaviors or events and to analyze spatial organization of campsites and camp activities.

Background

What are the key elements that make up family life in a camping setting? By describing those relevant to the *concept* of family, we can look at specific kinds of family groups through a common eye. If there are key elements that make up family life, we can try to describe how these elements operate within families in the parks. To understand family camping, we must first understand the family as a social group.

Several sociologists have attempted to lay out framework for investigating family life (Parsons and Bales 1955, Burgess et al. 1971). Social work researchers, concerned with the practical problems of troubled families, also have made this attempt (Geismar 1964). Burch (1964) touched upon family organization in his analysis of sex-typing in camping settings. This study of families in the parks embraced three key variables of family life: *family maintenance, family interaction,* and *family activities.*

When families go camping in outdoor recreation areas, the demands of *family maintenance* continue to shape much of family behavior. One of the primary maintenance functions is that of shelter. How is the maintenance of family shelter organized? Is the responsibility of shelter building sex-typed? How are camping shelters spatially located? Another primary aspect of family maintenance is food preparation and meals. Mealtimes require obvious organization and division of labor and therefore provide an excellent event for analysis. A third important function is protection— usually by parents and of children. This activity is highly visible in parks, especially at interest points and campgrounds that include natural hazards. How the protective function is carried out is an important element of each family's camping pattern.

Understanding *family interaction* is also critical to understanding families in parks. Meeting maintenance requirements often initiated a division of labor within the family group. Members were assigned (overtly or by norms) certain roles and behaviors. For example, fathers were often in charge of shelter building and campfires; mothers were in charge of cooking and child supervision. This division of labor formed the primary relationships and interactions within the family group. Parsons and Bales (1955) argued that there is a universal tendency toward "instrumental" roles for men and "affective" roles for women. An expanded view of role differentiation is presented by Blood and Wolfe (1971) in their work on family task performance. Blood and Wolfe argue that who does what is determined by both norms and by availability. If the normal performer is not available, then roles become more and more diffuse as tasks switch from member to member. Thus, an important aspect of family organization is how roles are assigned to family members. Do traditional sex-typed roles become more diffuse in the outdoor recreation setting? How do these roles interrelate?

Another major theme of family interaction explored in this study of families in parks is the fundamental question of group cohesion—the extent to which an individual's roles include interaction with other members of the group. Hess and Handel (1974) point out that two conditions characterize the family group; the members are intimately connected to one another, yet they are also separate. Each member must establish his or her own personality and identity and, at the same time, integrate personal behavior into that of the group. Each family must develop its own balance of connectedness and separateness.

The outdoor recreation setting is ideal for examining family cohesion, for the disruptive influences of employment often are left behind. Burch writes:

Camping differs from other play in that the campers, though isolated from the commitments of everyday life, pursue many of the routines of everyday life. The family unit for the duration of its engagement is a relatively self-sufficient unit containing the resources of existence without immediate, direct dependency on others (1965:605).

The third major element of family life in outdoor recreation settings is *family activities,* those units of group behavior that involve all family members to one degree or another. Families' activities may be agency initiated—developed by park management for visitors—such as interpretive centers, organized interpretive trails, and evening campfire programs. They may also be park-inherent—available due to the natural features of the area—such as mountain climbing, playing in streams, and fishing. Finally activities may be family initiated—developed by families independent of park resources—such as reading, badminton, listening to music, and so forth. Do different types of family groups gravitate toward different kinds of recreational activity? Are these activities organized in discernible patterns?

Another important aspect of family activities is their potential for ritualistic content. Bassard and Boll (1950) describe family rituals as beginning with "recurrent family behavior." As an activity is staged over and over again, definite forms of interaction and a specific cultural content are built up. The family ritual is a social process, one with the possibility of strong emotional overtones. Its importance to family cohesion is easily apparent.

Yet rituals serve other functions besides binding the family together. For young children, the material context of the ritual—the specific patterns of behavior—become pathways to social participation in the family group. The rituals become tools for the transmission of family culture. We know from previous research (Burch and Wenger 1967, among others), that childhood outdoor recreational experiences affect leisure choices in adulthood. Yet at a more psycho-social level, we are relatively ignorant of how this takes place. One possibility is that the rituals act as "culture carriers," and are reenacted (in different forms, perhaps) in adulthood. Because knowledge in this area is incomplete, an analysis of family ritual in camping settings was undertaken.

Results

The Nuclear Family

The fundamental unit of American family life is the nuclear family (Reiss 1972). Past studies of recreational use (Field 1972) have chosen not to differentiate between family types, making conjecture on the proportion of nuclear families difficult. However, it was very clear that nuclear family groups were the most common social group in each of the campgrounds studied.

The nuclear families observed in this study occupied primarily single-unit shelters—a tent, camper or trailer that housed the entire family. Occasionally, nuclear families were found using two shelters, with parents sleeping inside a trailer or camper and the children in a small tent nearby. Rather than a requirement for family maintenance, these extra units often seemed to be "adventure places" for the young.

For nuclear families, shelter building was primarily a responsibility of the father. Several fathers observed in field situations continued shelter building long after the demands of maintenance and convenience were satisfied. The tent was readjusted or the campsite reorganized. Burch (1965, 1971) describes this behavior as "symbolic labor"; such efforts also serve as creative outlets for the men who engage in them.

In the nuclear family, the protection function took two basic forms—preventive and active. Much of the protection that parents provided for young children was preventive. Campsites were chosen for their relative safety. Active protection also was plainly visible within nuclear family groups. Two important factors were evident: active protection was sex-typed as a female activity, and such protection often helped produce tension within the family.

> Father with movie camera takes pictures of daughter feeding the squirrels. Parents encourage her to feed them, while the father shoots several feet of movie film. Mother calls her back repeatedly from the lake rim. Father tells her to stay put so he can film. Father switches to Polaroid camera and tells her not to be afraid. The mother calls her back angrily, and finally both daughter and father come back over the rim wall (observation notes, August 24).

"Trophy-taking" (Burch 1965, Hendee et al. 1971) in the national parks, such as this father's attempt at filming his daughter, often involved some sort of real or imagined risk. To the extent that the urge for trophies conflicted with protection, tension was created. While trophy-taking was sex-typed as a male activity, active protection was definitely a female responsibility; hence much of the tension created was between mother and father. Another source of conflict was the close confinement between nuclear family members in their shelters.

These tensions, no doubt, appear regularly in the home. Yet part of the reason such conflicts occur in the campground is that, for the nuclear family, the balance of connectedness and separateness leaned heavily toward connectedness, whole group interaction cooperation, and family cohesion. The nuclear family when camping is concerned with togetherness, combined with sometimes opposing roles; conflict and tension are bound to occur. This orientation toward togetherness was not the case for all kinds of family groups. Observations suggest that nuclear families are involved in all manner of activities in outdoor recreation settings. Familiarity with the park and its recreational opportunities helped determine the most frequent kinds of activities. Families that had low familiarity with a park tended to involve themselves in agency-initiated programs such as campfires, nature walks, and visitor centers; families with high familiarity (often locals) tended toward park-inherent or family-initiated behaviors. This phenomenon was repeated in several areas consistently. Family activities seemed to change as familiarity with a recreation setting increased. As newcomers gained experience, knowledge, and equipment, dependence on agency-initiated activity seemed to decline.

Multiple Families

Multiple family groups—two or more unrelated nuclear families camping conjointly—represented a discrete kind of family group observed in the study areas. Some were families who have communal living patterns at home and bring those patterns with them when they visit a park. Others were traditional nuclear families who joined together specifically for outdoor recreation. Maintaining a multiple family group may entail more adults caring for a larger number of children, and many multiple families were able to develop ways to deal with these larger numbers of individuals. Kitchen areas were larger than for nuclear families, and meals often were all-group activities.

Shelter tended to be in separate nuclear units, partly due to a desire for adult privacy and the fact that recreational shelters designed for multiple families are not readily available. The shelters usually were arranged on campsites in patterns similar to those exhibited by nuclear families, but again this may be due to a lack of alternatives. Almost always, a single campfire circle served the entire group.

The key element in the cohesion of multiple family groups was the sharing of the protective function by all adult members of the group. It was "watching out for Ed's kids" and "taking care of the Wilson boys" that enabled multiple family groups to function in the parks. Protection of children was often sex-typed as in the nuclear family. Strong discipline was left to a child's parents; shared protection did not imply complete interchangeability of roles.

Multiple families had a wide range of family activities, similar to nuclear groups. The multiple family often involved itself in park-inherent activities that lent themselves to large group participation (beach hikes, organized games). Most of these activities reinforced the cohesion of the group. Teams were never chosen along nuclear family lines; children were told to "listen to Mrs. Charles" and "do what she says."

Parent and child roles were diffused considerably in the multiple family, similar to the process as it operates in communes or other group homes. The ability to engage in adult activities and momentarily share the caring and protective function with others enabled adult relationships other than mother-father dyads to develop.

It has been suggested that the nuclear family is heavily oriented toward connectedness while camping in parks. There is also togetherness in the multiple family; togetherness is what makes communal life. Yet because of the diffusion of norms involved in such conjoint endeavors, the enforcement of a single norm for group cohesion may be somewhat less severe.

The Extended Family

Nuclear families do not exist in a social vacuum, isolated from other kin. Researchers such as Litwak (1961) and Parsons and Bales (1955), while in disagreement as to the extent of kin relations, agree that the "modified extended family" is functioning in modern America. The modified extended family is a kin network of individuals and nuclear family groups banded together by affectional ties and choice (Sussman and Burchinal 1962, Litwak 1960). Sussman and Burchinal found that the major activities linking family networks are mutual aid—both financial and emotional—and social activities. This suggests that leisure may be a major factor in extended-family relationships. In fact, Dotson (1951) found that extended family get-togethers and joint recreational activities dominate urban working-class leisure pursuits. Hence it was reasonable to expect extended families in the parks. Shelter was a combination of nuclear family units and adventure places. Because of park regulations and site design, extended-family shelters were spread over several numbered campsites. However, it was imperative to most extended groups to be situated as close to one another as possible. Camping "close" often meant parking recreational vehicles off designated areas; soil compaction and vegetation trampling also were prevalent.

When a large extended family took its position in a developed campground, a central campsite often became the extended family "commons." Nightly campfires, family conversations, and large group meals were often held at this site. The extended family commons became the center for family maintenance and activity and usually was accompanied by overuse of the immediate area. Sites peripheral to the commons were used to varying degrees. Most meals were taken in nuclear subgroups.

Within the extended family, protection was handled in ways similar to that suggested for multiple -family groups. Protection was shared, with each adult member having a measure of parental responsibility and authority over the kins' children. Unlike the multiple-family group, more parental transfer of discipline was evidenced. Older family members often looked after children, freeing young parents for other activities.

Many of the extended families observed were engaged in more than recreational camping. They were staging an intricate and important ritual—a family reunion. It is hard to overemphasize the importance of this change in motivation. An extended family that stages a family reunion in a park likely has developed emotional ties to the recreational area that the park, the campground, even the campsite represent. These recreational places become traditional family settings; these camping activities become family rituals. Many of the extended family reunions examined had been held repeatedly in the same place, often at the same campsite. Many return each year at a specific date. They have developed attachments to areas administered by recreational agencies that transcend the meanings that managers and casual visitors use to order behavior in the park.

Family activities for the extended kin network tended to be family initiated, and there was little participation in agency-initiated programs. Team games were popular and often carried much ritualistic content. For extended families celebrating reunions in outdoor settings, much of family activity carried with it the social weight of tradition.

As could be expected, the extended family involves a complex network of social relationships. For extended family groups that included several generations, interaction revolved around the patriarch and/or the matriarch of the clan. Relationships tended to be directed upward, with identity and status gained by generation and age. Marriage-related members (a brother-in-law or sister-in-law) had equal standing; in the families observed they were always full participants.

Competition between generations was encouraged and most large extended families had contests of one kind or another. However, competition between members of the same generation was treated differently. Often, each member developed a special role that gave unique status. One young adult male might be "the top clammer of us all" and another "the frisbee champion." In this way, every member gained attention and status without undue family competition.

It must be remembered that while the extended family is camping in parks the kin network is not the only social structure that affects camping behavior. Each nuclear subgroup spent considerable time with its own members, and their behavior was similar to that already discussed. The tension-producing conflict of trophy-taking versus protection was not as evident in the extended-family subgroups, but this may be due more to familiarity with the park than to a unique social structure. For a family group returning to the same area many times, both the anxiety of protection and the desire for trophies may be significantly reduced.

The Partial Family

Just as membership in the family can be expanded from the nuclear group to the kin network, death, disruption, and divorce can reduce the family to partial status. Single-parent families were observed in the study areas; in-depth interviews were conducted with several such groups. Maintaining a partial family in a national park campground requires the same basic maintenance roles as the nuclear counterpart requires. Most of the observed partial families camped in single-unit shelters. There were fewer "adventure places" for youngsters; the partial family was sheltered together. Unlike nuclear families, shelter building was decidedly not a sex-typed activity, primarily because a single parent was the family head. Blood and Wolfe's (1971) theory of availability was clearly demonstrated as the female family leader took charge of setting up shelter, and children of both sexes pitched in to help.

This diffusion of work roles was evident in other forms of family maintenance. Food preparation became a family activity, and the entire group participated. The pressures and responsibilities of protection were especially evident in our observations of partial families and interviews with single-parent families. Without another parent (and often without another adult) to help, a single parent was left to assume the entire protective function alone. The difference from the organized protection of the multiple family was striking.

Partial families were largely dependent on agency-initiated programs for family activities. Many partial families stayed close to their campsites, talking, playing cards, stoking the fire. These times were not necessarily temporal bridges between other events: sometimes the activity continued for several hours. Partial families often had low familiarity with park areas, and their dependence on agency-initiated programs limited the range of activities in which they participated. Social relationships also were somewhat limited. Without a spouse to share in the protection, socialization, and emotional support of the children, the single parent often had little chance for social contact outside of parent-child relationships.

To the partial family, the question of connectedness and separateness is fairly moot. Separateness is a fact of partial family life outside the park. Hence, inside the outdoor recreational area, partial families tended to concentrate heavily on the connectedness of family life. Unlike the nuclear family, such a concentration did not run the risk of alienating individual family members. On the contrary, partial families welcomed the chance to use camping as a means for unifying and solidifying the family group.

Implications for Interpretation

From the research just described, several general conclusions about family camping are possible. First, families can be classified into four types—nuclear, multiple, extended, and partial. Each has a distinct membership. Information that allows for the classification of a family unit is relatively easy to obtain. The typology is not restricted to recreational research but can accommodate family groups in most settings. Second, this framework is especially useful in examining family camping. Each family type has developed distinct adaptive strategies for dealing with the maintenance, interaction, and activities involved in outdoor recreation, and specifically family camping.

Third, knowing into which type a family falls may help identify the social organization and behavior of that family. Knowing that a large, multigenerational extended family is about to enter a campground, we can predict the kinds of activities they may likely pursue and how the group might be organized internally. Such sociological knowledge can be useful in dealing with a range of interpretive situations. An example is the issue of protection. In protecting their young, families often had little familiarity with a park and its accompanying hazards. This left protection in the hands of park management. New ways to reinforce safety messages through interpretation that involves parents might be effective in reducing accidents within the parks.

Interpretive efforts that cater to the family group are especially appreciated by park-visiting families. For example, an interpretive program that generates dialogue between parent and child is especially appropriate for partial families; programs that provide parents with interpretive information can utilize the teacher-learner roles of parents and children. In such cases, the interpreter allows the family to interpret and acts as a catalyst for such encounters. It might even prove successful to have extended family groups and reunions present programs, encouraging visitor participation and dialogue between families within the park.

The data suggest that families having little familiarity with a recreational area are largely dependent upon the park agency to provide things to do. This needs further investigation; if it is true, there are important implications for interpreters. Some activities and written materials might be geared toward first-time visitors with the purpose of increasing familiarity; programs in areas with high numbers of repeat visitors might be altered or even discontinued.

Finally, this study suggests an intriguing path of discovery. It is concerned with how outdoor recreation fits into the general scheme of all-around family life. Are the behaviors and patterns of organization observed in campgrounds different from what goes on at home, school, or on the job? Are there behavioral differences between families that go camping and those that do not? Research that seeks to synthesize our knowledge of family camping and general family life can offer answers to these questions, and such answers may be useful to interpreters.

Interpretation for the Elderly
(1978)

Gordon Bultena

Donald R. Field

Renee Renninger

The fact that the national forests and parks today are serving a diverse clientele is important to an objective appraisal of the interpretive interests and needs of visitors. It has been found, for example, that national parkgoers are drawn from all age and social class levels, from several racial and ethnic groups, and from rural and metropolitan areas; they display widely varying levels of education, unique cultural and experiential backgrounds, and diverse motives for visiting parks (Cheek and Field 1971, Outdoor Recreation Surveys 1968). Despite this diversity, there has been a tendency for public agencies to plan programs for the mythical "average visitor," and thus to lose sight of, and perhaps give inadequate attention to, the unique interpretive needs and interests of visitor subgroups (Field and Wagar 1973).

This chapter reports findings from a study of the interpretive interests and involvement of one segment of the parkgoing public—retirees. Although older persons have been found to be less dedicated parkgoers on the whole than middle-aged or young persons, retirees who visit national parks often do so with considerable frequency and make relatively long stays. It can be anticipated that older persons will become an increasingly important audience for park interpretive efforts given their growing numbers in the national population, earlier retirement, increased affluence, and more social legitimation of their participation in leisure-oriented lifestyles.

Study Design

Information was obtained in this study from behavioral observations of, and interviews with, older persons (aged 60 and older) visiting Olympic, Rainier, and North Cascades national parks. A sampling design was employed whereby sites in each park were visited repeatedly in 1975. Data were obtained on older persons' attitudes and behaviors germane to their participation in organized interpretive programs (e.g., nature walks, talks, demonstrations, campfires). A total of 105 interpretive programs in the three parks were observed for purposes of obtaining information on the behavior of older participants. Opinions about these programs were solicited through informal interviews with participants.

Interviews also were conducted with 100 older persons in park campgrounds to elicit their observations and feelings about ongoing interpretive programs and to identify their interests and personal needs for interpretation. This camper population was felt to comprise a viable audience for park interpretive efforts, but it appeared to us that many older campers were not availing themselves of existing interpretive opportunities. Interview data were not collected from older visitors using local accommodations or from day users, except as they were contacted while participating in the formal interpretation programs.

Findings

Personal Characteristics

Retired parkgoers displayed several common characteristics. Most were relatively young, recently retired, and despite problems with chronic disorders, saw themselves as being in good health. They led active lives and displayed very positive attitudes toward their present life situations. They were high spirited, adventurous, and desirous of acquiring more knowledge about the historical and natural features of the parks. All were strongly committed to conservationist goals and specifically to the necessity of preserving parklands for future generations. They diligently sought to obey park regulations and showed disdain for persons who would violate rules or engage in depreciative behaviors.

Most retired persons contacted in this study were visiting the national parks as couples, with or without other friends or family members. Widows, widowers, and singles were most often observed in multigenerational groups or peer groups in day use areas or in organized commercial tours. Although the most common group type was the senior couple, numerous two- and three-generational groups (comprised of grandchildren, children, siblings, younger friends, and age peers) were observed. Group composition was important to involvement of the aged in park interpretive programs, as is later discussed.

The activities of these older respondents, unlike many of the younger park visitors, were generally unhurried and open ended.

Although most had basic travel itineraries, they did not feel bound by these schedules and opted to stay in campgrounds until local sightseeing and recreational opportunities had been exhausted.

An important facet of campground culture was the frequent formation of friendship ties and helping patterns between age peers. Ephemeral social communities evolved as new parties arrived in the campgrounds and others departed. New arrivals typically were greeted by age peers and introduced around. Although striking differences in personality and degree of sociability were observed, retired persons consistently regarded each other with mutual trust, respect, and understanding. Reciprocal exchanges of information, services, and goods were common. In some instances, this took the form of assisting age peers on the park trails by carrying personal items or aiding their passage over difficult terrain. Nearly all respondents, however, were in sufficiently good health to navigate the self-guided walks and many sought out the more demanding front-country hiking trails.

Often the sightseeing activities and day trips of respondents were coordinated with those of newly found friends in the sharing of transportation. In some instances, new friendships were apparently maintained beyond the park setting, as visitors integrated their future travel plans and/or arranged home visits. A further finding was that many of the aged were involved in larger social networks that provided them up-to-date information on highway conditions, places to eat, things to see, and desirable places to camp. One result of this "grapevine" is that many older visitors became well informed about the content of interpretive programs, and even the names of the best naturalists, prior to their arrivals in the parks.

Attitudes Toward Interpretive Programs

Observations of daytime interpretive programs (fixed displays, talks, and nature walks) revealed that older persons regularly made up from 25 to 35 percent of the audiences. This figure jumped to about 65 percent at some popular sites. Interestingly, the representation of older persons in these programs was consistently underestimated by park managers, suggesting that the numerical prominence of this user group is not correctly perceived by officials.

While most of the respondents rated their participation in interpretive programs as enjoyable, many also expressed concern that the program formats were not effectively meeting their needs. A common criticism was that programs were primarily geared to first-time visitors and often were superficial and uninformative. Because of longer stays and more extensive parkgoing experience than many younger persons, some older visitors were already familiar with current interpretive content. Also, given their strong environmental commitments and prior knowledge of park flora and fauna, many sought more in-depth, challenging presentations than they felt were being provided.

The experiences of older persons on nature walks suggested some additional problems. First, older persons sometimes were left behind, especially on elevated trails, as interpreters and younger visitors rapidly proceeded from one observation site to the next. Interpreters usually appeared oblivious to this problem. It was not uncommon for older persons, just catching up, to find that the formal remarks had been concluded and the group was prepared to move on. Older persons also tended to be shunted to the fringes of their groups as younger, often more aggressive, members sought access to park naturalists. Older persons sometimes experienced difficulties hearing in these situations and in gaining the attention of interpreters to ask questions.

A second complaint was that groups tended to be too large for sustained wildlife observation and for personal interaction with naturalists. Finally, groups sometimes were seen as affording too little opportunity for members to interact between themselves. The respondents saw opportunities for camaraderie with other visitors as a particularly desirable, but often unrealized, by-product of their participation in formal interpretive programs.

Evening slide presentations and campfire programs held mixed appeal for older campers. Some felt that the information presented was superficial and redundant; some resented disruptions of young children and/or felt the programs conflicted with their activity schedules. For instance, it was not uncommon for respondents to be early risers and to retire early, or to devote evening hours to

interaction with friends or the pursuit of hobbies or camp maintenance.

The composition of travel parties was important in the decisions
of older persons to participate in evening programs. When grandchildren were present, retirees took considerable satisfaction in
escorting them to evening programs and in sharing their excitement
with a new activity. In fact, retirees were found to devote considerable time and effort to acquainting their grandchildren with camping
and outdoor craft skills. In the absence of grandchildren, the evening
interpretation programs held less attraction for respondents, although they were frequently reviewed as a vehicle for becoming
acquainted with other campers.

Summary and Conclusions

Several conclusions about the efficacy of interpretive efforts for
retirees are suggested by this study. Although observations were
limited to three national parks in the Pacific Northwest, it is likely that
the findings have relevance for interpretive programs in other parks
as well. It was revealed that:

1. The prevalence of older persons in daytime interpretive
programs was considerable, but their numbers were regularly
underestimated by park officials.

2. Existing program efforts, while often positively evaluated by
respondents, were not fully congruent with their felt needs. Often
retirees were already familiar with the information being presented.
Also, because their visits were generally longer than those of younger
people, many older persons had exhausted the range of interpretive offerings in the local area.

3. Retirees' special needs on nature walks often went unob-
served by interpreters, and they informally expressed dissatisfaction
with this activity. The large size and rigid pace of interpretive groups
were points of particular concern.

4. An important motive for older persons participating in
interpretive programs was the opportunity for interaction with
others, especially age peers. Yet the formal, structured format of
many programs seldom provided the time or opportunity for much
interpersonal contact.

5. The content and scheduling of evening programs often precluded active participation by older persons, for several reasons.

Interpretation for the Aged

Given the numerical prominence of older persons among national park visitors, it appears that their special needs and interests should be more systematically solicited and carefully considered in planning interpretive efforts. Several suggestions follow with regard to possible directions of interpretive programming for this age group.

First, the image that park interpreters have of older visitors should be surveyed. There are many stereotypes about older persons that, if adopted by interpreters, could produce improper programming for this user group. Inservice educational programs may be required to sensitize park personnel to the characteristics, felt needs, and interpretive orientations of older visitors.

Second, consideration might be given to providing age-graded programs designed exclusively for older persons, as is now sometimes done with children. These programs could effectively speak both to the unique information needs of older visitors and could also be designed to facilitate opportunities for the desired social interaction with age peers. Age-graded programs also would remove a frequent irritant of age-integrated programs—disruptions by young children.

Third, new, in-depth interpretive presentations should be prepared for repeat visitors, who often have considerable knowledge about park history and natural ecosystems. In some cases, these presentations could be keyed to written materials that might be available on loan in the parks.

Fourth, comprehension of interpretive materials by the older population might be enhanced by more reference to aging processes and life-cycle patterns in nature (e.g., geological time, forest succession, lake eutrophication). The use of aging as a focal point for presentations would assist audience comprehension of the materials and better sensitize older visitors to the fact that life-cycle patterns are as much a part of natural ecosystems as they are of social systems and human life.

Fifth, the older visitor represents a virtually untapped resource for interpretive programming. Some persons probably have made visits to the park in its formative years, have had unusual park experiences, or have insights into park history that could be shared with newcomers. Programs could be periodically scheduled at which audiences would be encouraged to reminisce and share experiences about their earlier visits to the parks.

Sixth, some older persons have hobbies (e.g., painting and photography) that might aid others' appreciation of park phenomena. One aged respondent, for example, was found to have an extensive set of slides on local birds that had been photographed in their natural habitat. The photographer, a self-educated ornithologist, had presented numerous programs on birds to groups in his home community. Special interpretive programs or craft fairs could be held at which hobbies could be displayed. In some instances, older visitors might be encouraged to participate in special living history programs in the parks.

Finally, greater use might be made of roving rangers to meet the interpretive needs of older visitors. These rangers could partly utilize the social networks that form among retirees to gain access to this population. By deliberately seeking out retirees, interpreters not only would be able to better ascertain their special interests and needs, but also to identify the personal skills and resources that they might bring to broader and more dynamic interpretive programming in the parks.

A Sociological Look
at the Japanese Tourist
(1981)

Gary E. Machlis

Donald R. Field

Mark E. Van Every

Introduction

In the past decade, the United States has increasingly become a destination for international tourists. Technological achievements such as wide-bodied jet aircraft, improved economic equality between the world's industrial populations, and reduction of governmental travel barriers have contributed to this increase. Americans, who in the 1950s and 60s toured the world in large numbers and often controversial style, are now finding themselves hosts to people from other lands. This shift in travel patterns among the world's citizenry is not without its consequences for outdoor recreation places in the United States. Parks, forests, and historic sites once used predominantly by American citizens are now being visited by foreign tourists. These travelers add a unique element to the growing diversity of user populations. For the interpreter, they signal a new "need to know," as the successful planning and conduct of interpretive programs may now require an understanding of visitor publics widely different from traditional users.

This chapter focuses on Japanese tourists. Japan represents the third largest source of foreign visitors to the United States (after Canada and Mexico), and the U.S.A. is the most popular travel destination for the Japanese (U.S. Department of Commerce 1972). Hence, Japan represents a potentially important source of foreign visitors to U.S. parks and historic sites. Further, Japan is the only non-Western industrialized society; its cultural base is much different than other tourist-exporting nations. The purpose of this chapter is to provide information about Japanese travelers, the Japanese tourism industry, and Japanese society, and to suggest how such information can directly aid interpretive programming.

A sociological profile of visitors is a first step in such an effort, for it can outline the "natural history" and behavioral patterns of diverse publics that frequent outdoor recreation sites. Several variables seem important. Machlis et al. write:

> When visitors enter a park, they reflect certain *sociodemographic characteristics* such as age and family life cycles, and these factors may influence participation. Visitors depend upon a set of *human institutions* to help organize their recreation experiences—transportation systems, tour operators, travel agents, clubs, associations

and so forth. Finally, they rely upon *key cultural elements* to guide their individual action. Examples would include ethical systems, attitudes toward Nature, and norms for proper conduct (1981:201).

Our description of Japanese tourists is organized around these three variables: sociodemographic characteristics, human institutions, and key cultural elements.

Methods

There is no paucity of general tourism statistics. Dwyer et al. (1979) list twenty-two major U.S. organizations collecting tourism data, and this does not include many state, private, and site-specific efforts. Abundant aggregate information is available about the characteristics of tourists, destinations and origins, reasons for travel, methods of transportation, travel expenditures, and so forth. However, few studies provide specific information on interpretation-related activities.

While we could not locate specific studies dealing with Japanese tourism to U.S. parks and historic sites, several statistical reports can provide an overview of Japanese tourism to the United States. The first is *Tourism in Japan* (1979, 1981) published by the Japanese National Tourist Organization (JNTO). The second is a survey conducted by the U.S. Travel Service (1978), which reports 1977 data for 2,533 surveyed Japanese travelers. A third source is a similar study conducted by the U.S. Department of Commerce (USDC) (1972). Several works provided qualitative information on Japanese society (Reischauer 1978, Nakane 1970, Vogel 1963) and the role of leisure in Japan (Lebra 1976, Linhart 1975).

Sociodemographic Characteristics

General Visitation Patterns

Japan's rise as a major industrial power has resulted in a steady increase in the number of Japanese traveling abroad. In 1967 there were 267,538 overseas travelers; by 1979 there were over 4 million (Table 1). Tourism is a major factor, as 83.6 percent of all 1977 travelers were involved in pleasure activities (JNTO 1979).

The United States is the major destination of Japanese overseas visitors. Within the United States, Japanese vacation travelers are

Table 1. Number of Japanese traveling abroad, 1967-1979.

Year	Number of travelers	Percentage change over previous year
1967	267,538	+26.0
1968	343,542	+28.4
1969	492,880	+43.6
1970	663,467	+34.6
1971	961,135	+44.9
1972	1,392,045	+44.8
1973	2,288,966	+64.4
1974	2,335,530	+2.0
1975	2,466,326	+5.6
1976	2,852,584	+5.7
1977	3,151,431	+10.5
1978	3,525,110	+11.9
1979	4,038,298	+14.6

Source: Immigration Bureau, Ministry of Justice (JNTO 1979, 1981).

concentrated within the Pacific Rim (Guam, Hawaii, and the Far West), though a sizeable portion visit the East Coast. Table 2 shows that while 72 percent of all Japanese travelers surveyed visited U.S. islands, less than 5 percent visited the Mountain West or New England regions. Hence, it is the western national parks and eastern historical areas that are likely to have the largest numbers of Japanese visitors.

A study conducted by Japan Air Lines (cited in USDC 1972) suggests that national parks are important locales for Japanese tourists. When asked what activities they would be interested in undertaking on a trip to the mainland, visiting national parks was mentioned by 22 percent of all travelers (Table 3). Several alternatives (experience the scenery, visit historical places, visit museums, and so forth) are likely to involve interpretation as well, hence 22 percent is a conservative estimate of the proportion of Japanese visitors interested in interpretation-related activities.

Table 2. United States destinations of 1977 Japanese travelers.

U.S. destination visited	% of travelers surveyed[1] (N=1,096)
Mainland	51
New England	4
Eastern Gateway	19
George Washington Country	6
The South	6
Great Lakes Country	7
Mountain West	3
Frontier West	8
Far West	47
U.S. Islands	72
Guam	11
Hawaii	61

Source: U.S. Travel Service (1978).
[1]Percentages do not add to 100, since many travelers visited more than one destination.

Table 3. Activities Japanese travelers would be interested in undertaking on a trip to the mainland U.S.

Activities	% of travelers surveyed
Experience the scenery	44
Visit several cities	41
Visit historical places	34
See the "wild west"	32
Make purchases	31
Take a restful vacation	24
Enjoy the nightlife	22
Visit museums	22
Visit national parks	22
Gamble	21
Get to know the American people	21
Visit the Rocky Mountains	20
Spend time on beaches	18
Go skiing	9
Go to sports events	9

Source: USDC (1972).

Awareness of specific national parks is surprisingly high among Japanese international travelers, and their relative interest (the percentage of those aware of a place that are interested in visiting it) is also quite strong. Table 4 shows that while Niagara Falls and Disneyland rate highest in awareness (89 percent), Grand Canyon generates the highest relative interest (63 percent).

Demographic Characteristics

The Japanese traveler to the United States tends to be a young adult male with at least some college education. Yet, as Table 5 shows, travel to the United States is not restricted to an elite, highly educated class. Most visitors, 58 percent, are in the 18-34 age group, and the median age is 30 (U.S. Travel Service 1978). Since the Japanese often combine business and pleasure trips, reliable figures will include business travelers. In 1979, visas for pleasure accounted for about 84 percent of the visitors, while business visas encompassed about 12 percent (Bolyard 1981). Even so, 39 percent

Table 4. Awareness of and interest in specific attractions among Japanese travelers, 1972.

Attractions	Heard of	Interested in visiting	Relative interest[1]
	%	%	%
Niagara Falls	89	53	60
Disneyland	89	39	44
Statue of Liberty	86	28	33
Rocky Mountains	84	30	36
Cape Kennedy	80	25	31
Grand Canyon	70	44	63
New England	56	14	25
Yellowstone National Park	41	17	41
Banff National Park	20	11	55
Everglades National Park	16	5	31

Source: USDC (1972).
[1]Computed only among those aware of each attraction.

Table 5. Characteristics of Japanese travelers to the U.S.A.

	Percentage (N=1,096)
Sex	
Male	56
Female	44
Education	
Elementary/primary	5
High school	34
Technical/junior college	17
College/post graduate	45
Occupation	
Professional/executive	20
Clerical	27
Student	11
Sales	9
Self-employed	17
Unemployed/retired	12
Other	5

Source: U.S. Travel Service (1978).

of all 1977 travelers had less than a college education, and 50 percent were clerical workers, students, unemployed, or retired. These numbers vary greatly according to destination: a high proportion of males visit the frontier West; educational levels are higher among mainland visitors.

While 58 percent of total travelers claim to speak or read English, Reischauer (1978) suggests that fluency is much lower, due to the methods of English training used in Japanese schools. Vacation travelers claim the lowest English capability (49 percent), an important factor in interpretive planning for Japanese visitors.

Data on the kind of social units common to Japanese tourists is incomplete but suggests that the organized tour group is important. Table 6 illustrates that in 1972 and 1976 a large number of Japanese vacation travelers to the United States were involved in organized tours. In addition, over one-third of the visitors were in groups of four or more. However, the number of visitors involved in tours decreased from 1972 to 1976, while the number traveling alone or outside of tours has increased.

Human Institutions

Travel in Japan

Japan is an island country, a modern economic power, and a rapidly changing but traditional society. The Japanese are curious about other people and have a history of travel. Off-island travel began with the dramatic voyages by priests and grandees to China and Korea; they were followed by the rich and intelligentsia until the closing of borders in 1936. During World War II, wartime visits and duty tours exposed many Japanese to other cultures. Currently, the young adults of Japan are traveling in increasing numbers.

Table 6. Characteristics of trip, Japanese visitors to U.S.A., 1972 and 1976.

	% of Japanese visitors	
	1972	1976
Type of fare purchased		
First class	3	4
Regular economy/coach	22	32
Discount/excursion	18	18
Charter	3	4
Tour package	55	43
Inclusive tour travel		
Yes	71	65
No	29	35
Size of traveling party		
1 person	13	18
2 persons	39	36
3 persons	12	10
4 or more persons	35	36

Source: USDC (1972), U.S. Travel Service (1978).

Travel is becoming a status symbol in Japan for several reasons. As in most industrialized countries, manufactured goods are valued possessions in Japan. Lebra (1976) lists the "3 C's" as a consumptive goal: car, cooler (air conditioner), and color television; tourist travel competes with these other luxuries. The U.S. Department of Commerce (1972) suggests that travel has become a fourth consumptive goal for several reasons: Japanese ownership of manufactured goods is extremely high, cars are expensive relative to travel, and Japanese society provides for an extended youth before marriage. This population has time and money for touring.

Surprisingly, expenditures for travel remained fairly constant for 1975-1979 (Table 7). Only 2.3 percent of total household expenditures in 1979 were used for travel, while all leisure-related items accounted for 22.8 percent of the total.

Table 7. Average household expenditures for leisure-related items.

	1975	1976	1977	1978	1979
			Thousands of Yen[1]		
Dining out	68.1	71.1	73.8	78.8	84.9
Culture and recreation	87.4	90.8	93.2	95.4	97.6
Travel	47.1	45.9	44.8	48.4	47.9
Total household expenditures	1,895.8	1,919.0	1,935.6	1,974.4	2,028.7
Percentage of total household expenditures spent on leisure-related items	21.5	21.4	21.5	22.2	22.8

Source: JNTO (1981).
[1]Adjusted for buying power using 1975 as a base year.

Leisure in Japan

Japan is beginning to evolve work/non-work patterns common to industrialized societies: a traditional summer vacation, weekend free time, and a daily cycle managed by the industrial work clock. The five-day work week has been officially encouraged in Japan since 1973; in 1978, 44.7 percent of all firms had adopted the system (JNTO 1981). However, strong occupational differences are still present. The professional and salaryman (manager) have nonwork cycles amenable to tourism; the businessman may travel for business and recreational reasons at the same time. Leisure cycles in Japan are in a state of flux (Vogel 1963).

Tourism must fit into these evolving cycles, and the Japanese system of holidays is expected to provide more time for longer trips. Excluding weekends, the average number of annual holidays is 16.5 days (JNTO 1981). Major holidays include New Year's Day, Golden Week (which begins on the Emperor's Birthday, April 29, and ends on Constitution Day, May 3), and Vernal Equinox Day (March 20), which is evolving into a long weekend (USDC 1972).

Countering this increase in leisure is the Japanese attitude toward time spent away from work. Several authors (Vogel 1963, Lebra 1976, Linhart 1975) suggest that the Japanese worker is prevented by custom and obligation from taking days off which he or she has accrued. In 1969, 40 percent of Japanese employees used less than half of their allotted holidays with differences in this figure according to sex, age, and occupation (Linhart 1975). Only two strata in Japanese society have the full right to enjoy their leisure—youth (not part of the production process) and the elderly (retired from active work).

Further, traditional Japanese forms of leisure seem incompatible with the aggressive activity of the modern tourist. Linhart (1975) suggests that Japanese leisure is more passive than active, and that this orientation has been slow to change. Table 8 profiles 1975 leisure activities of the Japanese people. The most popular pursuits include reading books, enjoying TV and radio, and talking with family members. Significantly, travel abroad, participated in by only 2.7 percent of respondents over a long-term period, was the most desired activity mentioned (25.7 percent).

Table 8. Leisure activities of the Japanese people.

	Daily leisure time		Long-term leisure period		Leisure activities desired	
	Multiple answers					
	%[1]	Rank	%[1]	Rank	%[1]	Rank
Enjoy TV/radio	87.7	1	19.0	2	0.1	
Read newspapers	76.5	2	8.1		0.1	
Chat with family	49.6	3	7.4		1.0	
Read books	49.2	4	9.9	6	3.3	10
Mix with friends, acquaintances, or neighbors	35.1	5	6.1		1.7	
Mix with relatives	26.7	6	11.8	5	1.2	
Take a nap	24.2	7	8.0	10	1.6	
Listen to records or taped music	23.5	8	6.3		2.1	
Dine out or go shopping	22.1	9	12.5	4	1.4	
Educate children	21.2	10	2.6		1.8	
Go to a movie, watch sports	16.8		9.6	7	3.9	8
Participate in sports	13.0		9.5	8	8.8	3
Take a drive	6.9		8.6	9	1.8	
Take a day trip or day hike	10.8		17.8	3	5.7	6
Take an overnight or longer trip in Japan	10.6		43.3	1	24.6	2
Enjoy handicrafts, horticulture, or collecting stamps	19.3		5.3		3.9	8
Engage in artistic activities	12.3		4.2		5.2	7
Study to acquire qualifications or techniques	6.8		1.9		8.7	4
Learn to perform tea ceremony/ flower arrangements, cook, or sew	8.5		1.9		8.2	5
Travel abroad	0.6		2.7		25.7	1

[1]N=1,052

Source: A survey conducted by the Better Living Information Center 1975, cited in JNTO (1979).

Yet a description of Japanese leisure activities by Reischauer provides a different picture:

> Japan is a land of mass spectator sports and mass activities . . . Ski slopes are hazardously crowded in winter. The Shonan beaches near Tokyo will attract over a million persons on a hot summer weekend. An endless antlike chain of people on the slopes of Mt. Fuji turn mountain climbing in summer into a mass sport. Sightseeing crowds, mostly organized groups of school children and village and town associations, inundate famous beauty spots in the spring and autumn sightseeing seasons and all but obliterate them from view or even existence (1978:202).

Hence, Japanese attitudes toward vacations, tourism, outdoor recreation and travel abroad seem somewhat unclear.

The Tourist Industry in Japan

The tourist industry in Japan is highly dynamic, expanding rapidly, and developing a tie to Japan's basic economic structure (USDC 1972). Japanese attachment and dependency upon employers is widely acknowledged; what company one works for is more basic to one's identification than what one does (Lebra 1976). Vogel notes:

> In Japan, the basic mode of integration into the economic order is not through occupational specialty, but through the firm (1963:264).

The Japanese worker is likely to travel in groups either organized by his or her firm or in groups of similar workers. This close relationship of work and play has resulted in the centralization of the Japanese tourist industry. Most big industrial firms have their own travel agencies, and in 1972 six major producers accounted for 50 percent of wholesale travel activity (USDC 1972).

There are at least four major kinds of managed tours in Japan, excluding independent travel arranged by a travel agent. *Package tours* are fully managed tours, where all arrangements and many activities are organized by the agent. The group size is often quite large (as high as 300 persons). The proportion of Japanese travelers using package tours varies by destination; it is high for Guam (79.9 percent) and Hawaii (53.8 percent), while lower for the U.S.

mainland. For young travelers, package tours provide low bulk fares; for older tourists there is the security of a preplanned trip.

Affinity groups are tours organized by firms, industries, and cooperatives, where members either know each other or have an occupational relationship. For example, the Association of Agricultural Cooperatives has its own travel agency, with an annual production of 10,000 tour passengers (USDC 1972). Farmers participate in tours of special agricultural interest, visiting attractions such as the produce terminal in San Francisco or the Farmer's Market in Seattle and Los Angeles. Affinity groups vary in size.

Special study tours are a kind of affinity group, but with an even more occupational oriented framework. These tours are intense programs of travel, geared to learning new methods, viewing industrial sites, and conducting trade interviews. These groups usually have between ten and forty people. There is some resistance to these trips in the United States. USDC (1972) reports that Japanese travel agents report a growing reluctance among U.S. manufacturers to receive such tour groups for plant visits.

Incentive travel tours are benefits provided by employers to workers, either through outright grant, low-cost loan, or company-managed saving program. Workers have a wide variety of choices, and travel agencies may include these tourists in their package tours. Group size varies but is usually over forty-five, in order to take advantage of bulk air fares.

Key Cultural Elements

Japanese tourists bring a variety of social norms with them on trips to the United States. These norms, derived in part from key elements of Japanese culture, can serve as guides to Japanese tourist behavior. However, such norms are surely not ironclad. Reischauer notes:

> Though a homogeneous people culturally, the roughly 115 million Japanese display great variation of attitudes and ways of life by age group and according to their diverse roles in society. A teenager and an octogenarian, a day laborer and a corporation executive, a bank clerk and an artist show about as much diversity in attitudes as their

counterparts would in any Western country. Almost anything that might be said about Japanese in general would not be true of many and might be flatly contradicted by some (1978:124).

Four elements are discussed: belongingness, empathy, dependency, and occupying the proper place (Lebra 1976).

Belongingness

Japan is a social society. What would strictly be a private matter in an individualistic culture tends to be a group enterprise in Japan. We have mentioned that the Japanese white collar worker's recreation is often organized by his or her employer (Linhart 1975). The Japanese individual feels more comfortable in a group than alone, and it is not surprising that Japanese tourists prefer group tours to individualized travel (USDC 1972).

This sense of belongingness begins well before an expected trip or vacation. Travel begins with a "separation party," where friends and relatives wish the tourist well and offer gifts. An obligation to return the gifts is accepted, and Japanese tourists often spend considerable vacation time making these purchases. Table 9 shows that 21 percent of tour travelers' expenditures are for purchases; the number is lower (13 percent) for individual travelers.

Table 9. Distribution of expenditures by Japanese travelers, as percentages of all expenditures, 1972.

	Tour travelers		Individual travelers	
	Pacific area	Intercontinental	Pacific area	Intercontinental
Tour price/primary transportation	53	61	39	52
Local transportation	2	4	5	6
Lodging[1]	1	2	14	12
Food/drink	2	5	10	10
Purchases	32	21	21	13
Miscellaneous/sightseeing	9	7	11	7

Source: USDC (1972).
[1]Outside the framework of the tour.

Empathy

Empathy rates high among Japanese virtues. In a group-oriented culture such as Japan, decision making often requires consensus, and confrontation tends to be avoided. Nonverbal communication is highly valued and widely practiced and, in such a homogeneous country, applicable to many social situations. Reischauer describes the general process:

> Varying positions are not sharply outlined and their differences analyzed and clarified. Instead, each participant in a discussion feels his way cautiously, only unfolding his own views as he sees how others react to them. Much is suggested by indirection or vague implication. Thus, any sharp conflict of views is avoided before it comes into the open. The Japanese even have a word, *haragei*, "the art of the belly," for this meeting of minds, or at least the viscera, without clear verbal interaction (1978:148).

Conversations are punctuated with agreements and gestures of approval; to the Japanese, an American host may seem not to be listening because of his or her silence while a Japanese guest is speaking.

Dependency

Much has been written about the dependency of Japanese children upon their mothers, and the impact of this relationship on Japanese society (Vogel 1963, Lebra 1976). Other dependent relations exist; the employer-employee relationship is likewise based on dependency and service. This conflicts with American ideas of autonomy and individual equality. Many Japanese tourists to the United States are often put off by the self-service operations of American tourist sites; others find freedom with their lack of involvement in dependency relations.

Occupying the Proper Place

The Japanese are sensitive to rank order (i.e., "occupying the proper place"). Japanese language, social customs and values are all organized to illustrate the rank order of interacting individuals. When Japanese tourists visit countries with egalitarian ideologies (like the United States), the host/guest relationship may be influenced by this limitation. Lebra writes:

The cultural dearth of ways to express horizontal or status-neutral relationships forces the actor to make a binary choice between respectful, formal behavior and disrespectful, informal behavior (1976:53).

Japanese tourists may express "disdain" toward "backward" peoples, including Asian neighbors. Lebra (1976) makes note of the rude behavior exhibited by Japanese tourists in Southeast Asia. For tourists in the national parks, slight gradations in occupation may signal rank order, and it is a common custom of Japanese tourists to address a host by his occupation (Mr. Park Ranger, Ms. Travel Agent, etc.).

Applying the Information to Interpretation

How can such information aid interpretive efforts? We would suggest that better understanding of Japanese tourists would be useful in 1) visitor management, 2) information services, 3) the planning of interpretive programs, and 4) the conduct of interpretive programs.

Visitor Management

Visitor management can be crucial to effective interpretation. The high percentage of Japanese tourists who travel in tour groups (Table 6) represents an obvious opportunity; the cooperation of tour organizers can help dispense visitors to less crowded areas, can help promote safety, and can allow park interpretive staff to plan ahead. The centralization of the tourist industry in Japan suggests that contact with major wholesalers might allow the forecasting of future trends in Japanese visitation. Another suggestion would be to develop a "travel wholesaler's planning guide" to popular parks and historic areas. Such a guide could aid in development of the travel itineraries, bookings, and brochures used in Japan and could further coordinate the flow of tour groups and interpretive programming.

The data on travel expenditures (Table 9) suggest that "trophy-taking" (buying postcards, souvenir shopping, and so forth) are major components of the Japanese tourist's park experience. Hence, concessionaires and historical associations may need to be included in planning for Japanese visitors.

Information Services

The fact that the Japanese tourist is unlikely to be fluent in English, or to have had much experience in U.S. national parks, makes the provision of basic information extremely important. All visitors require information concerning shelter, food, medical attention, regulations, and so forth. To serve the Japanese tourist, several alternatives exist: the necessary information can be translated into Japanese, presented in English with ideograms, or a translator can be made available. Parks with growing Japanese visitation should have access to a translator, in case of emergency.

For more detailed information (such as the natural history of an area), arrangements can be made with nearby universities and language institutes to translate key publications. These translations can be handed out along with English versions of park guides and materials. An often overlooked approach is to purchase a small quantity of relevant Japanese reading materials from overseas publishers. In any event, many Japanese *are* fluent in English, and often tour group leaders can aid interpreters in communication.

The high awareness and relative interest in national parks shown by Japanese tourists reflects the use of parks as attractions in tourism advertising. Travel posters extolling the pleasures of an American vacation often include pictures of Grand Canyon, New York Gateway, Niagara Falls, and so forth. It is unclear, however, what information is actually communicated to potential visitors. Efforts to provide Japanese tourist organizations (such as JNTO) with up-to-date, accurate, and relevant information could result in increased visitation, greater cooperation by tour groups, and higher satisfaction of tourists' expectations.

Planning Interpretive Programs

Our profile of Japanese tourists presents several problems to the interpreter interested in "connecting" with foreign visitors. First, Table 8 suggests a passive orientation to Japanese leisure, and interpretation-related activities (such as visiting an art museum or zoo) rate somewhat low. However, Reischauer's description of Japanese outdoor recreation, and the high participation in day trips and hikes (17.8 percent over a long-term period), indicates an active, outdoor-oriented leisure. Wise interpretive planning might include both active and passive exhibits, opportunities for both quiet contemplation and participation in group activities.

A second problem is the combination of high education (Table 5), and a strong language barrier. Merely simplifying introductory material is often not appropriate. Translations of introductory material may be inadequate for Japanese tourists interested in natural or social history. A clear solution, whenever possible, would be to supply tour groups with material before an interpretive program, and to use the tour leader (often fluent in English) as an interpreter.

We have described several kinds of Japanese tour groups and suggested that participants often have an employer, occupation, or interest in common. Knowing ahead of time the kind of tour group to visit a site can be of great benefit to the interpreter, and he or she may use this information in choosing a subject, selecting a medium, and organizing a program. The difficulty lies in developing a link with the wholesale travel agents, and in the fact that 35 percent of Japanese tourists to the U.S. in 1976 did not prepurchase tour activities (Table 7).

Conducting Interpretive Programs

The conduct of interpretive programs for Japanese tourists may require special forethought. Japanese tour groups of fifty or more people are common, and such large audiences may be unworkable for programs that demand quiet, have limited staff, or are held in small spaces. Yet, other kinds of programs (campfires, movies, self-guided trailwalks) are amenable to bigger groups and should be satisfactory. Analyses by Reischauer (1978) and Lebra (1976) suggest that Japanese are generally group-oriented and have much experience in group activities. It may be more difficult to engage tour group participants in individual involvement, such as handling an antique reproduction, expressing an opinion on park facilities, or deviating from the group itinerary.

Besides a group orientation, several key elements of Japanese culture are of importance to the interpreter. Japanese manners consider quick individual decision making impolite, and the interpreter who is dependent upon immediate audience feedback may be disappointed. A traditional respect for rank may be misunderstood as insincere deference to uniformed personnel. The obligation of the traveler to return to Japan with gifts obviously requires large amounts of time spent shopping, rather than attending interpretive programs. Most importantly, almost all available data point to the high motivation of Japanese travelers for learning about other environments and cultures. Table 3 showed that 44 percent of Japanese travelers are interested in "experiencing the scenery"; Table 4 illustrated the high relative interest in visiting national parks; Table 8 showed the general Japanese interest in travel abroad. Hence, Japanese visitors to national parks may be quite eager to benefit from interpretation.

Conclusion

This chapter has taken a sociological look at Japanese tourists and has tried to outline the sociodemographic characteristics, human institutions, and key cultural elements that help shape their participation at interpretation-related recreation sites. Elsewhere we have written:

> Simple as it may sound, the matching of an interpretive approach with the appropriate audience is perhaps the most difficult challenge facing those responsible for the array of public contact programs now offered by the National Park Service and equivalent preserves (Machlis and Field 1974:19).

As the number of foreign visitors to parks increases, this job becomes more difficult and challenging. Interpretation for foreign visitors has a special urgency: it offers an opportunity for crosscultural and world understanding.

Cruise Ship Travelers to Alaska
(1981)

Barbara A. Koth

Donald R. Field

Roger N. Clark

Introduction

Cruise ships emerged as a major form of recreation travel in Southeast Alaska in the 1950s, but their popularity soared in the 1970s. In 1979, 70,000 passengers visited Alaska via this mode of travel to national park and forest lands bordering aquatic resource systems. The purpose of this article is to describe this leisure experience and to identify interpretive alternatives appropriate to each phase of the social event. It is not our purpose to introduce new or novel interpretive techniques, and some of the methods discussed actually are in current use on Alaskan cruise ships. Instead, this chapter suggests that the interpretive audience can be reached more effectively by coordinating and matching message content and method with trip phase.

The cruise ship as a leisure setting offers unique opportunities for interpreters to interact with a recreational public over an extended period of time, rather than during a single event. The long-term nature of this leisure experience allows presentation of interpretive material in phases appropriate to the level of interest and accumulated knowledge of passengers. A "building block" approach is possible, where material delivered to the audience at later stages is contingent upon earlier presentations and knowledge achieved by the message recipients. Details are added to the background initially provided. At the conclusion of such a trip, passengers would possess a complete set of information.

Additionally, the cruise ship offers opportunities for using a variety of techniques and topics to effectively deliver the interpretive message. Travel to Southeast Alaska has the potential for integrating the five types of tourism outlined by Smith (1977). *Ethnic, cultural,* and *historic* tourism, respectively, focus attention on Tlingit and Haida native lifestyle as a function of occupation and transportation networks, on past Russian influence, and on native/white interaction. While the *environment* (scenery and wildlife) provides a backdrop for observing these human factors, *recreational* tourism is the lure onboard, as passengers participate in various play activities and scheduled entertainment events. Whereas the majority of other vacation locations can be defined by fewer factors, in this cruise ship situation all five elements provide the impetus for travel; this calls for unusually diverse interpretive programs.

Background

The cruise ship industry in Southeast Alaska is very regular in terms of visitation. Six companies and nine ships operated during the 1979 season, and round-trip visits ranging from 7 to 14 days in duration departed from Los Angeles, San Francisco, and Vancouver, B.C. The majority of ships visit the southeastern locales in the following sequence: Ketchikan, Juneau, Skagway, Glacier Bay, and Sitka. One-way travel on the ships can occur as passengers connect at transfer points (Skagway, Juneau) with commercial tours to the Interior and Yukon. After completing these itineraries travelers can return home via aircraft, coach, or cruise ship.

At present, numerous onboard events are scheduled with emphasis on entertainment. The use of educational material varies dramatically from ship to ship, ranging from a proliferation of movies, slide programs, public address systems, and personal talks to a complete lack of any interpretive offerings. At Glacier Bay National Monument, National Park Service rangers come aboard for the day to describe the glacial environment.

Methodology

Webb et al. (1966) argue for use of supplemental research methods (e.g., participant observation and other unobtrusive measures) in addition to reliance on the traditionally employed questionnaire. By joint use of survey and observation methods, it is possible to minimize biases and define areas of consensus in the findings from each method. Observation provides firsthand information on the interrelationships between activities, participants, and meanings within a leisure setting.

During the summer of 1979, researchers sailed on three roundtrip, seven-day cruises and made informal observations to determine the nature of social interaction during the cruise. Impressions gathered through those informal observations form the basis of this chapter. Observers focused on the combination of spatial, temporal, and behavioral variables and their relationship to information flow.

Spatial elements were identified by mapping the dominant use of facility areas by passengers. Temporal variations in activity patterns by time of day and length of cruise were recorded, and behavior and the development of social networks were noted as they influenced informal information transfer. A field journal, informal interviews, and directed conversation formed the basis for subsequent analysis. Federal personnel associated with provision of interpretive services, cruise directors, crew members, and travel agents were utilized as informants to crossreference observed patterns.

Phases of Cruise Experience

The cruise ship experience is here categorized into five phases based on observations of travelers' activity patterns, relationship to the Alaska environment, and social contacts during the trip. The development of the cruise as a social event includes several stages: 1) planning and anticipation of the trip and travel to departure port, 2) embarkation, 3) early sailing northbound, 4) visiting ports and Glacier Bay, and 5) traveling toward home port. This phasing is similar to the stages of a recreational experience defined by Clawson and Knetsch (1966): anticipation of event, travel to the site, the on-site experience, travel from the recreational setting, and recollection. Our analytical phases for cruise ship travel to Alaska and their relationship to the Clawson and Knetsch's typology are presented in Table 1.

Planning, Anticipation, and Travel to Departure Port

The planning and anticipation phase includes pretrip activities from preliminary information gathering to packing and leaving home. The time lag between confirmation of reservations and departure may exceed one year for some individuals. Steamship companies provide introductory information regarding shipboard matters, payment, embarkation location, and itinerary material during this period.

Passengers can take a variety of modes of transportation for travel to the departure port. "Block booking," where travel companies reserve a block of accommodations for many clients departing from the same geographical region, is common. Travel agents book passengers on the cruise ship who have not met previously but share

Table 1. Comparison of phases of recreation experience.

Alaska cruise ship	Clawson and Knetsch
Planning and anticipation of trip and travel to departure	Anticipation of event Travel to the site
Embarkation Early sailing northbound Visiting ports and Glacier Bay	On-site experience
Traveling toward home port	Travel from the site
Recollection at home	Recollection

similar itineraries on chartered flights or buses to the port of embarkation. Upon arrival, check-in procedures at the pier complex require standing in line and waiting in public areas prior to boarding.

Embarkation

Upon embarkation there is an extravagant welcome by ship officers, a proliferation of complimentary drinks, much picture taking, and incessant attention from employees. During boarding, passengers begin to learn the informal rules by which shipboard behavior is governed, and one of these norms allows for unlimited passenger communication. This is achieved in part by creation of an atmosphere of luxury where details of ship arrangements are handled by company personnel and the passenger is free to meet new acquaintances. Travelers perceive commonalities with others onboard due to this treatment, and communication channels remain open throughout the duration of the cruise.

Early Sailing Northbound

The early sailing northbound is characterized by a familiarization process, including discovery of ship facilities, introduction to traveling companions, and a desire for information providing an overview of natural and cultural aspects of the trip. The ship is passing along the largely undeveloped coastline of British Columbia, and observation of scenery and sighting of marine mammals are popular activities during this phase. Reinforcement of group social bonds is primarily facilitated by the scheduled events taking place daily. Activities on the first portion of the cruise are of an introductory nature, familiarizing passengers with each other, the crew, and ship facilities. These include a Welcome Aboard/Get Together Party, the Captain's Dinner, a singles' party, lessons for the games played in the casino, and various team games of a humorous nature. Ongoing entertainment events are numerous and include, for example, nightly dancing and music, costume contests and games, and instructional classes. These offerings vary from ship to ship, but there is a constant variety of simultaneous offerings.

Visiting Ports

Upon reaching Alaskan waters, the schedule changes to alternate onboard and shore activities as port visitation occurs. Several hours are spent in the port of call, with the majority of passengers taking a short bus tour providing an overview of local culture, history, and environment. While shore time is limited, it is possible for passengers to participate in other self-initiated activities (e.g., shopping, walking tour) in the remaining time allotted. After reboarding, passengers participate in scheduled evening events. All travel, with the exception of cruising in Glacier Bay, is within Tongass National Forest. At Glacier Bay, National Park Service naturalists provide reading material, present a formal program outlining the park's natural and cultural history, and identify locations of interest over the public address system. No stops are made during this segment of the trip.

From our observations, it seems that intensity of interest in attractions in ports decreases after visitation to the initial ports, and little interaction with residents is noted during shore time. Utilization of outdoor deck space when traveling between ports is infrequent as compared with prior phases of the trip. Glacier Bay represents the high point of the itinerary for round-trip passengers and is the sole location during this phase where an interest in scenery is observed. However, one-way passengers board during port visitation, so behaviors specific to embarkation and early trip phases are superimposed upon the predominant pattern.

Traveling Toward Home Port

While traveling to the home port, no stops are made en route. Numerous shipboard events are scheduled, including those which highlight trip activities and travels. Observation of scenery and wildlife sighting cease to be important daily events during the later stages of the trip, as do all factors associated with the outside environment. Having seen a sampling of locations and events which represent Alaska, focus shifts to entertainment and social events. Upon disembarking many passengers interact with their families and oncoming passengers.

Interpretation Alternatives

Planning and Anticipation and Travel to Departure Port

Pretrip expectations often shape the nature of tourists' impressions and post-trip satisfaction. For many passengers the cruise to Alaska represents fulfillment of a long-term desire, and interpretive possibilities abound to fill the "at home" informational gap when anticipation is high. Since many ships are booked to capacity one season in advance, the time between reservations and departure is substantial. Material presented at this phase facilitates planning for port and shipboard activities.

At this stage, passengers' communication is limited solely to correspondence with the company with which the cruise is booked, with traveling companions, and perhaps with prior visitors. Information provided during the anticipation phase could serve as a basis for entry into discussions upon boarding and help avoid future discontinuities and lowered satisfaction levels by creating realistic expectations.

Prior to embarkation, passengers might receive with ticket mailings pertinent weather and clothing information and addresses to write for additional information of interest (e.g., federal agencies and park units, chambers of commerce). Familiarity gained by reading relevant material appears to be a major source of satisfaction, and the provision of a bibliography could direct passengers to appropriate library sources.

Providing a pocket diary for keeping a social record of names and cabin numbers of new friends would aid in group formation. The diary also might be a means of dispersing relevant information, such as brief descriptions of major animal species that might be seen en route. The species described in each diary could vary, so that information exchanges would be encouraged. The social record could be provided at one of two key phases in the trip—trip planning or embarkation. Name tags and identification buttons for passengers (as provided by some tour companies) would allow for instant recognition while traveling.

Embarkation

During embarkation passengers focus on the ship and port of embarkation. Since this phase occurs rapidly and alternative activities are rigidly constrained by company procedures, informal self-initiated interpretation must prevail. Travelers might receive a looseleaf notebook which could serve to organize materials gathered during the trip, such as the social record, pamphlets, publications, and maps assembled by the passengers. The notebook would serve to direct information gathering, and upon completion it would contain a record of trip activities and participants.

Many sites at the pier complex are conducive to initial or continuing exchange of information among passengers, including waiting rooms, lobbies, agent offices, outdoor areas with views of the various ships, and check-in boarding lines. Miniexhibits and posters highlighting anticipated sites and events are possible at such places.

Early Sailing Northbound

While traveling north to Alaska, scenery, wildlife, shipboard events and all factors associated with the trip experience are of importance. These elements provide an overwhelming variety of stimuli, which passengers sample to become familiar with the new environment. Enthusiasm is high, the quest for information constant. However, as the passengers travel *through* the areas of interest, they actually experience little of the outside environment. Clark and Lucas (1978) compare this encapsulated travel to an "isolation booth" experience.

Passengers' intense interest in fishing boats, shipping traffic, and residents' relationship with the environment is an attempt to experience the authentic Alaskan environment. A trip log that includes a sequential map of the travel plan keyed to a periodically updated central map would serve this goal. The trip log could serve to pinpoint the position of the ship, which is of constant interest to passengers, and to identify settlements and waterways. The trip log also could include historical and cultural information, details of settlement patterns, and factual information regarding the major industries—forestry, fishing, and mining. Incorporating wildlife checklists, marine mammal surveys, and eagle counts would allow the "collection" aspects of the trip to be fulfilled.

An orientation movie and/or program on Alaska that provides an overview of the trip experience, anticipated stops, and wildlife should occur early in the cruise when passenger interest is highest. The amount of material presented at this time can be substantial; its range should be broad and include a great variety of topics.

Visiting Ports

During the several days of visitation to various ports of call and Glacier Bay, passengers' attention swings back and forth from information on ports to the social events onboard ship. After several days of traveling, the settlements passed, shipping and fishing fleet activity, and scenery cease to be novel, and little interest in them is noted for the majority of passengers.

In conjunction with land managers, the cruise ship company could develop a series of posters drawing attention to features on the trip; these could be rotated as the trip progresses. The ship's newspaper could be planned to highlight key elements of the trip. Bulletin boards prominently displayed could allow for information exchange among passengers and discussion of trip details. "Cruise cards" describing Alaskan scenery, wildlife, and history could be placed at the center of each table at evening meals, along with other information. The cards could be collected by travelers, especially if prepunched for insertion in their trip record notebook.

Because vicarious experiences with the resource are important for some, a key location for consolidating and verifying information is necessary. The ship's library could be stocked with relevant reading material on Alaska, including brochures and interpretive material on the Alaskan Interior that would be of interest to one-way passengers connecting with tours to these locations. Use of the trip log may prolong passenger interest in the ship's travel corridor by increasing the amount of information available. The pattern of decreasing interest observed currently occurs where no interpretive efforts are made; this pattern may change with provision of comprehensive interpretive programs.

More formal approaches at this phase include periodic updates given over the public address system regarding wildlife sightings and ship position. This and any other information, regardless of source, was promptly relayed to uninformed individuals, researchers observed. A similar phenomenon might be evident if prepared audio programs were broadcast over the ship's radio channels, so that passengers could listen in their cabins if they chose. Automated slide programs also could be set up in a central lounge.

Some passengers indicated they were unaware of activity alternatives in the ports of call. This gap could be filled by formal presentations or an informal question-and-answer meeting prior to each visitation. Such programs should be given by knowledgeable staff members or agency interpretive personnel. If a complete cruise with a single passenger group is not possible, interpreters could be present on one segment of the trip for each ship. After the manner of Alaska Marine Highway programming, each trip leg also could be theme-related. Travel up Lynn Canal to Skagway could focus on gold rush history and the Chilkoot Trail, while cruising to Sitka could highlight Russian-American history in the area. At present, onboard interpretation does not focus on the unique character and diversity of each location.

Successful employment of matching techniques in part depends on recognition and use of informal group processes that diffuse the interpretive message beyond those initially exposed to the material. A message is not received by an individual in isolation from social memberships: rather a person performs in a role appropriate to one's position in the participating group. In a leisure setting where an interpretive program is presented to groups, some persons may discuss topics for other group members, provide links between groups through information exchange, or transfer information to nonattenders during informal conversation. Attendance at structured programs may not accurately reflect the true impact of the information provided; secondary effects can be encouraged by development of unstructured interpretive aids peripheral to the core program.

Traveling Toward Home Port

Travel to Alaska includes both an informational and social component. Information-gathering behavior is evident in the earlier stages of the cruise; certain attractions and species sightings are viewed as compulsory. Upon accomplishment of this "task," however, social goals predominate.

On the cruise home, the natural environment merely provides a backdrop for shipboard social events. Alaska is recounted in conversation and programs which serve as the recollection phase of the trip. Interpretation at this stage should thus focus on techniques which consolidate the information obtained and review the places visited. Booklets relating various Alaskan themes can fulfill the "take-home" phase of cruising. This provides an opportunity to collate the information received and makes it more easily recalled with the passage of time. In a study of tourism in Amish communities in Pennsylvania, Buck (1978) noted that reading publications subsequent to visitation reinforced the event and allowed for vicarious enjoyment.

Various interpretive themes have been proposed throughout this article. In summary, the following topics are suggested: industries, lifestyle, navigation aids, history, transportation networks, weather, tides, marine shorelife, whale migration, salmon spawning, native culture, U.S. Forest Service and National Park Service management, geology, flora, pipeline construction, and glacial geology.

Additionally, passengers returning from travels to the Interior and Far North could be encouraged to share their experience with passengers who did not visit these sites. The post-trip recollection

Table 2. Description of cruise ship environment and interpretive options at each phase.

Phases of trip	Relationship to Alaska environment	Social networks formed	Level of interest	Message content	Alternative methods
Anticipation, planning, and travel to departure port	Create images of Alaska, preparation for trip	Cruise ship companies & traveling companies	Builds toward departure; overview	Clothes, weather, bibliography, addresses	Pamphlets, guides, books
Embarkation	Shipboard environment	Initial group introductions	High; introductory	Shipboard facilities and events	Social record, mini-exhibits, posters
Early trip	All trip elements are stimuli	Group formation	High; introductory	Scenery, location, and wildlife	Trip log, maps, orientation movie/program, trip record folder
Ports/Glacier Bay	Alternating port/shipboard focus	Communication established among new friends	Moderate; focused	Community/Glacier Bay	Ship newspaper, cruise cards, library, P.A. system, audio programs, movies, agency interpreters
Traveling toward home port	Social events	Friendships stabilized	Low, synthesis	Recollection & consolidation	Booklets and pamphlets, other passengers

phase at home would be furthered by later viewing of the trip record collections, and could be shared both among participants and with relatives and friends. The ability to easily recall highlights of the trip experience by accumulated material may increase the retention period and prolong overall satisfaction. Table 2 consolidates our description of the cruise environment and summarizes the level, message content, and method for interpretive alternatives.

Summary

Different interpretive options arise throughout the cruise ship experience, and this chapter has examined opportunities for matching different social phases and activities with appropriate interpretational material. Existing information networks involving the travel industry, resource agencies, and cruise participants all can be used as instruments for knowledge gathering and exchange. On a cruise ship the passengers are together for a relatively long period of time, and social networks and information channels become comparatively stabilized. This process is not unique to cruise ship travelers, however. There are other clientele populations which would exhibit similar behavior patterns. Organized group tours and extended hikes are two examples where potential development of social structure might occur. The self-contained nature of the cruise ship allows for progressive disclosure of interpretive material that builds upon previous presentations, and programs geared to this philosophy may also be appropriate for long-term repeat visitors to a recreation site.

Trip phasing occurs for all leisure activities. By coordinating interpretive efforts for a site or activity, material could be designed for use during a specific phase in the recreation process (e.g., pamphlets distributed to aid vacation planning), or for use during several phases. Current interpretive efforts focused primarily on the on-site experience need to be reexamined in light of the stages involved in a recreation experience. Preparatory information will assist potential visitors in selecting a site consistent with their desired experience, while material provided after site visitation may promote a continuing dialogue between recreationists and managers and provide feedback and evaluation.

The amount of information available changes behavior at recreational settings. On a cruise ship, passengers utilize fellow travelers as information sources in the absence of interpretation. By continued analysis of observed activity patterns, interpretive offerings can be matched to current behaviors, and periodic updates and modifications can make this program sensitive to both short-term and long-range management goals.

Monster Time and Other Ethnographic Insights at Wupatki National Monument

(1989)

Robert T. Trotter, II

Introduction

Humans carry their cultural values everywhere they go, and act out of those values, whatever they do. This makes it useful to know the diversity of beliefs and values people bring to a subject when designing an interpretation program. National parks, museums, and all other cultural events are venues where interpretation specialists must accommodate their messages to a wide variety of beliefs and behaviors in order to get information across to the public. Ethnography has been widely used as a research method in the social sciences and is becoming an increasingly important mechanism to assist interpretation programs. James Spradley provides a cogent definition of ethnography:

> Ethnography. . . is a systematic attempt to discover the knowledge a group of people have learned and are using to organize their behavior (Spradley and McCurdy 1972:9).

This chapter presents a case study of the ways in which ethnographic research can be used to improve cultural and prehistoric interpretation. The author and his students were invited to do an ethnography of visitor behavior at Wupatki National Monument near Flagstaff, Arizona, in order to improve the interpretation at the park[1]. When the findings from that research were shared with interpretation specialists around the country, we discovered that much of our specific data can be generalized to other parks, to

---

1. The basis for this chapter is a field school conducted during the summer of 1989 at Wupatki National Monument as one element in an existing cooperative agreement between the Monument and the Anthropology Department at Northern Arizona University. The project was funded by a grant from the U.S. Department of Education and included a companion archaeological field school at Wupatki Ruin. In addition to the research questions being answered by the field schools, the two field schools were designed to provide research training to undergraduate minority students, to encourage those students to seek graduate careers. Both field schools lasted seven weeks. Six students received ethnographic field training. Their instruction included direct observation and recording of visitor behavior, interviewing techniques, computer-based field note development and management, ethnographic analysis, and the presentation of ethnographic data. Their research education was directed by the author and supported by two anthropology graduate assistants, Ms. Duffie C. Westheimer and Ms. Lisa M. Leap. The students were asked to address

museums, and to other organizations that interpret human prehistory and other aspects of human culture to visitors from many different backgrounds.

The chapter is organized as follows. First, the research methods employed in the study are briefly described, along with a brief background on the Monument. Next, a general profile of visitors to Wupatki is presented. Since a significant portion are international visitors, a detailed profile of one group is included, to demonstrate the understanding that can be gained through the ethnographic approach. Next, visitor behavior is described, focusing upon the gender roles, family dynamics, and vandalism found at the site. Visitor needs and expectations are then explored, and the chapter ends with the implications of these results for interpretation.

Research Methods

Our ethnographic research design was directed at understanding the behavior of visitors in and around the visitor center at Wupatki Ruin and at two other outlying archaeological sites which are easily accessible to visitors. Decisions on where to concentrate our research and the kinds of information to collect were guided by two initial steps in the research process.

First, the author conducted two focus group sessions with park management and personnel, to determine the most pressing information needs that could be met using an ethnographic research approach. The Park Service personnel decided that their greatest needs were in the areas of interpretation and the control of behavior deleterious to the park resources. They requested that the research effort determine how long people stay at the ruins, where they go, what interests them, what types of interpretation work well, and

---

the general interests of Park Service personnel while selecting their research topics. The focused topics that they chose were visitor interest and beliefs about the monument (Cha 1989), the interaction between Park Service and visitor beliefs about boundaries and permissible behavior (Hopkins 1989), family dynamics at the park (Winkfield 1989), visitor center information services and employee interaction with visitors (Brown 1989), German tourists at an archaeological park (Orozco 1989), and behavior at outlying sites (Valero 1989).

how visitors generally behave. They decided that they would most like to know the answers to two questions. What do people really want to know about the ruins? Why do people vandalize the ruins?

Second, a two-week period of general observations was undertaken. This exploratory research phase allowed us to discover and monitor the most common patterns of visitor behavior. The ethnographers periodically timed visitors, unobtrusively followed their movements through the ruin, listened to public conversations, and asked a few preliminary questions. From these observations we devised questions to ask the visitors to gain more in-depth information about their experiences in the park. We pooled and discussed our findings, to provide everyone with the broadest view of visitor behavior at the park. From this preliminary work, we selected individual topics for additional observations and ethnographic interviewing. The next four weeks were spent completing these specific research assignments. At the end of the research project, team members presented their findings to Park Service personnel and provided written reports for further reference.

Background on Wupatki National Monument

Wupatki National Monument receives approximately one quarter million visitors each year. The heaviest visitation is during the summer and on holidays during other seasons. The park maintains a steady, but reduced, flow of visitors at all other times. Wupatki is known for its rich archaeological resources, which include 2,668 sites with historic significance within a 53-square-mile boundary. It is administratively and ecologically tied to nearby Sunset Crater National Monument.

Wupatki is designated, by park personnel, as an "on-the-way-to" park. While it is a destination park for local residents, a significant portion of its visitors are either on the way to or are coming back from the Grand Canyon or other parks in the southwestern United States. Some visitors are on a grand tour of archaeological monuments in the southwestern United States, with Wupatki being wedged among better known archaeological parks such as Canyon de Chelly or Mesa Verde.

Wupatki is not easily accessible. Visitors must enter at the South Entrance, pass by Sunset Crater National Monument, and drive an additional 18 miles into the desert to Wupatki. Or, they must come in the North Entrance and drive an approximately equal distance to reach the visitor center from that direction. The total loop is about 36 miles and tends to discourage the more casual type of visitors. In fact, every day we observed potential visitors turning around and leaving the park, after having driven 15 miles and being within a mile of the first ruin in the park. It takes about 45 minutes to simply drive through the Wupatki boundaries, without stopping at any of the available sites, so visitors feel they have spent a great deal of time in the park, even when they don't get out of their car.

General Findings on Wupatki Visitors

The student ethnographers found that Wupatki visitors are well educated and are commonly more interested in archaeological history than the general population. Therefore, the overall profile of visitors to the park differs from that of visitors to parks that are more easily accessible, and parks that are primary destination parks, such as the Grand Canyon.

Wupatki visitors are predominantly middle-class Anglo-Americans. This was first determined by direct observation of key social markers, such as dress, material items (cars, camera equipment, etc.), and speech patterns, and later confirmed by direct questions about background, employment, and educational status during interviews. The second largest contingent at Wupatki is of foreign visitors from Europe and Asia. The most common are those from Germany, Austria, and Switzerland. Numbers of French-speaking tourists also visit the park, as well as a sprinkling of people from Japan. One of the smallest contingents is of visitors from various minority groups in the United States. The students observed Black, Native American, and Hispanic visitors but they are the exception. This trend had been noticed by park personnel and was of concern to them. One of the questions we had hoped to address was why the number of Native American and Hispanic visitors is so low, but the small numbers prevented any extensive exploration of this issue.

The average length of stay at Wupatki Ruin and the visitor center is less than thirty minutes. In this time visitors typically move from the parking lot into the visitor center, look at the displays and make purchases, and then move beyond the visitor center to the archaeological site itself. About 10 percent of the visitors circumvent the visitor center and go directly to the ruin. Beginning at the overlook to the ruin, people choose among several routes which shorten or lengthen their stay.

Some visitors never make it out of the visitor center. They use the toilet facilities, make purchases, ask directions, and return to their cars. It is not uncommon for some of the teenage visitors to not even get out of the car in the parking lot, while members of their family group visit the ruins.

About 20 percent of those who visit the ruin walk out to the overlook, read part or all of the trail guide, and return to the visitor center or directly to the parking lot. The rest go at least part way into the ruin. As many as one-third of the visitors miss the sign that points the direction to take around the ruin, corresponding to the trail guide numbers. They end up going around the ruin in reverse order. Most accommodate rapidly by reading the trail guide backwards, but this does cause some confusion.

There are several decision points during the tour where visitors either continue on or skip some part of the tour and return to the visitor center. The first decision point is at the overlook, which provides a panoramic view of the main ruins, an amphitheater, a ball court, and a small geological formation called the blow hole[2]. Some people stand at the overlook and read the Wupatki trail guide without getting closer than about 100 yards to the ruin. The second major decision point is whether or not to visit the amphitheater. This

---

2. The blow hole is a small crack in the ground, which has been bricked over with a small grate to prevent accidents. Under the opening are thousands of cubic feet of cracks in the rock formation below Wupatki. The blow hole gets its name from the fact that the cyclical heating and cooling of air at Wupatki causes air to either blow strongly out of the hole, or to be sucked into it with considerable force. Visitors often stand on top of the crack, to allow the outflow to act as a natural air conditioner on very hot summer days.

adds 50 yards to the tour, and it is a moderate climb. At 5,000 feet in the desert heat, these decisions are important. The third decision is whether or not to go from the end of the major ruin complex down to the ball court and blow hole. This adds at least 150 yards to the trip, with no shade available. Those who do visit the lower part of the monument are among the group whose visit lasts longer than the average. In almost all cases it is common for the visitors to read the sections of the trail guide that describe the areas they are not visiting, while looking at them from a distance.

German Tourists in the Southwestern Desert

The general demographic surveys done in the park, along with visitor logs, indicate that approximately 20 percent of the Wupatki visitors have a Germanic cultural background. One of our student ethnographers developed an interest in these visitors when he observed that almost every rental car in the visitor center parking lot that had California license plates disgorged a group that was speaking German (Orozco 1989). He began to wonder why Germans were the most frequent tourists, rather than an even mixture of people from other European countries. British and Japanese visitors were present on an irregular basis during the summer, and they tended to arrive by bus. The Germans arrived every day by the car load.

One of Orozco's findings was that many of the German visitors had developed an interest in American Indian cultures, and in U.S. prehistory, on the basis of reading children's books written by a German author named Karl May. May wrote a large number of highly romantic books about Indians, and their treatment by the dominant U.S. culture, at about the turn of the century. Many of the visitors, especially those over forty, came to the Southwest with expectations of experiencing contact with Indian groups, and to play out childhood dreams. The younger visitors were less likely to expect things to be as Karl May portrayed them, but nonetheless, many had read his books and gained an interest in the region because of them. Orozco also found a general desire on the part of these visitors to have a greatly expanded German language trail guide. Most of the Germans visit a variety of archaeological sites

throughout Arizona, New Mexico, Colorado, Nevada, and California. They are very well educated, as a group, and have a high level
of interest in U.S. prehistory. They commonly read books about
the Southwest prior to traveling to the region, and purchase other
books during their travels. They also receive large volumes of materials from German travel agencies. The existing interpretive
materials at Wupatki, and most of the other archaeological parks
they visit, provide far less detail than they would prefer.

Visitor Behavior

Gender Roles and Family Dynamics

Visitors play out a number of middle-class American cultural
patterns as they tour the ruins. The most visible patterns are
consistent differences in gender roles, age-related role behavior, and
differences in the family dynamics of visitors. These cultural
differences have important implications for interpretation.

After exiting the visitor center, tourists pass a box on a post
which contains trail guides for a self-guided tour of Wupatki Ruin.
Most single individuals pick up the trail guide, and tour each
numbered station independently of other visitors. If the visitors
come in a group, then one or more members of the group pick up
trail guides and move around the ruins more or less in contact with
one another, depending on the composition of the group and the
factors described below.

Couples and families with children tend to take a single trail guide
(although children occasionally demand to have their own separate
guides). Usually one of the children or one of the adult males in the
family takes the trail guide out of the box and carries it to the first
station, an overlook of the ruin. At the overlook, the trail guide is
handed over to the "central female" in the group, who begins to read
the guide to everyone in the contingent. We designated this person
the "central female," because in groups where more than one adult
female was present only one normally took on the role described
below. She was typically the oldest female, unless the oldest was in
her sixties or older. This woman seemed to take the lead in sharing
information about the ruin with the rest of the family. At the same

time, the "central male" took on the role of photographer, recording the visit with either a still or a video camera. If he used a still camera, he simply alternated between taking photographs and listening to the female who was reading the guide. If he used a video camera, he normally recorded the sound of the trail guide being read as he panned across various scenes in the ruin that corresponded to each section of the trail guide. This division of labor continued throughout the ruins.

This gender-typed behavior is not universal. Males occasionally read the trail guide out loud to the family or group, and some women did a considerable amount of photography. But these were less common. The few times we observed males reading to families, most sounded as if they did not have much practice reading out loud. This probably ties into the fact that it is much more common in American families for mothers to read to their young children than for fathers.

In a single-sex group, it is most common for everyone to take a trail guide, but to proceed around the ruin together. Occasionally, especially where the group was two or three females, one individual would read the trail guide out loud, in the same manner as in a family group. However, it was more common for individuals to read silently at each marker, and then to make comments to one another or ask additional questions raised by the trail guide at that point in their collective experience.

Overall family dynamics were explored through interviews (Winkfield 1989). We found that families differed greatly in the amount of control exerted over various members of the group. They also differed significantly in the purpose they expressed in visiting the monument and this often correlated closely with observed behavior in relation to social control.

The behavior of children in these family groups depends on the level of social control that the parents exert on them. At one end of the spectrum the children stand with the guide book reader and the photographer at each station, listening and participating in a group experience of the ruin. At the other end of the behavioral spectrum, the children range far ahead of the parents, paying no attention to the adult roles being acted out around them, and often straying from the trail boundaries. If the family was visiting the monument as one stop on their vacation, they tended to maintain far less control of the children, even encouraging behavior beyond the boundaries of acceptable behavior in the park. But if one of the main purposes for the visit was to instill a sense of history, to educate the family and the children in particular, then the parents tended to show respect for the ruins and to demand the same respect from their children. These families seemed to be more concerned about the preservation of resources than those whose purpose was solely entertainment or relief from the boredom of a long drive. These differences have some direct bearing on interpretation in the parks.

The behavior in the educationally oriented families was relatively consistent. These families nearly always took a copy of the trail guide, and deliberately kept the family together as the guide was read at each numbered point. If the family had small children, one or both parents normally held their hands or carried them. These parents tended to be proactive in teaching the children proper behavior before they had a chance to misbehave, explaining to them, for example, why they should stay on the trails and not disturb the ruins. These families also tended to be very responsive to the presence of rangers and were eager to talk with them and ask additional questions.

The behavior of families lacking an educational orientation differed in nearly all respects. There were far fewer attempts to keep the family together; individuals were allowed to experience the ruin on their own, at their own pace. Far less behavioral control was exhibited, and it was nearly always reactive. When the trail guide was read, it was rarely to the whole family group. These differences in family dynamics suggest that at least two different approaches to encouraging appropriate behavior in visitors and their children need to be attempted by Park Service personnel.

The following sections provide specific case study material derived from the ethnographies. These include findings on vandalism and monster children; visitor needs, expectations, and interpretive preferences; and the implications of our research.

Vandalism

All of the ethnographers were alerted to watch for, categorize, and understand vandalism at the monument. This sometimes created a delicate balance between participant observation and intervention. We needed to see what was happening, in order to record it and understand it for appropriate park staff intervention in the future. We also were concerned for protection of the resource.

One of the students focused on the issue of social and physical boundaries in her ethnographic research. Hopkins (1989) describes boundary ambiguities and misbehavior of visitors in a tour of Wupatki Ruin. She also identifies nine forms of ruin abuse, and provides profiles of the location and frequency of these forms of vandalism, along with recommendations for reducing both their severity and their frequency. Table 1 is an adaptation of Hopkins's findings on vandalism.

The anthropological literature would predict that the strongest agreement about the size, shape, and purpose of social boundaries in the parks would exist among Park Service personnel, since they share a single corporate culture, while visitors do not. It would also predict that many of their beliefs about these boundaries would not be shared by visitors until, or unless, visitors are educated about them.

This is a classic situation, found in many instances where a professional group controls special cultural information and interacts with a public which lacks access to this information. It is common for the professional group to believe that their cognitive patterns are shared. This is why doctors confuse their patients when they use medical jargon instead of normal social language. In the same vein, we discovered a Park Service culture that includes a relatively well shared cognitive map of the "proper" boundaries at the monument. As predicted, it is not adequately shared by visitors. Hopkins found this creates problems of a number of varieties, including confusion over boundaries in the monument.

No culture is completely homogeneous. We found variation in beliefs about appropriate boundaries among various groups of individuals working in the park. The full-time and seasonal staff

Table 1. Types of vandalism at Wupatki Ruin.

Perpetrators	Type of vandalism	Frequency
General public	Walking on impacted areas, off trail; leaning on ruin walls	Extremely common
Children	Walking in ruins; climbing walls; picking up and throwing objects; graffiti	Extremely common
Touchers	Touching artifacts; sitting on walls; walking on walls	Very common
Photographers	Walking off trail; posing people in restricted areas	Very common
Curious	Walking off terrain into restricted ruin areas	Quite common
Nature lovers	Walking far off trail	Common
Collectors	Walking off trail; going into back country; picking up artifacts, rocks, & other specimens without permission	Uncommon
Graffitiists	Writing marks or ruining surfaces	Uncommon
Miscellaneous	Trespassing cattle; offroad vehicles, etc.	Common

shared professional orientations and standards that tended to make them relatively consistent in defining both physical and behavioral boundaries. More variation was noted between these people and the volunteer staff. But all of the staff controlled tacit knowledge that was not easily accessible to visitors. As one of the students stated, inconsistencies in the beliefs of the staff, combined with a lack of definition of some of the boundaries, make it easy for tourists to be legitimately confused about what is or is not permitted.

Loopholes also allow deliberately destructive individuals to manipulate the situation, since the staff is anxious to maintain positive relationships with the public. Hopkins cites the example that the people who visit the outlying ruins, where there are few clear boundaries, expect to have the same freedom of access at the main ruin. They occasionally become angry when confronted by official requests to not behave at Wupatki in ways that were uncontrolled at Wukoki or the Citadel. The inconsistency of the controls placed on visitors leads to confusion and other more serious problems, permitting deliberately destructive individuals to manipulate the situation, since the staff is anxious to maintain positive relationships with the public. The information provided in Hopkins's report acts as an excellent model for similar studies at other sites and could be useful for establishing and maintaining workable boundary controls for archaeological parks.

Monster Time at Wupatki Ruin

One type of vandalism that occurred regularly in the park became the focus of much interest during our research. We discovered that Wupatki Ruin had a special time of day that we labeled "monster time." This was a very predictable form of child misbehavior which occurred in the ruins every afternoon.

Monster time begins at approximately 3:00 P.M. and lasts until 4:00 or 4:30 P.M. During that time period at least one child, and frequently more, would be observed actively climbing all over the ruin and getting into areas that were far outside of appropriate visitor boundaries, despite the numerous signs requiring visitors to stay on the paths, stay off the walls, and not disturb the ruins.

We developed a basic profile of the "monster child." The most common monster was a young Anglo male, between the ages of 10 and 13, distinguished from non-monster children by several characteristics. Monster children tend to wear clothing that has bright colors, or they are dressed all in black. Their t-shirt normally has a logo with a rebellious message. The monster child visits the ruin with his parents, but quickly leaves the family group. Monsters move very rapidly into the ruin and begin cutting trails, walking on walls, and moving into restricted rooms in the middle of the ruin. They continue to exhibit this behavior, ignoring any parental comments, throughout their visit. The monster always appears to be very full of energy at a time when the rest of the family is dragging. The parents tend to lag far behind, probably because they have been cooped up in a car with a monster child for the entire day, or longer if they are traveling on a family vacation. In no case did we observe family members effectively controlling the monster's behavior. Most of the time their parents were not close enough to comment to them anyway, let alone close enough to control their behavior. The only condition that appeared to deter monster behavior was the immediate presence of a uniformed ranger.

Monster children tend to take signs very literally, as a manipulation device. For example, we interviewed one monster child after he had jumped three walls and was climbing up into the middle of the ruin. He belligerently stated that he had strictly obeyed the sign that said, "please stay off the walls." He had carefully jumped the walls and not touched a single one of them. Another child said, when asked to get off a wall, that the sign which said to stay off the wall was in an entirely different part of the ruin (about 25 feet away), not right where she was sitting. She felt the sign didn't apply to this particular place.

This instance of a female monster child was unusual. Monster children are rarely female. We did observe instances of female monster behavior, but almost all were accompanied by males that fit the primary monster profile. Their behavior in most cases appeared to be tagged to male monster behavior, rather than being self initiated. Most girls were simply accompanying a monster male on his run through the ruins.

The ethnographers also noted monster behavior at the outlying sites, but it was not as easy to confirm the timing of these events. It did become apparent that some of the children who performed monster activities at Wupatki exhibited the same type of behavior at outlying sites. This was confirmed by direct observation when students moved from one site to another at the end of the day, first observing monster behavior of a particular child at an outlying ruin, and then, when they returned to the visitor center, observing the same child in the Wupatki ruins. It was also confirmed by indirect evidence as the students compared notes which allowed them to recognize similar individuals who were observed in two different locations by different ethnographers.

Visitor Needs and Expectations

The student ethnographers spent several hundred hours interviewing visitors about their interests and interactions with the monument. In addition they recorded natural conversations between visitors, between visitors and Park Service personnel, and between visitors and other visitors. This allowed us to explore the types of questions that visitors would like to have answered about archaeological ruins in general, and Wupatki in particular. This appears to be an excellent guide for the development of interpretive materials, and for training Park Service personnel for interpretive duties. The areas noted below are described in more detail in several of the ethnographic reports, and especially in Cha (1989).

Lifestyles

One of the major topics of interest to visitors is finding out details about the lifestyles of the people who lived at the site. Their questions provide an excellent profile for the development of trail guides at any archaeological park, and for the types of interpretive material that can be transmitted by park personnel.The most common things visitors wanted to know were:

1. The physical characteristics of the people at Wupatki. What did the people look like? How big were they? (Some thought they must have been very small because of the small doorways at Wupatki, not realizing that small doorways lose less heat during the winter).

2. Their resources. What did they eat? Where did they find water? (This was a very common question in this desert environment.) How did they get the food they ate? Did it all come from hunting or agriculture or both?

3. What kind of rituals did they perform?

4. What was their language?

5. What were their religious beliefs?

Many people wanted to know about the cycles of daily life at Wupatki. They wanted to know what kind of game the people hunted, and where they found it. They asked when and where the crops were planted and when and how did the people at Wupatki harvest them. They wanted to know how all the different kinds of

foods were cooked. Others wanted to know if the environment and
the climate were the same or very different from those at Wupatki
today. Some were surprised by the amount of technological
knowledge that went into the construction of the ruins and wanted
to know more about it. Visitors also wanted to know the architec-
tural history of the ruin, and how many people lived in it (and in the
surrounding area) at any given time. They wanted to know who the
people at Wupatki were related to, who they traded with, and
whether or not they engaged in warfare. They also wanted to know
where they went when they abandoned Wupatki, and why that
abandonment occurred.

Architecture

The visitors were fascinated with the architecture at Wupatki
Pueblo. The men, in particular, were interested in learning about the
construction methods used in the ruin. They wanted to know how
the stones were shaped, how the walls were laid, what was used for
mortar, and what kinds of tools the people used for construction.
The women were more interested in domestic activities. They asked
where people did various tasks, and how the rooms were set up for
comfort and utility. The women also made far more comments about
the aesthetics of the architecture and were interested in how people
would create beauty in their lives.

Visitors realized that the ruin had been stabilized, and some
people wanted to know how they could easily distinguish between
the parts of the ruins that have been reconstructed and what remains
of the original buildings. In one case, a visitor thought that Wupatki
had been built by the Park Service, for her entertainment, much
like at Disneyland. This was an extreme example of the types of
beliefs visitors take into the monument, but there are many other
pieces of misinformation that needed to be handled appropriately.

The Setting

Tourists wanted to know why the people who built the ruins
picked the particular sites they did, instead of nearby sites that
looked more interesting or useful to them, or at least seemed equally
advantageous as a home site. They wanted to know why they picked
sites that were close to but not right on top of their water sources.

They also wanted to know how the volcanic eruptions had affected people at the ruins.

Burials

The trail guide describes a room with a small open grave as one of seven infant burials found in the ruins and states that burying stillborn infants inside the pueblo was a common practice for the Sinagua, the prehistoric group who built Wapatki pueblo. This marker triggers more questions than any other. Burials and funerary practices are an area of strong interest for Anglo-American visitors. People wanted to know where the other six burials are, and whether they are all in one room or not. They also wanted to know more about the beliefs of the people, especially those related to this custom. On the other hand, this particular part of the trail guide is considered highly inappropriate by many Native Americans. They feel it is improper to display or discuss such things in their culture, and doing so is insensitive of their cultural values. This is a type of cultural difference that the Park Service will increasingly need to address in the future, in order to provide the most sensitive interpretation of archaeological resources.

Visitor Preferences for Interpretive Methods

Visitors expressed clear views about their preferences for different forms of interpretation (see Cha 1989, Valero 1989). In general, the strongest preference was for a trail guide that allowed for a self-guided tour. The trail guide allows people to go at their own pace, to control their experience, but to have relatively dense information. It was preferred over both permanent signs and ranger-guided tours.

Interpretive signs received both positive and negative comment, depending on their function. The most popular were small signs (about the size of a 4 by 5 card) which gave the names of various plants and their uses. These were scattered unobtrusively at various locations and drew consistent positive interest and comment from visitors. On the other hand, large interpretive signs, such as the single sign at Wukoki (one of the outlying ruins), were often ignored or actively disliked. People disliked having to crowd around a sign with other groups who might be making comments the visitor did not like, and noted that it was difficult to read the sign in the glare of desert sunshine. Visitors also pointed out that one cannot get as much information on a sign as in a brochure. If the Park Service put up as many signs as would hold the information in a trail guide, the place would be littered with signs.

Ranger-guided tours received both positive and negative comment. The trail guides were preferred by many, but others (perhaps those who learn better verbally than visually) gave the guided tours high marks. Other people seemed to merely tolerate ranger lectures in order to have the opportunity to ask their own questions about the ruins. In all cases, the visitors preferred short general lectures, followed by plenty of time to ask individual questions.

Whenever we observed park personnel on patrol, they were stopped by visitors and asked numerous questions. This is probably one of the most subtle and effective of all of the interpretive and educational modalities available to the Park Service. Brown's (1989) report indicates that there is wide variation in the quality, quantity of interpretation, and sometimes the style of these "interpretive patrols" between Park Service professionals and volunteers. But in all instances people expressed serious interest in this personalized form of interpretation. It appears to be one of the key forms of education that the Park Service can provide, but it is also the most sensitive to budget reductions and to movement from a professional to a volunteer work force in the parks. This is an area where there should be an expansion rather than a contraction of resources in the future.

Implications from an Ethnography of Interpretation

Using ethnographic techniques, we allowed the visitors to identify important interpretation issues. We observed their behavior, listened to their public conversations, and then asked them directly what they thought about the monument. We followed up on the leads they gave us in these interviews with more observations and more interviews on those subjects. Thus we were not only attempting to discover information that park personnel felt was important, but were also afforded the luxury of discovering issues that were imbedded in visitor behavior, but had not been previously identified as critical to interpretation. The following are some of the implications of our findings.

Our family-oriented research identified an increasing use of video technology for recording visits to cultural sites. This raises the possibility that all interpretive guides should be reviewed not only for their written content, but also for their oral characteristics. It is obvious that the visitors have discovered an interesting way to create their own semi-professional quality "voice-over" effect for their personal video travelogues, by combining cooperative male and female roles in the park. Interpretation specialists should take advantage of this new use of media to get their messages across to not only individual visitors, but also to all of those audiences back home who will be given the opportunity to see their neighbors' tour on the visitors' home VCR.

Our observational studies demonstrated that there was a very consistent pattern of behavior where guided tour markers are used. Individuals stop at each marker in the interpretive guide (whether it is written or taped) at least long enough to determine whether or not this was a place where they wanted to linger. This produces an excellent passive system for grouping people at key points in the system. The numbered markers on the guide also keep visitors focused on moving around the ruin in a consistent and predictable pattern to stop in designated areas, rather than encouraging them to get off the trail or to stop at points where they would cause difficulties for the flow of visitors. This tendency should be taken into account in developing both guides and other interpretive materials. It means that there can be some very subtle combinations of information and visitor flow management combined to create positive visitors' experiences in a park. Markers should not be placed where they will cause confusion or impede flow, but they can be used to "side-track" part of the visiting contingent during peak times and can be used to make overall interpretation management easier.

Monster time seems to be a very widespread phenomenon. We have received numerous comments about similar behavior at other parks. It seems most likely to occur in institutions that have a large amount of territory that is not under direct observation from the institution's personnel. The data from our direct observations and interviews of "monsters" causes us to recommend that patrol times be changed in those institutions to anticipate the need for control of monster time. Since this is often the most uncomfortable point in a long day, prior to our observations this was a point at which there was very little patrolling going on. However, a modification in patrol schedules was effective at Wupatki in cutting the number of instances of monster behavior.

A request surfaced from the educationally oriented families that is worthy of serious attention as an interpretation policy. Many of these families felt that it would be very useful for the park to have a children's trail guide, in addition to the adult interpretation guide. This would be a guide written at an appropriate reading level (most suggested second or third grade) and containing the same type of information (or parallel information) about the ruin that could be found in the adult guide. Wupatki has a very nice workbook for children, which received praise. But the workbook does not provide much information about the ruin. It provides a series of educational activities that keep some children busy during their visit. It is more commonly used by the parents to keep their children occupied on the road after the visit, since it includes some drawing and word exercises that can be used as a game. However parents, and some of the children, suggested that the creation of a trail guide that has serious educational content about the ruin itself, but is written at a level that the children could read and understand, would provide a better all around educational experience for the children. It would teach them directly about the people who lived at Wupatki, as well as being an excellent vehicle for telling the children why it was important for the Park Service to preserve this type of heritage. We would recommend that similar services be considered for other institutions as well. These educationally oriented families are the future support for cultural institutions, and should be supported wherever possible.

The results of the research on the outlying sites (see Valero 1989, Cha 1989, Hopkins 1989) at Wupatki indicated that it would be useful to increase the amount of interpretation at remote locations, for several reasons. Better interpretation would create clearer boundaries for visitors, using the full range of passive controls that are available for such sites. These controls could include well marked paths, increased use of signs to indicate boundaries, and the use of a trail guide. This would provide much better interpretation of the resources for the visitors, and would reduce accidental harm to them.

Another of our recommendations comes from our exploration of German visitation to archaeological parks. It would be useful for the interpretive division of the National Park Service (or any group with high levels of German visitation) to do an analysis of two or three of Mr. May's most popular children's books. This would allow for the development of interpretive materials for German visitors which could better meet the expectations of this audience, and at the same time would serve to clarify issues that are raised by the specific historical and romantic views portrayed in his books.

It would also be advantageous for U.S. cultural institutions to provide better interpretation for foreign visitors. For Wupatki, the German language material is a single typewritten page, rather than a full translation of the trail guide (with both pictures and words). This eliminates the opportunity for these visitors to learn about and compare various sites, unless they read English. This also means that major parts of the Park Service story and its policies go unheard for as many as one in every five visitors to this park and many others. It would appear that there is an unmet need for better interpretation materials in other languages, for the most frequent foreign visitor groups.

All in all, ethnography turned out to be a valuable tool for determining visitors' beliefs, their ideas, their knowledge, and their behavior. It allowed us to discover generic data that can provide information useful to the protection and interpretation of all archaeological parks, and promises to be an important tool in looking at similar issues in other venues.

Children and Gender-Based Behavior at a Science Museum

(1990)

Gary W. Mullins

Kristin Benne Kremer

Introduction

Centers of science, technology, and industry, and museums in general, play an important role in our society. They are both collections from the past and windows on the future. The social setting and design of these exhibits is thought to influence how visitors interact with these media. This chapter is concerned specifically with how gender bias may influence children's interaction with exhibits in a science museum.

In a typical scene at a science museum, neon lights flash, children pull a variety of levers to light up a giant scoreboard, or a parent tries desperately to get a three-year-old to unhand a rabbit at the live animal exhibit. Children's science museums are places for casual learning, not overly structured in content, yet exciting, dynamic, and educational (Falk and Balling 1980, Lucas 1974). A multitude of sciences are interpreted here. Activities are intended to help children gain new information about the world they must understand if they are to succeed.

These museums are also windows for observing social behavior as is the case in this study. Children and adults bring their social skills and bias to the museum setting, just as they do to other social settings. The interest in social behavior in this interpretive setting is to explore relationships between the gender of children and their participatory behavior toward interpretive exhibits.

Background

The literature relating to gender, sexism, social norms, rules, and other aspects of normative theory is immense and subject to a variety of interpretations. Most recognizes that boys and girls are different genetically and for the most part are nurtured and socialized differently as well. Sex is what we are born with and gender is what we are socialized into. The research reported herein assumes children are taught gender-consistent or appropriate gender-based behaviors (or "gender behavior") by their culture, their community, and their social groups.

Children learn what is traditional and proper from sources such as parents, guardians, siblings, playmates, mass media, and religious and community leaders. They also learn this in school and in informal educational settings such as zoos, parks, and museums. From the cradle, they tend to be taught different skills or traditional gender traits associated with being masculine or feminine. For example, toys and games chosen for children by parents and schools often encourage traditional gender-consistent behavior deemed appropriate by the dominant society. The toys typically selected for young females encourage "fantasy and role-playing and foster the development of verbal and social interactions skills" (Barr 1985, p. 1). In contrast, young males are taught to manipulate and tinker with objects fostering the development of important problem-solving skills (Barr 1985, Shapiro 1990).

A 1978 study (Fagot, in Skolnick et al. 1982) reported observations of 20- to 24-month-old children and their parents at home. Young females were given approval for doll play, dressing up, watching television, and staying close to parents. Young males were positively rewarded for activities such as playing with blocks or competitive games and were chastised for doll playing. By the time children reach school they have had very different experiences. Literature reviewed by science equity specialists report females enter preschool with verbal, fine motor, nurturing, one-to-one, role rehearsal, adult modeling, and impulse control experiences. Males enter school with spatial, gross motor, inventive, managing, group, career and life option, direction, instruction and selfworth experiences (Greenberg, in Sprung 1987). Masculine-oriented skills such as competitiveness, exploration, and spatial awareness better prepare young men to enter the competitive and challenging world of science and technology than do the more traditional feminine skills taught young females (Barr 1985, Weitzman 1979, Carter 1987).

Boys and girls, and men and women, for the most part have historically tended to occupy different social positions and have behaved somewhat differently. One of the questions raised in arguments surrounding gender bias and sexism is the appropriateness of such a phenomenon in our present-day culture in the United States.

At issue in this study is not whether these norms or rules are appropriate, but how people's life choices are affected by the skills gained or not gained as the result of their childhood socialization process. Childhood play behaviors, governed to some extent, at least, by societal norms, lead to the acquisition of different sets of skills. The skills acquired, and the behaviors a child becomes accustomed to, are believed to influence career decisions (Barr 1985, Shapiro 1990). By 1987, almost 50 percent of the U.S. work force were women but only 12.8 percent of scientists and engineers were women (Dix 1987). Gender behavior is often considered one factor leading to this disproportionate representation of men in the sciences and engineering.

The Museum's Role

Museums are places where the sciences, and other disciplines, are interpreted; they are a place where children can be "connected" with science. To accomplish this it is important for a museum staff to understand children's behavior as well as the subject matter being interpreted.

In traditional school settings, young females generally possess positive attitudes toward science until early adolescence (Erb 1981, Kahle 1983a). At this time, many young females designate science as "men's work and boring," with too many facts to learn (Kahle 1983b). Even in the elementary science classroom males receive preferential treatment in the quality and quantity of attention they receive and the types of feedback they are given (Barr 1985). This may lead some young females to begin to doubt their competency in science and shy away from taking risks, screening themselves out of further science courses, further widening the gender gap in science (Linn 1981).

Although these trends have been documented within schools and the home, science museums have not investigated to any great extent the effects of children's gender behavior on the museum learning experience. Science museums need to know if their learning environment is a comfortable one for all children and actively encourages their participation across all exhibits. Because children will ignore activities which they feel involve inconsistent gender behavior (Carter 1987), science museums could maximize the impact on the visitor by better understanding the role of gender behavior in the elective learning environment.

Family interaction research conducted at science museums and zoos has indicated certain gender behavior differences do occur. For example, Rosenfeld's (1980) study of families at a zoo found that adult males consistently led the family groups. Diamond (1980) observed families in two science centers and found mothers most likely to be family management oriented. Mothers in that study were least likely of all family members to choose exhibits and most likely to follow other members. Cone and Kendall (1976), in a study of families visiting a science museum, observed fathers ignoring their daughters. They suggest this could be partly responsible for the relative passivity of young females in the museum setting. They hypothesize science museums may be a "male environment" and definitely are social settings with strong occurrences of both generational and sex-stereotyped roles. Staff of the Children's Museum in Boston have observed that "boys and girls racing through the exhibits are similarly active, similarly rambunctious, and similarly interested in model cars and model kitchens until they reach the first grade or so" (Shapiro 1990, p. 57). However, no research was found within the museum literature addressing children's gender behavior and its possible effects upon the science learning experience.

The question to be addressed eventually is: Are we who interpret in and design exhibits for museums doing anything to encourage or discourage the gender gap in science? A beginning place for this type of inquiry is to observe what children are doing in museums.

Methods

The case study reported here was conducted in 1988 at COSI, a Columbus, Ohio, center of science and industry. COSI is a large, nationally recognized facility attracting over 700,000 visitors per year. Exhibits are hands-on and highly participatory. Themes vary from computer technology to health and well-being to space exploration.

Participant observation was used to gather the data; 419 children, from kindergarten through third grade, were observed interacting with one of five different participatory interpretive exhibits. Children visiting the special area where the study was conducted were almost equally divided between males and females; the study sample reflected this balance. Children were observed directing jets of water at a designated object; making bubbles using a variety of sets of hand-held rings; engaging in face painting; viewing, petting, and holding small animals; and building a small-scale house.

The qualitative study recorded observations around a theme of gender behavior. This exploratory study follows Guba and Lincoln's (1985) guidelines for maintaining credibility, transferability, dependability, and confirmability in qualitative inquiry. Credibility was established by spending substantial time observing each exhibit and participant, debriefing of the observer by other researchers, and independent reviews of the raw observational data by an advisory group. The ability to generalize or transfer the findings to other settings was not the intent of the study; however, the observations made can provide other museums with a basis for studying children's gender behavior. Raw data auditors, a research diary, and a research committee's review of the analysis process, as well as a limited amount of quantitative data, aid in confirming the data and attesting to its dependability.

Observations were made in a special museum section called "Big Kidspace." Each child in the study was selected by alternating between male and female. The time spent at the observed exhibit by a child was noted. Children's interactions with adults and peers, as well as social group composition, were recorded at each exhibit.

The observations made provide a basis for further studies which may begin to better describe and explain the meanings attached to gender-related behaviors in interpretive settings. Because of the lack of baseline information about children's gender behavior in museums, an exploration of some key structural properties of the event is necessary before further inquiry can take place. The observations made in this study, although exploratory in nature, do provide some issues for consideration by interpreters.

Observations

Analysis of the observations centered on two questions:

1. Do young males and females, from kindergarten through third grade, interact differently with the exhibits?

2. Does the presence of adults or peers tend to encourage gender behavior?

Another question was implied: Where gender preference for an exhibit is evident, are there design elements within the exhibit that encourage the expression of gender behavior?

Behaviors at exhibits—The water jets exhibit consisted of a rectangular-shaped glass case with hanging red plastic targets. Six hand-held jets continuously streaming water were around the periphery and could be used to aim at the targets. At this exhibit 21 of 74 boys made reference to guns and shooting and held the jets as though they were guns shooting at a target. Boys stayed at the exhibit an average of 20 percent longer than girls. The overall participation ratio was 1.7 males to one female.

The paints exhibit consisted of a round table with mirrors and chairs. Paint and sponges were available for face painting. At this exhibit, which was designed somewhat like a vanity, seven out of 20 girls applied the paint like make-up and sought social approval, while 13 drew markings such as rainbows, balloons, and hearts. In contrast, 14 of 21 boys drew stripes and dashes, often without looking in the mirror. Only females were observed wiping off the paint as if dissatisfied with what they had drawn. Girls stayed at the exhibit nearly twice as long as boys did. The female-to-male ratio was two to one.

The bubbles exhibit had two tubs filled with soapy water and variously shaped metal rings for making bubbles. Seven of 48 females made negative comments or through their behavior showed disinterest in the exhibit because they might get wet; only one in 49 males made such gestures. Males spent an average of 30 percent longer at the bubbles exhibit. The male to female ratio was almost equal.

As could have been predicted, more girls than boys expressed nurturing skills at the small animals exhibit where animals were in glass cages approximately one foot off the floor to provide children easy access for holding and viewing. Fourteen of 49 females, as compared to only two of 49 males, were observed expressing affection towards the animals. The girls' behavior is gender consistent and is also consistent with Kellert's (1983) findings. Girls participated in the exhibit nearly twice as long as did boys. The ratio was 1.4 females to one male.

Behaviors also differed at the build-a-house exhibit; this was a miniaturized bilevel house with three rooms. Children's building items were curtains, carpet squares, foam bricks, and plastic pipes. Twelve of 28 males compared to only two of 28 females exhibited aggressive behaviors, knocking down and kicking building materials. Males stayed at the exhibit about 20 percent longer than females did. The ratio was 1.5 males to one female.

Adult and peer influences—The interactions of adults and peers with children at exhibits were observed. Adult women accompanied the young visitors three times more often than adult men did. Only 11.5 percent of the children studied were accompanied by both an adult male and female.

Women accompanied children to the paints exhibit in 44 percent of the cases observed; men did so only 7 percent of the time. Given that there were nearly three times as many women as men in the Big Kidspace area, men were underrepresented at the paints exhibit by approximately 50 percent. Two adult males were observed ignoring their young female charges at the paints exhibit.

At the animal exhibit, more women than men were observed teaching nurturing skills, but only to young females. Men were observed at the water jets exhibit with male children in 16 percent of the cases observed. Women were with boys in only 10 percent of the observations at the water jets exhibit. Given the adult ratio of three women to one man, a greater percentage of women would be expected here. Eleven adult females compared to one adult male were observed drying the children's hands at the bubbles exhibit. Adults were not permitted in the build-a-house exhibit area.

Observations of peer groups, where they existed, indicated that across all five exhibits peer groups tended to be the same sex most of the time. Male peer-group support of gender-consistent behavior was most evident at the water jets and build-a-house exhibits. Group comments and short games relating to guns and shooting were evident among groups of boys at the water jets; no groups of girls displayed this behavior. Nor did groups of girls display the aggressive, destructive behavior found among groups of boys at the build-a-house exhibit.

Groups of girls engaged much more in conversation and actions relating to nurturing than did groups of boys. The most interaction within groups, including those of both girls and boys, was at the bubbles exhibit where extensive peer teaching of the fine art of bubble making occurred.

Discussion

What meanings do we attach to these observations? Observations for the most part were of gender-consistent behavior, behavior that is rooted in and reinforced by culture, community, and social groups. Weitzman (1979) suggests that children express gender-role preferences and behave within the norms they have learned. In this case norms are seen as behaviors guided internally by what is known to be traditional and proper (Edgerton 1985, p. 8). Conflict theory literature suggests that the idea of norms as what is traditional and proper is only one perspective of normative theory (Turner 1978, Bernard 1983). Symbolic interaction theory, as presented by Stryker and Gottlieb (1981), for example, may provide another perspective for trying to ascribe meanings to the observations made.

At the water jets boys were playing games that increased their spatial awareness, improved their motor skills, and helped them learn about the dynamics of water. Aggressiveness and competitiveness were observed among boys at the build-a-house exhibit. Girls were not learning these skills as intensively as boys. Yet some of these skills are considered preparatory for entering the competitive and challenging world of science and technology (Barr 1985, Weitzman 1979, Carter 1987).

Girls at the paints exhibit were refining role-rehearsal, fine-motor, and adult-modeling skills. The animal exhibit provided girls opportunities to express and refine nurturing skills. Although these gender-consistent feminine skills are important to learn, the science and technology professional must also gain those skills and experiences often thought of as gender-consistent for males—spatial, gross motor, inventive, managerial, group, life option, direction, instruction, and self-worth (Greenberg, in Sprung 1987). Our observations may indicate that many girls screen themselves out of activities they have been taught are gender-inconsistent, thus unconsciously limiting their options to explore science as a career. Adults and peer groups appear to reinforce these decisions.

On the other hand there were indications that gender-consistent behavior is not an absolute. Some girls were getting wet at the bubbles exhibit and were being aggressive towards the build-a-house exhibit; some boys were learning nurturing skills with the animals. Verbal and social skills were being refined by young males at the bubbles exhibit. Some cross-gender skills were being learned.

Just as young females need to be encouraged to learn traditional male-oriented skills, young males need to be socialized to learn and appreciate what are often considered more gender-consistent female skills. As society moves toward a more egalitarian perspective on gender, cross-gender skills training will be increasingly important. The application of these new skills may help us more effectively use all of our human resources to better address the needs of our society and those of the entire world society.

Implications for Interpretation

What can the interpreter, the museum director, and the exhibit designer do to foster cross-gender skill acquisition and to make science more interesting? First and foremost, we can begin to ask what the social consequences of interpretive actions are. Although we may not wish to figuratively neuter our exhibits or seek a unisex way of thinking, we can seek to design exhibits, interpretive materials, and presentations that are attractive across genders. If a water jets exhibit has greater appeal for young males, we can have a comparable exhibit which teaches similar motor skills and water properties for young females. Or, even better, we can combine the concepts of the two separate exhibits to create one where youth can play and learn about science together. Found in interpretive products are the means and messages to help young people learn cross-gender skills and to lessen the stereotypical role modeling that may hinder children's life choices.

We can begin to address this issue of gender bias by building a philosophy in our own organizations that will promote recognition, understanding, and mitigation of gender bias both within our staff ranks and in the messages we deliver. Female interpreters, for example, can be assigned to interpret science for young visitors and be role models for girls to show that science and technology are not only subjects for males. Male interpreters can help boys, as well as girls, become aware that nurturing, fine-motor, verbal, and social skills are important to all and will be even more important in the twenty-first century.

To more fully understand how to recognize and appropriately deal with gender bias in interpretive materials will require interpreters to view their role more broadly than purveyors of information. As we interpret social actions we must understand from which bias or theory base we are filtering our observations. Explanations for gender bias range across the gamut from nature and nurture arguments to explanations of contrived systems for maintenance of male domination. In this article we have only begun to explore a topic that is most germane to the field of interpretation.

Given that interpretation reflects wider social processes, interpreters are faced with many complex issues, including gender-based behavior. The challenge before us is to recognize that interpretation is an important mechanism for society to gain information for decision making. Interpretation also may be an important part of the solution to problems such as sexism that society deems important to solve. Perhaps we are broaching the subject of interpretation as a social engineering tool. Certainly inequities and injustices exist in our society as they do throughout the world. How interpreters can address these are questions that need more scientific inquiry as well as moral reflection.

Interpretation and
Hispanic American Ethnicity
(1991)

James H. Gramann

Myron F. Floyd

Alan Ewert

Introduction

A few years ago, one of the authors of this chapter was meeting with the chief of interpretation at a national park in the western United States. During the meeting, the interpreter brought up the topic of Mexican American visitors and the fact that they did not seem to be as interested in the park's educational programming as Anglos were. The interpreter was not sure why this was the case, but was hoping to increase Mexican American participation. This was needed, he said, because it appeared that these visitors did not fully appreciate the park's unique natural values, and interpretation could help instill this appreciation in them.

The discussion of ethnic diversity among recreation users frequently follows this pattern, focusing on presumed differences between ethnic minorities and Anglo visitors and the consequences of these differences. Such discussions are usually infused with one of two overtones. In many cases, there is a sincere concern over how best to serve the needs of "nontraditional" users. However, in other instances there is a sense that many behaviors of these groups are inappropriate for the setting in which they occur and should be modified, either through interpretation or by other means.

In this essay we will address basic issues related to interpretation and Hispanic ethnicity. In doing so, we will try to deal with the concerns expressed by the chief interpreter. Before we proceed, however, we will make one key observation up front: many areas have yet to solve the problem of how to attract significant numbers of Anglo American visitors to interpretation, let alone Hispanic Americans. Because most attendees at interpretive programs are Anglos does not mean that most Anglos attend interpretive programs. On the contrary, our experience suggests that the chief reason that Anglo Americans outnumber other ethnic groups at many activities has little, if anything, to do with interest or cultural differences. Rather, it's because they outnumber ethnic minorities in the visitor population as a whole.

Who are the Hispanics? The U.S. Census Bureau is perhaps most responsible for popularizing the use of "Hispanic" as a label for all Americans of Spanish descent. Although the term has gained widespread acceptance among Anglo Americans, Tienda and Ortiz (1986) point out that common ancestral ties to Spain cannot mask the cultural diversity produced by centuries of settlement in widely separate regions of the New World. When defined by native origin (e.g., Mexico, Puerto Rico, Cuba, Panama, Spain), there are at least twenty distinct Hispanic groups in the U.S., and the term itself is subject to multiple interpretations. In some cases, it is reserved for persons of South American or Central American descent, excluding Mexico. In other cases, the term "Latino" is preferred, while "Hispanic" may take on derogatory connotations. In our research, we have found that most persons of Mexican origin prefer to describe themselves as "Mexican American," with smaller groups favoring "Chicano," "American," or "Mexican." In sections of the southwest, especially northern New Mexico (Knowlton 1972), descendants of the original Spanish colonists frequently are referred to as "Spanish American" or "Spanish," and strongly object to any inferred ancestral ties to Mexico.

Thus, the basic premise of this book, that visitors cannot be treated as undifferentiated blocs, applies as much, if not more so, to "Hispanics" as to Anglos. Where data permit it, we will point out particular aspects of internal variation among Hispanic Americans that are especially relevant to interpreters.

This chapter is divided into four parts. We begin with a description of demographic trends and how they are affecting the ethnic mix of the U.S. population, as well as visits to parks, forests, and other outdoor recreation areas. We then review basic research on the nature of leisure behavior and its role in maintaining ethnic identity in a multicultural society. Following this, we summarize available data on the recreation patterns and attitudes of Mexican Americans and other groups of Spanish origin, and conclude by considering how sensitivity to group differences might be applied to the delivery of interpretive services.

Ethnic Trends in the United States

The demographic outlook for the U.S. is clear: as a nation, we are becoming more ethnically diverse. In 1980, one in five persons in the United States belonged to a non-Anglo minority; by the year

2025, this proportion will be one in three (Spencer 1986, Wetrogan 1988). In some states the shift in ethnic balance will be so great that no single group (including Anglo Americans) will be able to claim majority status.

A major force behind the nation's demographic metamorphosis is the dramatic increase in Hispanic American populations. Between 1980 and 1990, the number of Hispanics in the U.S. grew 53.1 percent, compared to a 9.8 percent increase in the population as a whole (Table 1). Presently, Hispanic groups constitute the country's second-largest minority after African Americans, but are projected to exceed Blacks in numbers within two or three decades (Davis et al. 1983). Of the twenty or so Hispanic national-origin groups in the U.S., Mexican Americans are by far the largest, comprising 63 percent of the Hispanic population. The great majority of Mexican Americans live in the five southwestern states of California, Arizona, New Mexico, Texas, and Colorado, but large Hispanic populations are also found in Illinois and New York (McLemore 1991). In addition, a substantial number of immigrants from Central America, South America, and the Caribbean have settled in Dade County, Florida, where Hispanics are projected to make up 70 percent of the Greater Miami population by the year 2000 (Noe and Snow 1989/90).

Table 1. Change in ethnic composition of the U.S. population, 1980 to 1990.

	Number		% change	% of total population	
	1980	1990	1980-90	1980	1990
Anglo	180,602,838	188,128,296	+4.2	79.7	75.7
Black	26,091,857	29,216,293	+12.0	11.5	11.7
Hispanic	14,603,683	22,354,059	+53.1	6.5	9.0
Other	5,247,427	9,011,225	+71.1	2.3	3.6
Total	226,545,805	248,709,873	+9.8	100.0	100.0

Source: U.S. Bureau of the Census.

Ethnic Trends in Recreation Visits

In the 1960s and 1970s a major issue in leisure research and policy concerned minority group "under-participation" in wildland recreation. Early studies showed that a smaller proportion of Blacks took part in many types of wildland activities than did Whites (Mueller and Gurin 1962). This was usually attributed to the lower socioeconomic position of African Americans in a White-dominated society, although later research indicated that cultural preferences and perceived discrimination also played a role in maintaining distinct leisure patterns (Washburne 1978, West 1989). The creation of the nation's first "urban" national recreation areas in San Francisco and New York in 1972 was motivated in part by the desire to reach a constituency of urban, primarily Black, residents who had been largely inaccessible to agencies providing wildland recreation (Wellman 1987).

Although under-participation has not disappeared as a policy issue, research indicates that it may be less relevant in the case of many Hispanic groups. One of the first studies of recreation participation among Hispanics (McMillen 1983) compared Mexican Americans living in Houston with a national sample of the U.S. population. Very few differences in participation patterns were discovered. More recently, a nationwide study conducted for the President's Commission on Americans Outdoors (Market Opinion Research 1986) reported that the proportion of Anglos and Hispanics who participated "often or very often" in 35 different recreation activities differed substantially in only three of the 35 cases. However, Hispanics were somewhat less likely than Anglos to be frequent visitors to either state or federal parks.

The above results have been replicated in a series of regional and on-site studies. A telephone survey of households in Dade County, Florida (Snow 1989) found that even though Hispanics were somewhat less likely than other residents to have visited Biscayne National Park, 68.1 percent still reported at least one trip to the area. In Arizona, a survey of residents of the Greater Phoenix region (Gramann and Floyd 1991) found no meaningful differences between Anglos and Mexican Americans in the percentage who had participated in 18 of 23 outdoor recreation activities during the previous year. In addition, Mexican Americans and Anglo Americans were equally likely to have visited five of seven recreation areas on the Tonto National Forest, as well as two city parks and two National Park Service sites in central Arizona. However, as in previous studies, Mexican Americans were less apt to be regular visitors (defined as two visits during the previous year) to either national forests or national parks.

Despite the tendency for Hispanic Americans to be slightly under represented among regular users of certain types of outdoor recreation areas, other studies have reported high concentrations of Hispanic visitors to some wildland sites. A survey conducted on the Angeles National Forest in Southern California (Simcox and Pfister 1990) found that Hispanics of Mexican and Central American descent comprised 87 percent of the users at one dispersed recreation area, while in New Mexico 63 percent of visitors at a primitive campground on the Lincoln National Forest were found to be Mexican American (Irwin et al. 1990). In fact, Mexican Americans in general appear more likely than Anglos to prefer minimally developed camping locations over more elaborate facilities (Gramann and Floyd 1991, Irwin et al. 1990).

One factor that counteracts the overall pattern of less regular Hispanic use of state and federal recreation sites is the more stable residential pattern of Mexican Americans compared to the relatively mobile Anglo population (Keefe and Padilla 1987). Gramann and Floyd (1991), as well as Irwin et al. (1990), both documented rates of repeat visitation to specific national forest locations by Mexican Americans that exceeded those of Anglo Americans. In each case, the sites in question were minimally developed recreation areas (Roosevelt Lake on the Tonto National Forest and Sleepygrass Campground on the Lincoln National Forest).

Style, Taste, and Freedom to Be

As the ethnic diversity of visitors to wildland areas has increased, so too have concerns expressed by Anglo resource managers (including the aforementioned chief interpreter) about the style of minority-group recreation. This concern frequently reflects fears on the part of managers that the distinctive styles of some ethnic groups may result in inferior recreation experiences, facility damage, and resource degradation. By "style" we mean the unique quality of recreation behavior that arises from variations in group size, group composition, participation motives, preferred activities, and attitudes towards natural and cultural resources.

That differences in recreation style are noticed at all attests to the enduring nature of ethnicity in America. Ironically, many "modernization" theories of the 19th century predicted the disappearance of important ethnic differences in industrialized nations (Evans and Stephens 1988). Instead, homogenized mass societies would emerge, in part through the assimilation of ethnically distinct immigrant groups into host cultures. Although cultural assimilation does occur (Keefe and Padilla 1987), for most Hispanic groups it is a selective process, consisting of the addition of strategic Anglo traits (such as the English language) to their Latin heritage, rather than the total replacement of one culture by the other (McLemore 1991).

Recreation appears to play a critical role in the process of selective assimilation. This is because leisure, in contrast to other human activities, is chosen in comparative freedom. As a consequence, it is relatively unfettered by pressure to conform to majority-group standards. Cheek and Burch (1976) employ the term "taste" to describe unique styles of leisure that arise from group differences, while Kelly (1987) uses "freedom to be." Whatever the label, each term connotes the potential of leisure to serve as an avenue for expressing individual and cultural identity. The implication is that leisure time may be the one social space in American life where ethnic distinctions become most evident and persist the longest.

Leisure Style and Primary Relationships

Besides the expressive nature of leisure, there is another factor that contributes to the persistence of ethnic differences in recreation styles. A major sociological function of leisure is the creation and maintenance of "primary relationships" (Burch 1986, Cheek and Burch 1976, Kelly 1987). These consist of the network of warm and intimate ties exhibited in personal friendships and kinship bonds. They contrast with the impersonal "secondary relationships" characterizing interactions with persons known only by their social roles (e.g., bank teller, sales clerk, interpreter). Research shows that as much as two-thirds of adults' most common leisure activities are learned in primary relationships (Kelly 1977), and that these relationships form the most frequent context for leisure behavior (Cheek and Burch 1976, Kelly 1983). Equally as important, primary bonds tend to be "ethnically enclosed." In other words, people are strongly biased in their primary associations towards members of their own ethnic group.

Among Mexican Americans, the enclosed nature of primary relationships seems to be especially applicable to leisure partners. In a study conducted in three southern California communities (Keefe and Padilla 1987), just 10 percent of second-generation Mexican Americans and 7 percent of third-generation Mexican Americans were found to use leisure settings where most of the other users were of non-Mexican origin. In their Arizona study, Gramann and Floyd (1991) found that only 15 percent of Mexican Americans claimed primary ties mostly with Anglos. Given that primary bonds are a major context in which leisure behavior is learned and maintained, and given the strong social orientation towards one's own ethnic group, it stands to reason that ethnically based differences in leisure styles should persist.

Hispanic Ethnicity and Leisure Style

The preceding theoretical arguments are bolstered by research documenting differences between Hispanics and Anglos along several dimensions of leisure style. In this section, we will examine Anglo/Hispanic style differences in three important categories: size and composition of social groups; participation motives; and attitudes towards natural and cultural resources. Following this, we will discuss one additional issue of particular importance to interpreters: interest in interpretive programs and services. This will lead us into the concluding section of the chapter on the application of sociological research to interpretation.

Size and Composition of Social Groups

One of the most commonly noted distinctions between Anglos and Hispanics relates to the size and composition of recreation groups. Sociologists have long recognized the importance of group characteristics in shaping recreation participation (Field and O'Leary 1973). However, recent research indicates that associations between group type and activity participation that are typical of Anglo Americans may not apply to Hispanic Americans.

Although Hispanics and Anglos often visit the same types of areas, Hispanics tend to recreate in larger social groups. In a study of Chicago park users, Hutchison (1987) reported that the average size of Anglo parties was 2.5 persons, while that of Mexican Americans was 5.7. Among campers at a national forest in New Mexico, the average number of people in Anglo groups was 6.9, compared to the Mexican American average of 12.8 (Irwin et al. 1990). In Yosemite National Park, a recently completed study by the senior author recorded a mean party size of 3.1 for Anglos, while the average for Hispanic visitors was 4.4.

Larger groups among Hispanics often are the result of differences in party composition. Hutchison (1987) found that Mexican Americans using Chicago parks typically visited as part of nuclear or extended families. In contrast, Anglos and Blacks tended to participate as individuals or as members of single-generation peer groups. The study by Irwin et al. (1990) of New Mexico campers reported that 48 percent of Anglo parties had no children present, while among Mexican Americans this figure was only 8 percent.

Many interpreters and resource managers are reluctant to deal with large social groups. In fact, it is not at all unusual for recreation areas to regulate group size, either by restricting the size of parties that can enter an area without permission, or by limiting the number of people, groups, or vehicles allowed to occupy a campsite. In their study of campers in New Mexico, Irwin et al. (1990) reported that Mexican American groups exceeded designated campsite capacity by an average of almost 30 percent.[1] In situations such as this,

---

1. The capacity of sites in this campground (ten persons per site) evidently was dictated by the area's classification along the Forest Service's Recreation Opportunity Spectrum, which assumes that "primitive" experiences can only be obtained under relatively low use densities. Apparently, this stricture does not generalize to Mexican American culture.

managers are faced with the difficult choice of either defining essentially harmless behavior as illegal, or of ignoring unenforceable rules, thus devaluing the significance of all regulations. It would seem better to understand the cultural values of users and, so long as serious compromises to resource integrity or visitor safety do not result, adjust regulations to conform to established norms.

Participation Motives

A strong emphasis on the extended family is a recognized hallmark of Mexican American culture. Although close family ties are hardly unimportant to Anglos, Keefe (1984) notes that the two cultures differ on what is meant by "close." With regard to the extended family, Anglos are satisfied with intermittent meetings, supplemented by telephone calls and letters. In contrast, Mexican Americans place greater value on daily face-to-face contact. While this is important to nuclear family life among Anglos, it is less integral to the extended family.

Disruption of kinship ties is a frequent consequence of migration. For this reason, face-to-face interaction with nuclear and extended families is often less possible for immigrant Hispanics than for subsequent generations who have rebuilt local kinship networks (Keefe and Padilla 1987). Gramann and Floyd's (1991) Arizona study found that "doing something with your family" and "doing something your children wanted to do" were significantly more important as recreation motives among the most culturally assimilated Mexican Americans in their sample (who were all born in the U.S.) than among either Anglos or the least-assimilated Mexican Americans (who were mostly immigrants). This was true even after controlling for differences between groups in the number of young children in a family. Interestingly, the least-assimilated Mexican Americans seemed to compensate for their lack of local family ties by placing a greater emphasis on "meeting new people" as a reason for recreation participation.

In their study of visitors to San Gabriel Canyon on the Angeles National Forest, Simcox and Pfister (1990) also found that Hispanic groups placed a greater emphasis on family-related motives than did Anglos. In particular, Anglos were significantly less likely to rate "watching children play" as an appealing part of their recreation experience. In this case, the strongest family-oriented motives were expressed by Central Americans (mostly Salvadorans). This was especially true among the immigrant generation, suggesting that Central American immigration may involve more complete family units than is true of Mexican American immigration.

Attitudes towards Natural and Cultural Resources

When faced with recreation styles that they consider inappropriate, resource managers often voice concerns over possible negative impacts on natural or cultural resources. The implication is that some types of visitors lack strong positive attitudes towards the conservation of natural and cultural heritage. In fact, research reveals that the protective attitudes of Hispanic Americans are often as strong as, if not stronger than, those of Anglo Americans and other non-Hispanics. In part, this seems to result from historical differences in the development of Anglo and Hispanic culture in the Americas.

In the case of natural resources, Knowlton (1972) points out that early Hispanic settlers in North America identified very closely with the land. Although extensive private landholdings existed in the Spanish colonies, communally owned lands were regarded as especially important, both for human life and village welfare. The English concepts of private property rights and human dominion over nature were not necessarily antithetical to Hispanic culture, but the idea that one could monopolize vast acreages while others went landless was morally repugnant. This sense of the communal stake in the resource base appears to be reflected in the pro-environmental attitudes of many Hispanics today.

In the case of cultural resources, one of the major differences in colonial development along the Atlantic seaboard and in New Spain was the Spanish policy of using the Catholic Church to force Indians into Hispanic society (albeit at the lowest levels of servitude). Conversely, the English pursued a policy towards Native Americans that is best described as "exclusion and extermination" (McLemore 1991). As a result, the culture of Mexico and other Spanish territories became much more "Indianized" than that of the United States. Today, this is a source of great pride throughout Latin America, contributing significantly to the spirit of *la raza,* to the sense of emotional solidarity between *latinoamericanos* and separation from *norteamericanos* (Condon 1991). The consequence is that most Anglo Americans have evolved a less personal relationship to Native American heritage than is true of most Hispanics.

These historical influences appear to have shaped contemporary views towards environmental and cultural-preservation issues. Noe and Snow (1989/90) compared the environmental attitudes of various samples of Hispanics and non-Hispanics in south Florida, including visitors to Biscayne Bay and a general sample of households in the Dade County-Miami area. The non-Hispanic groups comprised Whites, Blacks, and Orientals, while the Hispanic samples presumably consisted mainly of Cubans and other Caribbean and Central American groups. In the general population survey, both Hispanics and non-Hispanics were similar in their agreement that humans must live in harmony with nature, that the balance of nature is easily upset, and that people are severely abusing the environment. These attitudes were held even more strongly by Hispanic and non-Hispanic visitors to Biscayne National Park, suggesting that interpreters who confine their activities to on-site programs in this park will "preach to the choir," whatever the ethnic background of their audience. In contrast to the view that Hispanics are less attuned to resource conservation than Anglos, non-Hispanics in the general population were much more likely than Hispanics to believe that humans should dominate and exploit the environment. This was reflected in non-Hispanics' agreement with such statements as "Plants and animals exist primarily to be used by humans" and "Mankind [sic] was created to rule over the rest of nature." Hispanics strongly disagreed with these positions.

Gramann and Floyd's (1991) survey of households in the Greater Phoenix area contained several questions measuring interest in cultural resources and their preservation. Mexican Americans expressed a stronger interest than Anglos in learning more about the prehistoric peoples of the Southwest, and also were significantly more likely to agree that "The Southwest's prehistory is part of me." However, this greater sense of kinship with the past did not always translate into stronger protective attitudes. For example, Anglos were more likely to think that artifact collecting on public and private land should be illegal, while Mexican Americans were more likely to agree that "The loss of prehistoric remains is a necessary result of progress." Despite these differences, Anglos and Mexican Americans were equally opposed to allowing landowners to excavate prehistoric burials on their property, and were in strong agreement that at least some prehistoric remains should be preserved for future generations. Both groups also were similar in their marked preference for visiting prehistoric ruins, rather than learning about them in a museum or book.

Interest in Interpretation

The chief interpreter described at the beginning of this chapter was concerned because he felt that Mexican Americans were less interested in his park's interpretive programs than Anglos were. In fact, research suggests that, if anything, Hispanic American visitors have a greater interest in interpretive and information services. For example, more Hispanic visitors to Biscayne National Park than non-Hispanics believed that the park did not provide enough information on the area's natural environment, history, or rules and regulations, and that the information that was supplied was presented in an uninteresting fashion (Snow 1989). In Simcox and Pfister's (1990) study on the Angeles National Forest, immigrant Mexicans and Central Americans rated insufficient information services as a significantly greater problem than did either Anglos or U.S.-born Hispanics.

The survey of Yosemite National Park visitors described earlier revealed that more Anglos than Hispanics were aware of Yosemite's interpretive programs. Despite this, a higher percentage of Hispanics who knew about the programs used them during their visit. Even so, a casual observer probably would conclude that Hispanics were less interested than Anglos in interpretive activities, because Hispanics constituted less than 5 percent of total park visitation. Thus, in any single program, it is unlikely that Hispanics would be represented in large numbers.

Yosemite visitors also were asked about their use of seven specific personal and nonpersonal interpretive services during their visit, ranging from conducted walks to exhibits in museums and visitor centers. In six of the seven comparisons, no statistically significant differences were found in the percentage of Anglos and Hispanics who reported using a particular service. In the seventh case, Hispanic visitors were significantly more likely than Anglos to have viewed interpretive films and slide presentations. While these findings obviously do not cover the entire range of situations that interpreters work in, it should be clear that any judgment that Hispanic Americans have less interest than Anglos in interpretation may be premature and inaccurate.

Implications for Interpreters

It is easy to both exaggerate and underestimate the difficulty of intercultural interpretation in a multicultural society. We say "exaggerate" because the barriers to communication often perceived by Anglo interpreters are in many cases illusory. In this chapter, we have shown that the presumed lack of interest among Hispanics in interpretation, as well as their supposed careless attitude towards natural and cultural resources, are either unfounded or no more of a serious barrier to communication than exists among Anglos. On the other hand, the difficulty of successfully "connecting" with a visitor population as diverse as Hispanic Americans should not be glossed over.

The Issue of Language

A basic concern of interpreters and visitors alike is the matter of language. The various Hispanic populations in the U.S. differ from many other American ethnic groups in that they have maintained many aspects of their cultural heritage through maintenance of the Spanish language. A common pattern among other ethnic groups is a decrease in the use of ancestral languages over time, such that in the third and subsequent generations English becomes the first language (McLemore 1991). The persistence of Spanish among Hispanic populations is related to several factors, not the least of which is the continuing influx of Mexican, Central American, and Caribbean immigrants. In addition, Hispanics tend to settle and remain in geographic areas where there is no great need to learn English for day-to-day living.

For interpretive purposes, it is important to distinguish between the ability to speak a language and facility in reading it. First-generation immigrants may acquire some knowledge of spoken English, but be completely unable to read the language. On the other hand, it is not at all uncommon for subsequent generations of Hispanics to speak both English and Spanish fluently, and yet have only limited ability to read or write in the Spanish language (Keefe and Padilla 1987). If this seems strange to Anglo readers, consider how effortless it is to learn spoken English as a young child, and yet how difficult it would be to decipher this page if you had not been taught how to read. This is exactly the experience of many Hispanic Americans who, as children at home, learn to speak Spanish fluently, but do not receive instruction in how to read or write it in school. For this reason, printing interpretive brochures, signs, or labels in Spanish, as common as this practice may be, is likely to be most effective at communicating with educated immigrants who were not born in the U.S. In some cases, this may include the oldest generation in extended-family groups although, due to limited schooling, these individuals often have difficulty reading either English or Spanish. Simcox and Pfister (1990) recommend that informational services should rely heavily on international symbols. This is especially appropriate in states where "official-language" laws require that signs on state highways or buildings be printed exclusively in English.

Taking Advantage of the Extended Family

The multigenerational nature of Hispanic extended families places a premium on programs and settings that are interesting to both young and old, the active and inactive, and speakers of both English and Spanish. The rarity of such programming may be one reason why many Hispanic visitors to Biscayne Bay and the Angeles National Forest expressed dissatisfaction with interpretive services. The senior author recalls an outing in New Mexico's White Sands National Monument in which a multigeneration Hispanic family arrived at an adjacent picnic site. The group drove up in a modified school bus, and while the grandparents listened to music in the shade of the site's ramada, the father lit the coals in the barbecue grill and the children took turns burying each other in the gypsum sand of a nearby dune. Whether by design or accident, this activity and setting afforded something of value to everyone in the group. (It also accommodated another "odd" party: the author and his American and Korean graduate students, who were feasting on take-out fried chicken from a fast-food restaurant!) One possible reason that Hispanic visitors favored the interpretive films and slide presentations at Yosemite National Park may have been that, like the picnic area at White Sands, the activity and setting offered something of worth to everyone in the group. In this case, even those who did not understand spoken English could receive interpretive information via visual images and expressive music.

Becoming Interculturally Competent

A colleague of ours, an Anglo with considerable experience in intercultural communication, tells the story of an encounter with a group of Hispanic men at a national forest recreation area. The men, who were drinking beer and talking in Spanish, had just finished changing a tire on their pickup truck when our associate approached them and asked for their cooperation in a visitor survey. Upon learning that he was a university professor, the Hispanics began questioning him about global warming and depletion of the ozone layer. We suspect that most Anglo readers will be as surprised by this story as the Hispanics were when they discovered that not all university professors are conversant with these subjects. This anecdote illustrates one of the most prevalent barriers to effective intercultural communication: the preconceptions and stereotypes that make us too quick to judge others. These preconceptions display themselves in an array of biases, running the gamut from redneck racism and bigotry to the relatively innocuous discomfort felt in the presence of those who are "different" (Brislin 1991). The story also illustrates the fact that no single ethnic group has a monopoly on stereotyping. Indeed, experimental research in educational settings consistently reports greater difficulty in reducing prejudice among minority-group subjects than among members of majority groups (Stephan 1985).

What does it take to be an effective intercultural interpreter? Unhappily, there is no simple recipe for achieving this goal. Nevertheless, some guidelines have been developed. Barna (1991) reviews many of these in an article on the stumbling blocks to intercultural competence. Important barriers include ethnocentrism (including the assumption of similarity instead of variation between cultures), differences in verbal language, misinterpretations of nonverbal language, lack of open-mindedness and empathy, and the presence of high levels of anxiety during intercultural contacts.

To Barna's list can be added an unwillingness to engage in "adaptive behavior" (Ellingsworth 1983). This is the capacity to accommodate the perceived foreignness of others by showing respect (through both verbal and physical behavior) for culturally based beliefs, values, and behaviors different from one's own. According to Ellingsworth, when one or more parties to an interaction cease engaging in adaptive behavior, communication may continue, but the potential for effective *intercultural* communication and understanding is lost. Unfortunately, during exchanges marked by differences in power or social status, as when interpreters lead visitors through an educational activity, the burden of adaptive behavior usually falls on the less powerful parties. Thus, it is expected that participants will adjust to interpreters; however, if intercultural interpretation is to be effective, a special effort must be made by interpreters to adjust to participants.

There really is no substitute for personal commitment to intercultural interpretation. One must understand and respect the culture of others if one expects to receive understanding and respect in return. In many cases, the process of seeking understanding will reveal that communication barriers thought to be insurmountable actually do not exist. In other cases, greater insight into the behavior and beliefs of diverse groups will suggest program changes that can significantly enhance intercultural competence. Achieving this goal is a two-way street, and requires adjustments by users as well as interpreters. However, this is unlikely to occur if interpreters themselves do not actively work to bring it about.

Little Darwins:

A Profile of Visitors to the Galápagos Islands
(1991)

Gary E. Machlis

Diana A. Costa

Introduction

To be a tourist in the postmodern world is to engage in small interpretive dramas infused with cultural meaning. A child at Disney World, a gambler at Las Vegas, a white collar worker on a sex tour in Thailand, and a backpacker in Katmandu all have dramatic expectations of what they will find, experience, and feel. Hence, tourism is *mythic*, and to grasp the mythic content of a tourist experience is to gain leverage in understanding the tourist, the tourist site, and ultimately tourism itself (for a detailed discussion, see Machlis and Burch 1983).

That tourism has become an important economic and social force is indisputable: tourist revenues rank third among all export industries and travel represents 10-20 percent of the world gross product (D'Amore 1988). One kind of tourism, recently labeled "ecotourism," has experienced particularly rapid growth in the late 1980s and early 1990s. Ecotourism (sometimes referred to as nature tourism) is essentially recreational visits to relatively natural sites, where the attraction is an opportunity to learn about and appreciate nature and local cultures.

Ecotourism is not immune from the dramatic requirement for mythic experiences. Sometimes the myth chasing is subtle, as when modern-day river runners float down the tamed Colorado River through the Grand Canyon, following the route of the one-armed Powell as he navigated the then wild and unknown river. Sometimes, ecotourism can be ironically comic: well-parkaed tourists flying to Antarctica to linger a few minutes at the Pole; high-tech bicycle tours through low-tech countrysides; eager graduate students and faculty on collecting tours through tropical rain forest; treks, pilgrimages, expeditions. Again, to understand the dramatic meaning of ecotourism is to gain usable knowledge about the tourist and the resource.

In this chapter, we describe contemporary visitors to the Galápagos Islands through the lens of Darwin's historic visit in 1835; modern tourists are revealed as "little Darwins." Hence, the chapter serves two purposes: to profile current visitors and their views of the islands, and to illustrate the importance of understanding the dramatic liturgy of tourism.

The chapter is organized as follows. First, we describe and place in historical context Darwin's visit to the archipelago. Second, we briefly review the evolution of tourism in the Galápagos: its recent and explosive growth creating among managers and conservationists a need to know more about these visitors. Third, we describe the purposes' and methods used in a survey of Galápagos tourists conducted in 1990. Fourth, we present a profile of visitors, drawing on data from the survey. Fifth, we interpret the results in the context of touristic myth: the visitors at least partially defining their experience through the mythology of Darwin's visit. And finally, we discuss the implications of our findings, both for the future of tourism in the Galápagos Islands and for our theoretical argument.

Darwin and the Galápagos Islands

Charles Darwin was certainly not the discoverer of the Galápagos Islands, nor did he lead the first scientific expedition to the archipelago. The first visitors might have been Indians from Peru, or Inca voyagers, though evidence is not clear (Steadman and Zousmer 1988). Indigenous settlement had not preceded European discovery, as was more commonly the case in the "New World." The Bishop of Panama, Fray Tomás de Berlanga, officially "discovered" the islands in 1535, providing the King of Spain with first-hand descriptions of the giant tortoises and iguanas, and the extraordinary tameness of the birds (Jackson 1989).

Following European discovery, a cycle of pirates, whalers, furseal hunters, naturalists, soldiers, convicts, fishers, farmers, park managers, scientists, and tourists have visited and exploited the archipelago. By the time Darwin reached the islands in 1835, whalers had decimated the tortoise population, exotic species had already been introduced (goats on Santiago), a colony had been established on Floreana, and the archipelago had seen military action (the U.S. warship *Essex* destroying the British whaling fleet) and had been politically annexed by Ecuador.

The voyage of the *Beagle* was in its fourth year when it reached San Cristóbal in September of 1835. Captained by Robert FitzRoy, the *Beagle*'s mission was cartographic and scientific. Richard Marks, in his book _Three Men of the Beagle_, describes the unique motivation of such expressions of imperial power:

> . . .these English sailors of the Royal Navy, led by inspired aristocrats, assisted by scholarly plutocrats, were remarkable for their caliber. . .They operated in peacetime; they were the generation after Nelson; they fulfilled a mission of noblesse oblige, furthering civilization's comprehension of the physical world—and they did what they did without the lure of gold or the lust of conquest (1991:67).

Darwin himself represented the British fascination with science as a tool and responsibility of empire. Raised in an upper-class family for a career in medicine or the clergy, independently wealthy (through profits from the Wedgwood china enterprise), Darwin at 22 was on board the _Beagle_ at his own expense and for the purpose of natural history. He was well into his journey and scientific routine of collecting and note taking. He was feeling a rising confidence in his skills, and rising doubts concerning his creationist beliefs. The Galápagos stunned the young scientist. Writing in _The Voyage of the Beagle,_ he remembers:

> In the morning (17th) we landed on Christmas Island, which like the others, rises with a tame and rounded outline, interrupted only here and there by scattered hillocks—the remains of former craters. Nothing could be less inviting than the first appearance (1860:269).

To Darwin (as well as to others), the central character of the Galápagos Islands was their uniqueness, their isolation, and the tameness of their wildlife:

> The natural history of this archipelago is very remarkable: it seems to be a little world within itself; the greater number of its inhabitants, both vegetable and animal, being found nowhere else. As I shall refer to this subject again, I will only remark, as forming a striking character on first landing, that the birds are strangers to man [sic]. So tame and unsuspecting were they, that they did not even understand what was meant by stones being thrown at them (p. 270).

Darwin spent nineteen days on shore upon four islands and eighteen days cruising within the archipelago. On 23 September he visited a penal colony, and talked with the inhabitants about the hunting of tortoises. On the 29th he climbed a volcano and down into its caldera. On 8 October he went ashore for a week of collecting, and visited with several Spanish tortoise hunters, spending the night in their shelter, and going out on their small boat. He made sure (even in pre-tabloid Britain) that the macabre was represented in his public recollections:

> . . .the scene was both picturesque and curious. A few years since, the sailors belonging to a sealing-vessel murdered their captain in this quiet spot; and we saw his skull lying among the bushes (p. 275).

Darwin was fascinated by the giant tortoises, repeatedly describing them in otherworldly terms, as ancient, "antediluvian." Yet he was also exuberant, playful, mischievous, touristic:

> I was always amused, when overtaking one of these great monsters as it was quietly pacing along to see how suddenly, the instant I passed, it would draw in its head and legs, and uttering a deep hiss, fall to the ground with a heavy sound, as if struck dead. I frequently got on their backs, and then, upon giving a few raps on the hinder part of the shell, they would rise up and walk away; but I found it very difficult to keep my balance (p. 278-279).

And again, with an iguana, even more playful:

> I watched one for a long time, till half its body was buried; I then walked up and pulled it by the tail; at this it was greatly astonished, and soon shuffled up to see what was the matter; and then stared me in the face, as much to say, 'What made you pull my tail?' (p. 283).

And, naturally, Darwin the naturalist ate his subjects. He supped on tortoise, of course, but also on iguana and birds. He is repeatedly fascinated by the tameness of the birds and other wildlife, their unusual lack of fear:

> There is not one which will not approach sufficiently near to be killed with a switch, and sometimes, as I have myself tried, with a cap or hat (p. 285).

Darwin ended his recollection with a careful discussion of the origin of such behavior, growing more somber by the sentence. He concluded with a grim statement of relations between strangers, a foreboding expression of consequences:

We may infer from these facts, what havoc the introduction of any new beast of prey must cause in a country, before the instincts of the aborigines become adapted to the stranger's craft or power (p. 290).

And then, in the late fall of 1835, without a single specimen of the adult giant tortoise and with his collection unknowingly mislabeled, Darwin and the *Beagle* steered for Tahiti.

Tourism in the Galápagos Islands

Travel in the Galápagos has undergone numerous changes since Darwin's visit. Protection was first legislated by Ecuador in 1934. During the first ten years following the establishment of Galápagos National Park in 1959, tourism was incidental and uncontrolled. It was difficult for tourists to reach the archipelago, and those who did depended on islanders' willingness to transport them within the islands.

The arrival in 1970 of the first cruise ships (one with capacity for 58 passengers) brought large, organized trips to the islands. A national park entrance fee was instituted in 1972, higher for foreigners than Ecuadorians. In 1973-74 the Galápagos National Park Service started the demarcation of actual visitor sites, where visitors could come ashore under strict guidance and supervision of private tour guides. A management plan for the Galápagos was developed; it set the maximum number of tourists at 12,000 per year, which was soon exceeded. Daily tours, with visitors staying in hotels and going on day trips, were first begun in 1977 and have since expanded. Visitation during this period steadily increased, except during the energy and fiscal crises of 1974 and 1979-80 (see Figure 1).

In 1982 the master plan was revised, and the visitor limit was increased to 25,000 per year. In less than five years this limit was again systematically being exceeded. The archipelago gained recognition as a Biosphere Reserve in 1984. The San Cristóbal airport was opened in 1986, doubling the arrival capacity of the islands. Visitation increased dramatically (see Figure 1): 155 percent between 1980 and 1990. In 1990, over 45,000 visitors came to the Galápagos Islands.

The Study

With this dramatic increase in visitation came the political pressures to both continue the growth of ecotourism and protect the environment and wildlife of the archipelago. Knowledge of visitors became advantageous for park managers (to evaluate services), conservation biologists (to document human impacts), tour companies (to plan marketing strategies), and policy makers (to decide on future tourist development). A visitor study was commissioned by the Charles Darwin Foundation, and conducted by the University of Idaho. The objectives of the study were to describe the demographic characteristics of visitors, and to document their opinions and perceptions concerning their visit to the Galápagos Islands.

Front-end interviews were administered and questionnaires distributed to an interval sample of 457 adult visitors leaving the Galápagos Islands between 25 July and 10 August, 1990. Hence, the data reflect only summer season visitors. Visitors completed the questionnaires before embarking through the Baltra or San Cristóbal airports; since approximately 99 percent of the visitors leave through these locations, the population is well represented. A 100 percent response rate was achieved; nonresponse bias is nonexistent. The

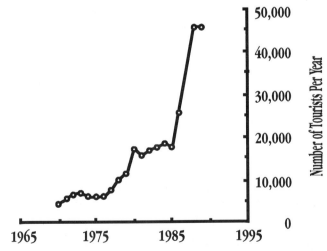

Figure 1. Growth in tourism within the Galápagos Islands.
Data from Anonymous 1988.

data were analyzed using SAS (for a detailed description of the study methods and results, see Machlis et al. 1990).

A Profile of Visitors

Figure 2 shows a wide range of age groups visited the Galápagos Islands, the most common being adults aged 26-55 (76 percent). Fifteen percent of visitors were adults 56 or older; a similar proportion (16 percent) were between 18 and 25 years old. Non-Ecuadorian visitors comprised 72 percent of all visitation. Figure 3 shows that most visitors came from the United States (30 percent), followed by Ecuador (28 percent), and several European countries (39 percent). Figure 4 shows visitors had a varied level of education. Fifty-two percent held bachelor's or graduate degrees, followed by visitors with some university education (22 percent), secondary education (14 percent), and vocational degree (6 percent).

Figure 5 shows that 74 percent of visitors organized their visit to the Galápagos Islands as packaged tours, 12 percent traveled independently, and 14 percent used some combination of packaged and independent travel. Figure 6 shows the proportion of visitors that participated in selected activities during their visit to the Galápagos Islands. Common activities were observation of animals and plants (99 percent), guided walks (97 percent), photography (94 percent), and visiting the Charles Darwin Research Station (89 percent). Visitors also went shopping, swimming, and sunbathing, and engaged in evening entertainment.

At the end of the questionnaire, visitors were asked a series of open-ended questions regarding their visit to the Galápagos. Table 1 shows the number of responses for selected categories. The variety and tameness of animals was most commonly mentioned.

Discussion

In the above data, and in additional comments made by visitors, there is at least some evidence that the mythic character of Darwin's visit is being reenacted. The visitors are largely American and European; almost one-third have taken advanced graduate courses or have a graduate degree. Their travel is packaged rather than independent (and on board the tiny *Beagle*, under FitzRoy's

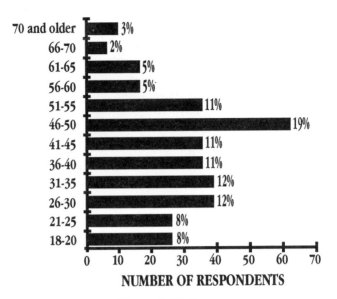

Figure 2. Visitor ages.
N = 452 individuals. Percentages do not equal 100 due to rounding.

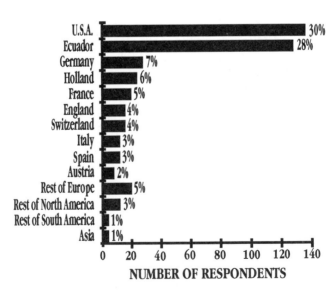

Figure 3. Visitor nationalities.
N = 455 individuals. Percentages do not equal 100 due to rounding.

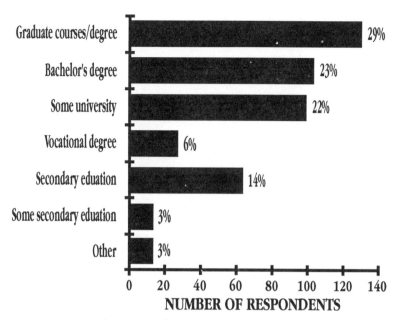

Figure 4. Visitor education levels. N = 455 individuals.

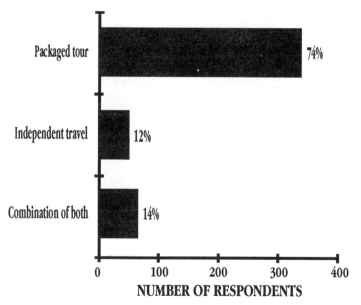

Figure 5. Trip organizations. N = 455 individuals.

command, was not Darwin's?). Their activities reflect Darwin's visit. All spend time observing fauna and flora, hiking, recording observations (in contemporary terms and technique, "photography"). And visitors are drawn to the unique character of the island's ecology: a variety of fauna, the tameness of animals, observing endemic species, all are valued experiences. As they describe in their own words:

> I did not expect the islands to be so beautiful, so peaceful or so clean. I was amazed. . . I was not prepared for the vast variety and intimacy with wildlife.

Like Darwin, they are pleased and astonished by the tameness, the unique behavior of the archipelago's wildlife:

> How amazing it was for the birds to land just beside you.

> Actually seeing the birds in their mating rituals and displays was a thrill of a lifetime.

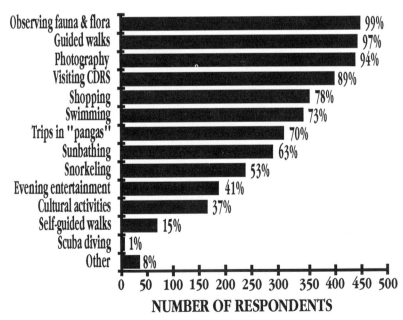

Figure 6. Visitor participation in each activity.
N = 457 individuals. Percentages do not equal 100 because visitors could report more than one activity.

A difference emerges, however: such pleasure is tinged with nostalgia and romanticism at err with Galápagos history:

> I most liked the experience of a place where there is virtually no trace of man or his [sic] interference and the resulting natural raw state of everything, and the animals' lack of fear.

> To see all the animals so close and friendly. Islands without people, like it was in the past.

And while Darwin rode the giant tortoises, ate iguanas, and slapped at finches, the contemporary visitors cannot. The result is plaintive:

> I want to touch the animals.

Implications

What can be made of these behaviors and remarks; what do they mean for tourism in the Galápagos? First, they reflect the dramatic requirements of ecotourism: to tour the natural world remains a cultural act. A visit to the Galápagos is what Turner (1969) calls a "liminal" moment; a set-piece composed of nature and cultural history or fable.

Second, the dramatic liturgy of ecotourism serves as a guide for the development and marketing of environmental education and on-site interpretation. Visitors to the Galápagos Islands made numerous suggestions on such matters:

> Emphasize Darwin and the *Beagle* more. A lot of visitors are very interested in this aspect—and have scientific backgrounds. Darwin was a giant of sciences—emphasize it.

> Maybe a show-video of the life of Charles Darwin, a brief description of all the islands, an explanation of the weather and the ocean currents. This would be like a scientific film of explanation. Perhaps shown at the airport as people wait, as can be found in many museums.

Third, to be a "little Darwin" is to care, in some cases deeply, about the preservation of the Galápagos Islands. When visitors participating in the survey were asked for proposals regarding the

Table 1. *Visitor responses to the question: "What did you like most about your visit to the Galápagos Islands?"[1]*

Comment	Number of times mentioned
Personnel	
Knowledgeable and respectful guide	13
Good guide	4
Services and facilities	
Boat accommodation	16
Boat trips	11
Food	5
Guided walks	4
Travel agency organization	3
Trails	2
Natural features	
Variety of fauna	130
Fearless animals	66
Seeing penguins, sea lions, iguanas, tortoises, etc.	49
Beautiful and unique environment	42
The flora	27
The landscape	26
Snorkeling and swimming with marine life	25
Closeness to nature	24
Observing endemic animals living naturally	20
The beaches	19
Observing fauna	19
Bird watching	17
Naturalness of environment	10
Volcanoes, lava, geology, topography	7
Activities	
Interacting with locals and fellow tourists	25
Snorkeling	24
Visiting different islands	6
Learning	4
Photographic opportunities	4
Scuba diving	3
Resting	3
Walking	2
Hiking	2

[1]N=785. Visitors could make more than one comment.

archipelago's future, six suggested better hotel accommodations and 104 called for limiting the number of tourists. Some realize the irony:

> Cut down the number of tourists—but that is difficult and perhaps I would not have been able to visit the Galápagos had the numbers been limited.

Hence, the dramatic appeal and ritual of ecotourism can, if managed, serve as an engine of conservation, encouraging tourists toward a kind of "low-impact touring" that buffers the almost inevitable expansion and excesses of the industry.

And lastly, the evidence of human drama, even in such a nature-dominated ecosystem as the Galápagos archipelago, illustrates a larger truth: the relationship of *Homo sapiens* and environmental resources is one of choice, of will. David Steadman is a scientist studying the fossil record of the islands. During the 1980s he has relived, more than most tourists, the drama of Darwin's visit. And perhaps he has also understood it more than most:

> To be in the Galápagos is to encounter a degree of vulnerability so dramatic that visitors have always been struck by it, though not all react the same way. Vulnerability touches an ambivalent chord in human nature: sometimes arousing a passion to intervene and protect, at other times stimulating a perverse temptation to brutalize or exploit. In the Galápagos, nature and human nature are now intertwined. The drama is as old-fashioned as the conflict between good and evil and it will surely carry into the future: the more the nearly pristine vulnerability of the islands puts its spell on people, the more the Galápagos will become a battleground where man's [sic] best instincts will clash with his worst (1988:78).

Essays

The sociological perspective also can be applied to a variety of contemporary issues that affect interpretation. The articles in this section are not studies *per se,* but essays on a wide range of topics. In the tradition of Tilden's principles, their purpose is to provoke the reader to view interpretation in a social context, to adopt the sociological "way of seeing" discussed at the beginning of the book.

The first essay deals with a sociological process not widely discussed in earlier chapters—the interplay of myth, values, and behavior. Joseph Meeker's 1973 essay "Red, White and Black in the National Parks," first published in *The North American Review,* initiated a vigorous debate over the level of elitism found in U.S. national parks. Perhaps overlooked was Meeker's insight that the very resources interpreters interpret are often cultural symbols of great potency. In a heterogeneous nation like the United States, it should not surprise us that some American subcultures are ambivalent toward historic sites, national parks, and other traditional settings for interpretation. The challenge that this creates for interpreters is significant.

The second essay is what the author, Kenneth Nyberg, has described as "friendly banter." First given at the Association of Interpretive Naturalists workshop in 1977, "Some Radical Comments on Interpretation" was viewed by some as controversial. Nyberg examines interpretation as an institutional function and challenges "the fundamental character of interpretation." The essay is included here because its analysis of interpretation is sociological (much of the essay dwells on the social relations between the interpreter and visitor), and because it speaks from the viewpoint of what the sociologist Peter Berger has called "the disenchanted observer." If interpretation is to advance as that unique public service Tilden envisioned, such disenchantment is healthy reading.

"Interpretation in an Urban Society" is the third essay. Most of the United States population lives in cities, and the implications for urban interpretation that stem from this fact include a need to understand the role of nature in the city. The essay examines historical trends, the sociological functions of urban open space, and property rights, and argues that all are factors influencing interpretive programming in urban areas.

The fourth essay, "Thoughts on a New Interpretation" represents a significant widening of the scope of interpretation—a redefinition of what it means to be an interpreter and the responsibilities of the profession. As interpretive programs struggle to maintain budgets and operational levels, this call for a greatly *expanded* interpretive function is cause for reflection and debate.

The next essay has its own controversial history. "Interpreting War and Peace" first appeared in 1985 in a newsletter of the Association of National Park Rangers, and in an edited form in *National Parks,* the magazine of the National Parks and Conservation Association. Reaction among interpreters of war-related sites was strong and divided; all agreed the issue of interpreting war and peace is important. Events of the last several years—the opening up of Eastern Europe, the end of the Cold War, and the Persian Gulf War of 1991—only reinforce the need for interpreters to grapple with this issue.

"The Devil's Work in God's Country," the sixth essay, is an analysis of how modern democratic politics have influenced interpretation in the United States. Machlis argues that "in contemporary America, interpretation is a political act, and is increasingly intertwined with the chaotic democracy that is American politics." The implications for the interpretation of controversial sites (like Custer's Battlefield) and issues (such as the Yellowstone fires) are significant and likely to increase as the politicization of interpretation increases.

The final essay moves from the United States to a global perspective. In "Crossing Borders and Rethinking a Craft," Ham and Sutherland suggest that interpreters who want to be effective in developing countries must experience a dramatic shift in thinking. The United States model (largely interpreting for on-site visitors) does not necessarily hold for the expanding interpretive efforts that are becoming part of the world park movement. The essay suggests that very different audiences, and hence approaches, may be required. This final essay therefore repeats this book's central theme, that interpreters must sociologically understand their clients if they are to be effective.

Red, White, and Black
in the National Parks
(1973)

Joseph W. Meeker

National parks were created as an expression of deeply rooted but poorly understood values inherent in American culture and in the traditions of Western civilization. No one need be surprised if ethnic groups who do not share those values fail to see the parks as their founders did, or as the National Park Service might like them to. It is worthwhile to review some of the myths and images relevant to park lands in Western culture in order to measure their distance from the traditions of minority groups in America.

Nature as a Refuge

The Western world has long looked on nature as a symbol of peace and purity. The garden of Eden was a natural setting characterized by beauty, simplicity, and moral innocence until it was infiltrated by corrupting influences. Ancient Greek thought also idealized a "Golden Age" somewhere in the dim past, conceived as a garden where food was abundant and adversity unknown. Both the Greek and Hebraic roots of Western culture agree that man originated in a benevolent garden and that civilization is a debased condition intended to punish man. When he was expelled from the benevolent garden, man went forth to build the ugly and hostile cities where he now suffers.

Efforts to regain the lost garden as a refuge from urban life have long occupied our minds. We dream of safe natural settings which will provide the comfort and repose lacking in the city. Such nostalgia for nature is common in our time, but it is also found strongly among the urban aristocrats of ancient Rome. The Roman poet Virgil is remembered not only for the *Aeneid,* but also for his pastoral poetry which glorifies the peace and simplicity of the rural countryside in contrast to the anxieties of urban life in Rome. And Juvenal, a Roman satirist of the second century A.D., speaks of "Rome, the great sewer" because of its pollution problems, then proceeds with a long list of other Roman miseries, including degrading poverty in the ghettos, high taxes, inflated prices for poor goods and services, corrupt government, crime and vice in the streets, pressures of social conformity in the suburbs, and poor schools run by wicked teachers. Juvenal's advice to weary Romans is "Tear yourself from the games and get a place in the country" where life will be easier, safer, and more sensible. Our culture has long agreed with Juvenal and Virgil that city life degrades man and that the country restores his sense of dignity; in the city man is controlled, but in the country he controls. Rural settings have symbolized both the purity of nature and the power of man since the beginning of the Western cultural tradition.

It may seem a paradox that the love of nature has been strongest in those civilizations which have produced the largest cities and the most complex technologies. From ancient Rome to modern America, nature has been thought of as a refuge from the problems of civilization. Within that tradition, humans have expected to find in natural settings a reaffirmation of human worth and purity. Like Adam and Eve in their garden, park visitors often feel their personal sanctity when they enter natural surroundings, and they feel the loss of sanctity when they return to the profane life awaiting them in the city. Nature is not sacred, but humans feel sanctified by their contact with nature. Such attitudes are not found among the hunting and agricultural cultures of Africa and the American Indians, where *nature itself* is thought sacred, and humans participate in that sacredness according to their degree of integration with natural processes. The need to protect nature from human activities is thus strongest in those cultures where humans look upon themselves as separate from natural life, and where they see that civilization is dangerous to the natural settings they need for spiritual relief.

The Royal Privilege

The recreational enjoyment of natural surroundings has been until recently a privilege reserved for aristocratic classes. Since Roman times, only those with wealth and leisure have been free to escape the pressures of the city. The great park lands of Europe were originally established as royal game preserves and forests from which commoners were strictly barred. British common law held that wildlife and forests belonged to the crown, as Robin Hood discovered when he poached the king's deer. The American translation of this tradition specifies that wild lands and animals belong to the people as a whole, but the idea of state ownership was long established by European monarchs before America appeared on the scene.

Early settlers in North America looked upon the land as a natural refuge from the oppressive cities of Europe. America was thought of from the beginning as a gigantic garden or wilderness park where humans could regulate their lives according to the principles of nature rather than the whims of kings. America *was* a national park in the minds of our founding fathers, but one which existed for the benefit of all people rather than merely a handful of royalty.

Yet, strangely, the aristocratic view of gardens remained alive as our early history unfolded. The leaders of the American Revolution were members of a new kind of aristocracy that was also based on land ownership. They shared the view that a social utopia would be created if the values traditionally associated with gardens and farms could somehow be fused with the needs of civilized life. Thomas Jefferson envisioned a civilization which would draw its moral strength from the people's attachment to the land. In Jefferson's words, "Those who labor in the earth are the chosen people of God . . . whose breasts he has made his peculiar deposit for substantial and genuine virtue." Jefferson, of course, was not thinking of the American Indians or of the black slaves who labored in the earth of the plantations, but rather of farmer-landowners like himself—the pastoral gentlemen who owned and managed the American garden. Jefferson connected both moral virtue and political rights to land stewardship exercised by landowners. Slaves and Indians, no matter how close they might be to the land, were excluded from Jefferson's vision and from the Constitution which he and his fellow proprietors created.

Snakes and Machines in the Garden

Jefferson feared the intrusion of a snake into the American garden, and he knew that the snake's name was industry. Leo Marx's revealing book, *The Machine in the Garden* (1964), traces Jefferson's anguish as he fought the development of manufacturing and industry in the hope of preserving the garden qualities of America. Jefferson even argued that America should export raw materials to Europe for manufacture and import finished products rather than develop factories on the garden soil of America. He knew that the machine and the garden were incompatible.

Jefferson's hopes for retaining a garden America dissolved, Leo Marx tells us, when the War of 1812 made it necessary to develop manufacturing in the interests of national defense. Like Adam in the Garden of Eden, America then fell from its state of purity, and Jefferson wrote in his diary that "Our enemy has indeed the consolation of Satan on removing our first parents from Paradise: from a peaceable and agricultural nation, he makes us a military and manufacturing one." Expelled from the garden by the two-headed snake of war and industry, we proceeded to build more and more machines in the garden, but Americans have never lost their sense of nostalgia and regret for the pastoral peace left behind.

The middle years of the nineteenth century were devoted to the machine and to the conversion of the wilderness garden into an efficient farm. Power and wealth appeared along with cities and industry, and America became more urban each year as it overwhelmed the natural wilderness with mechanical progress. Those who still cherished the dream of a garden America then organized themselves to preserve some part of that vision from the encroachment of machine America, and the national park idea was born in 1872 at Yellowstone.

America's national parks are expressive of myth that has been present in Western culture for some 4,000 years. They are National Gardens of Eden where we can feel close to the origins of human life and to the peace, innocence, and moral purity that myth ascribes to the origins of mankind. They are also places to seek refuge from cities and machines, offering us the psychological relief (the literal meaning of re-creation) that makes it possible to continue our work in unpleasant urban surroundings. They are remnants of the Jeffersonian dream of a garden Utopia, comforting for the evidence they offer that there are still a few places where the machine has not yet spoiled nature. And somewhere within us they also feed our aristocratic ego by showing the world that we are rich and powerful enough to afford gardens. All Americans can think of themselves as kings who control vast game preserves.

The Roots of Minority Indifference

It is a source of some embarrassment and concern to National Park Service officials that the parks have never appealed equally to all people. Poor people, black people, and ethnic minorities generally show little enthusiasm for the park idea. Despite recent strenuous efforts to bring "Parks to the People," the parks remain essentially playgrounds for middle-class citizens. The reasons behind minority indifference toward national parks are largely unexplored, perhaps because indifference doesn't demand to be understood as strongly as hostility does. No minority groups really hate the parks, but none seem to care much about them either. Recent attempts at cultural self-appraisal by thoughtful black and Indian writers offer some insight into American minorities' lack of enthusiasm for parks.

First, it is important to remember that the Myth of the Garden is not part of either African or American Indian traditions. The mythologies of both cultures assume that the civilized structures of human life are perfectly compatible with systems of nature, and both emphasize that the adaptation of human affairs to natural processes is one of the essential responsibilities of civilization. Before Africa and Indian America were influenced by the intrusions of European civilization, neither had ever heard that nature is a place of refuge from the evils of civilization, or that the present state of humanity represents a fall from an earlier state of purity symbolized by the garden. It is thus no wonder that the great national parks created by white men in Africa and America have always been difficult for the natives of both places to understand. Their inherited mythology simply does not support the idea of separate value systems for nature and for humanity.

In addition to their varying cultural mythologies, the red man and the black man have more practical reasons to view the American wilderness differently than white Americans. For the past few centuries, both groups have learned in pain that their association with the land is a source of misery and humiliation, not peace or fulfillment. Black and Indian values today not only lack the pastoral garden imagery reflected in the national parks, but both are in some ways actively hostile to that imagery.

Black Prisoners on the Land

Shortly after his release from prison in 1968, Eldridge Cleaver wrote an essay called "The Land Question and Black Liberation" (1970), in which he pointed out that one of the more important consequences of slavery in America was that "black people learned to hate the land." The American land was a place of punishment and imprisonment for slaves, not the source of liberation that white settlers found. From a black point of view, Jefferson's idyllic image of the nobility of rural gardens was thus completely reversed. The history of black people in America has tied them to the land with hatred, not love, with servitude rather than ownership. That is why, according to Cleaver, "one of the most provocative insults that can be tossed at a black is to call him a farm boy, to infer that he is from a rural area or in any way attached to an agrarian situation" (1970:18). Since the end of official slavery gave blacks some mobility, they have "come to measure their own value according to the number of degrees they are away from the soil" (1970:18). The city and its symbols, Cleaver concludes, are more likely to attract black allegiance than any images of nature.

Black efforts over the past few decades have been concentrated on the struggle for social justice and political power, not for relief or a pastoral retreat from pain. When refuge is needed from that struggle, black people are not likely to look for it in any wilderness setting, but among other black people, where they can expect to find understanding and human compassion. Nature, parks, and wilderness are terms that rarely appear in black vocabularies. A search among scores of recent books by black authors reveals no reference or index entry concerning national parks or wilderness lands. For most black people, the word park refers to an urban setting containing basketball courts, baseball diamonds, and perhaps a lawn for picnicking. The only wilderness of any concern is of the kind found in cities, the wilderness of the ghetto.

The Humiliation of American Indians

Indians, too, need to be free of the images historically imposed upon them by the white man. Vine Deloria, one of the most articulate Indian spokesmen of recent years, summed up in a nutshell the traditional white view of both blacks and Indians: "Negroes were considered draft animals, Indians wild animals" (1969:171). White images pictured the slave as a domesticated animal laboring in the American garden, and the Indian was viewed as a wild brother to the deer, antelope, and other creatures who were at home on the range. When national parks were established to commemorate the white conquest of the American wilderness and its wild animals, Indians were of course included. So now we can see bears at Yellowstone, wolves at Mount McKinley, Hopis at Grand Canyon, and Navajos weaving blankets at many national monuments of the southwest.

The national parks are places of humiliation for Indians who are displayed and exploited there. The curio counters are piled high with cheap imitations of Indian artifacts to be sold as trinkets to white tourists, and in the evening the naturalist's lecture is likely to begin with a brief description of the quaint Indians and other animals who used the parklands before the white man arrived. Many of the parks specifically glorify the white conquest over Indians or commemorate the white appropriation of Indian lands. Even the few preserved Indian victories are monuments to white dominance, as at Custer Battlefield, where it is shown how the Indians won the battle while losing the war. As the plantations remind blacks of both past and present causes for shame, so the parks often recall to Indians the destruction of their cultural heritage.

Economic and Social Problems

It is small wonder, then, that neither blacks nor Indians show enthusiasm for national parks. The usual explanation for their disinterest, common among sociologists and National Park Service officials, is of course also pertinent: blacks and Indians are generally poor people who can ill afford the time or money needed for enjoyment of nature, and neither group is likely to find much pleasure in the hiking, camping, photography, and nature study which attract middle-class whites to the parks. But even if blacks and Indians could be "taught" to appreciate parklands in the same way that many whites do, and even if both groups could somehow be provided sufficient wealth and leisure to visit the parks regularly, only the protruding tip of an enormous iceberg of indifference would be melted. The larger influence of established cultural values which disagree with those of white Americans would remain untouched.

Can the great wilderness parks, then, be of any benefit to American blacks and Indians, as Park Service officials now say they would like them to be? Perhaps not, except in the relatively superficial matter of providing inexpensive recreational space without discrimination for those few blacks and Indians who may choose to use the parks on weekend outings. The deeper emotional and cultural needs of both groups are unlikely ever to be satisfied in the sense that the parks satisfy Americans of European ancestry. Neither blacks nor Indians are ever likely to find the Garden of Eden in Yosemite Valley as other tourists do. Attempts by the National Park Service to attract minorities to the parks assume that these groups will find them pleasant and meaningful in the same way that white middle-class visitors do, but that assumption is most likely false.

Social Protest in the Wilderness

The national parks fortunately have not so far been involved in the great struggles between races and economic classes that have characterized recent decades. It is possible to imagine, however, a sad day when the wilderness parks might become just one more symbol of white American exploitation, as white banks and businesses now are to many young people of racial minorities. The parks do represent white American values, not universal human values, and there is no reason for them to be held sacred by groups who may oppose those values. A bit of plastic explosive in Old Faithful would go a long way as a protest demonstration. The features preserved in the parks are delicate and difficult to defend against those who do not respect them. If it should ever become fashionable to bomb and burn the national parks, we will have reached a profound and perhaps irreversible level of cultural and racial warfare. The very values which Americans have attached to the parks have made them vulnerable symbols of white exclusiveness, and so subject to such attacks.

The national parks need not be thought of as Gardens of Eden tended primarily for aristocratic or middle-class relaxation, or as symbols of the white man's conquest over nature or his fellow man, or as playgrounds for relief or distraction from urban social ills. Their most important values may lie instead in the integrity of the wilderness ecosystems which are protected within them, quite apart from any emotional needs they may satisfy for the American people. Wilderness ecosystems are capable of maintaining their equilibrium without human laws or intervention, and they represent our best source of information about the necessary preconditions for long-term survival of complex living communities. It is perhaps time now to look to our parks for the knowledge inherent in their natural structures, rather than for relief from the private fears we bring into them.

Ecology vs. Justice

Social justice and environmental stability are the two urgent needs facing American policy in the remaining decades of this century. Often their demands seem mutually exclusive, as when minority groups demand new industrial developments which will produce more jobs and more pollution, or when attempts at population control are regarded by racial minorities as genocide.

As the implications of both movements begin to unfold more fully in public, positions of neutrality between them will be more and more difficult to hold. The National Park Service, like most federal agencies, has so far elected to respond to the demands for social justice made by racial minorities, for that demand has been voiced most powerfully. The parks are increasingly expected to respond to legitimate social demands, even if a few demands of nature must be sacrificed in the process. The pendulum of Park Service policy, which has always swung precariously between preservation and recreation, seems now to be caught increasingly on the recreation side, and the imperative of preserving park wilderness must suffer accordingly. But that is a hopeless position for park policy to take. For even if the parks could be made accessible to all oppressed people in America, many of those people would not want the parks.

Racial prejudice is an internal disease of society that has grown from faulty human attitudes toward other humans. Environmental degradation is the sad result of mistaken human attitudes toward the processes of nature. Ecosystems, like racial minorities, have now announced to the white man that they will tolerate no more of his garbage or exploitation. Both crises have been created by the inordinate egotism of white culture with its demand for symbols of power and dominance; yet the two diseases should not be confused with one another, for their treatments must be different.

The goals of social justice will not be served by converting our best remaining examples of environmental integrity—the national parks—into settings for mass recreation. Prejudice and discrimination must be overcome by improving the laws and customs that govern human social relationships, not merely by providing minority groups with the recreational escapes which have sometimes helped white men to forget their problems. Similarly, environmental disease cannot be treated if we sacrifice our few surviving healthy ecosystems to social purposes. We will desperately need parks and other wilderness lands to study for the knowledge they alone contain about the ingredients essential to equilibrium among biological species, including our own species.

Black people and Indians have much to teach white culture about both problems. Both groups have survived tenaciously against overwhelming odds, because they have learned better than whites how to encourage tolerance and brotherhood among humans and how to adapt human activities to the conditions of natural environments. Both know that men must change in order to agree with the world, not the other way around. That is a lesson the white man has yet to learn from his fellow humans and from the wilderness land that still persists.

Some Radical Comments on Interpretation:
A Little Heresy is Good for the Soul
(1977)

Kenneth L. Nyberg

"Do not say, 'Draw the curtain that I may see the painting.' The curtain is the painting."

Nikos Kazantzakis

In one of the more pretentious descriptions of environmental interpretation, Carr (1976) is reputed to have said that:

> ... not having an interpreter in a park is like inviting a guest to your house, opening the door, and then disappearing.

Unlike Carr, I rather suspect that not having an interpreter in a park is more like returning to your own home and not having a salesman there waiting for you. Indeed, it is the essential thrust of my thesis that environmental interpretation is not only largely unnecessary, but significantly more likely to produce harm than benefit.

There is a considerable body of literature addressed to modes and means of improving environmental interpretation. What is not considered is the fundamental character of the phenomenon itself, i.e., the more radical questions of "what is it, why is it, and what has accrued because of it?" As a beginning, I offer three short answers to these three short questions. The remainder of this essay will elaborate these considerations.

Regarding the first of these questions—what is environmental interpretation?—it appears that the interpreter does three things: the interpreter tells the audience what it already knows, or the interpreter tells the audience what it does not want to know, or the interpreter tells the audience more or less than it should know. The important thing to remember here is that the interpreter is forever "telling" the environment to others.

The second question—why environmental interpretation?—is even simpler to answer. Having considered the question of why we have interpreters at all, I have come to the only conclusion possible: that the interpreter exists as a service to the good Bishop Berkeley, so that if a tree should fall in the forest we can be sure that it does make a sound, because someone is in fact there to hear it.

The third question—what hath environmental interpretation wrought?—is considerably more complicated but can generally be answered by noting the plaques on every conceivable house. The interpreter, much like Lot, continues to glance over his shoulder just in time to see everything turning to salt. Before him lies plague, pestilence, and immeasurable debauchery in the cathedral.

There is something wholly audacious about the environmental interpreter's work. Much like the doorman treating the landlord as a tenant—and an undesirable one at that—the interpreter is involved in convincing the public that their land is in fact his, and if they are good they may visit it for a short period of time. The term for this in Yiddish is "chutzpah," which basically means "unmitigated gall." Not only is such gall unmitigated, but it is also undiminished. Having convinced the owner that he is not the owner, and having provided him with a new title ("visitor"), the interpreter than proceeds to convince him that he is ignorant, as well. The visitor does not see, taste, hear, feel, or smell what he sees, tastes, hears, feels or smells. Rather, he *mis*-sees, tastes, hears, feels and smells what is "really" there. Hence, the visitor does not see a pretty, leafy tree sprouting nutlike growth, nor does he even see the "Ohio Buckeye." Rather, the visitor misperceives what is, in fact, an *Aesculus glabra.*

In short, the environmental interpreter is in the business of "telling" reality, thus denying to all others present the inspiration of speculation. To remove, hinder, or displace this speculation is to destroy reality; borrowing from T. S. Eliot (1952:117), reality is:

> An abstraction
> Remaining a perpetual possibility
> Only in a world of speculation

and by telling it, no longer is the possibility possible. Telling reality negates reality and ultimately negates man himself. As the philosopher Heidegger (1961) notes, the fundament of man is brought forth in a threefold act of founding a world *(Grunden),* discovering the things-that-are *(Shiften),* and endowing them with a sense or meaning *(ontologische, Begrunden des Seienden).* The interpreter, by telling a meaning, diminishes discovery and ultimately precludes man's founding of a world.

Realities are nothing more than ways of knowing, things to be known. When the interpreter tells his reality, he does not share it on an equal footing. Rather, he tells it so that it now is to be someone else's reality. It is an act of epistemological violence, not simply saying "my reality is better than your reality," but "my reality *is* reality." All else is illusion or delusion.

Much like the priest who observed that it is almost impossible to have a religious experience during a church service, I am compelled to argue that an environmental experience is far more often precluded by interpretive programs than facilitated. Indeed, it has always struck me much like programmed love-making, complete with a coach. Whatever technical knowledge the coach can provide will hardly compensate for the loss of passion and intimacy. It is damnably difficult to enjoy what you are doing when some other person keeps shouting instructions.

Aside from meeting the quizzical demands of Berkeley's dilemma, the very real question remains; why environmental interpretive programs in the first place? It is important to remember that, unlike the proverbial chicken and egg, the interpreter clearly did not precede either the environment or the actor in it. And, improbable as it may seem, far more people have benefited from an uninterpreted river than from an interpreted one. If God had wished for there to be interpretive programs He or She would have properly labeled trees and rock formations in the first place.

Essentially, interpretation—the telling activity—was largely instituted to *provide* a need, not to meet one. Prior to interpretive programming, such responsibility was entrusted to various incompetents such as fathers, mothers, friends, or—worst of all—one's own imagination and scholarship. This occasionally led to such crises of consciousness and faith as confusing a Douglas-fir with a slash pine, sandstone for limestone, and the yellow-bellied sapsucker with the loon. Such *angst* was relieved by the presence of the interpreter. Now one did not have to make up something when one didn't know, or figure it out for oneself; someone was present to assume this responsibility. Not only could we now be sure that the tree is, in fact, a Douglas-fir, but we also were immeasurably enhanced—interpretive programs invariably enhance—by the knowledge that the average twelve-year-old Douglas-fir regenerates 11,156 needles every year, while the loon hardly any.

I do not mean to deny the fact that a great many people like interpretive programs; they prefer having their world told to them. Generally, however, people who like interpretive programs also believe the Northwest Passage was opened by Coleman and Winnebago. Their idea of a primitive campsite is one where the television reception is bad and the ice machine is at least 30 yards away.

The argument goes that we need interpretive programming to meet the increasing demand of visitor populations. One of the reasons for this increasing visitor population is greater numbers of interpretive programs. My suggestion is to cut off the snake's head and let the body die. Simply abandon every interpretive program; tear up every access road; dismantle every prepared campsite and refreshment stand; and remove every plaque, sign, poster, arrow, and restroom. What will occur? Basically, fewer people will attend parks, wilderness areas, and forests. Only those people truly interested will go, not as visitors but rather as indigents. After all, where is it written that everyone needs a wilderness experience, properly interpreted or not?

If you can imagine the consequences of my suggestion, then you know the "what," "why" and "benefit" of interpretive programming: pure Keynesian economics. Indeed, the only unquestioned benefit of interpretive programming is that it:

> May assist in the successful promotion of parks where tourism is essential to an area's. . . economy (Sharpe 1976:9).

In this regard, the intepreter becomes a lackey for the exploitive interests of the bourgeois, and—unless pay scales have improved immeasurably—like all lackeys, does not participate in the bourgeois' profits.

Do I truly view interpretive programming as encouraging Bad Faith (Sartre 1957), playing *reductio absurdum* with the natural environment, and unwittingly participating in capitalist exploitation? The answer is yes. A student and—until now, at least—a good friend, has argued that the interpreter should ". . . assume a role that supports public mental health services" (Philip 1976:12). I take this suggestion as final evidence that I am right. Interpreters perceive their role far too ambitiously. It is not simply outrageous, it is dangerous as well. They tamper with the lives—mental, physical and spiritual—of people. Interpreters take from people not only their definitions but their defining capabilities and processes too. Interpretation has moved from prophecy to priesthood; interpreters' proclamations no longer are prayer, but revelation. And the fundamental question is: do they know what they are doing?

By now, I suspect I read like Madalyn Murray O'Hare at the Southern Baptist Convention. In truth, my remarks are intended to challenge complacency. I believe it is useful to question the very basis of that which we do—to go to the roots, to be radical. This is true of science, life, and interpretive programming, as well. Quite often the journey itself is more important than the ultimate destination. Quoting one of James Agee's wonderful aphorisms, "the tigers of wrath are wiser than the horses of instruction" (1960:458), Zaner goes on to observe that:

> One learns little or nothing if he avoids the central tigers of his discipline or craft, even though remaining with the gentle, domesticated horses may seem safer. It is necessary, then, to enter the fray; not for me to pretend to instruct, which is for horses, but rather to take up the issues directly, inviting you to think through with me the sense of criticism and its demands on thinking (1970:178).

It is my hope that this essay serves as a catalyst for such a demand on thinking, and that interpreters devote time to the critical consideration of environmental interpretation: what is it, why is it, and what has accrued because of it? We need to confront the tigers—if only to grab them by the tail—and consider seriously this topic which I have only poorly delineated.

Interpretation in an Urban Society
(1981)

Gary E. Machlis

In 1979 more than 67 percent of the United States population resided in metropolitan areas, with 28 percent living in the central cities (U.S. Department of Commerce 1980). The city is home for a majority of Americans, and its consumption of food, energy, water, resources, and open space is significant. This suggests that nature in the city is both ecologically important and sociopolitically relevant. This essay is about nature in the city, how nature is interpreted, and how it can be interpreted for the urban population. An assumption is that interpretive programs in metropolitan areas require a knowledge of historical and contemporary urban trends.

The essay is organized into three sections. First, some of the unique characteristics of nature in the city are described. These vary by culture, but there seem to be regularities among metropolitan areas of Western industrial societies. The analysis then suggests implications of these trends for urban interpretation. Lastly, an attempt is made to define, in the broadest terms, the scope of nature interpretation in an urban society.

Nature in the City

Cities are complex systems comprised of people, social institutions, technologies, and natural environments (Hawley 1971, Berry and Kasarda 1977, Michelson 1976). The city is both an outward form—housing, streets, factories, parks—and an inward pattern of life—cycles of work and play, routes of travel, rules of conduct, and so forth. Imbedded in both the physical form and social patterns of the city are its "nature areas"—those places where flora and fauna are evident. If we focus on only the broadest trends, we can discern several unique characteristics of nature in the city.

There is limited interdependence between local nature and other components of the urban system. During the Neolithic stages of urbanization, the emerging cities of the Indus Valley and Fertile Crescent relied heavily on local ecosystems. These cities utilized organic sources of energy and local supplies of drinking water. Cultivated land was within walking distance of the urban center. Human and animal wastes were used as fertilizers. Low concentrations of inorganic refuse (such as glass and metal) were produced. The

Neolothic city survived off the bounty provided by local ecosystems and was limited by their capacity.

A variety of technological and organizational advances released the urban settlement from reliance on local nature. The paved road made transport independent of season; the granary and reservoir allowed the storage of food and water. Concentration of administrative and military power (its physical form exemplified by the buttressed wall) allowed the city to conquer other populations and draw resources from more distant ecosystems. The limits of local nature were overthrown, yet enclaves of natural phenomena persisted. Even in the Middle Ages, cities retained some portion of land within their walls for use as gardens.

In the modern city, the actual interdependence between the urban population and its natural areas is relatively small. The majority of food, water, energy, and other resources comes from locations geographically distant; the city relies on what Catton (1980) calls "ghost acreage." New Yorkers draw water from upstate, eat vegetables from California, and drink orange juice from Florida. The large natural areas of most cities are either limited to providing recreation (e.g., parks) or acting as a convenient sink for industrial wastes (e.g., riverfronts). The smaller areas are often engulfed by economic processes that limit their usefulness. Martindale describes the impact of speculation and development on the growth of American cities:

> The inorganic gridiron plan of city layout was adapted to speculation and sale, for the first step in the development of a new quarter of the town was the plotting of streets. . . As the pattern extended, it was accompanied by the destruction of the natural properties of open space. Low places and streams were filled in. The first step in preparing a site for real estate speculation was the clearing away of all or most of the natural features of the area (1960:172).

The ecological implications are significant: landfill, drainage construction, and pollution act to reduce the viability and diversity of urban wildlife (Howard 1974) and can eliminate taxonomically important species (Campbell 1974). In some twentieth century urban areas (such as European ghettos of the late 1930s or highrise developments of the 1950s), natural features simply disappeared.

The city tends to collect and display nonlocal nature. Metropolitan areas are centers of commerce, administration, education, and entertainment (Odum and Moore 1938, Zelinsky 1973). They concentrate and mix social elements from varied hinterlands. As an extension of this pattern, the city collects and displays nonlocal nature, and the urban population's interest often is in the exotic. Zoos and aquariums are examples. The ancient city of Rome was treated to an expanding menagerie of animals from conquered lands, and the Roman games consumed immense numbers of wildlife. At the dedication of the Colosseum under Titus, 9,000 animals were destroyed in 100 days (Hughes 1975). Feathers, bone, and hide were items of cosmopolitan fashion.

Nineteenth century cities also reveled in nonlocal nature. The great European and American circuses, major zoological collections, and arboretums were all elements of urban life. A variety of natural history lectures, poetry recitals, and travelogues were available as part of the Iyceum movement, and these also helped satisfy the urbanite's fascination with nature from somewhere else (Dulles 1965).

Besides the traditional zoo and aquarium, other collections are unique to metropolitan regions. Amusement parks and public housing developments tend to landscape with nonlocal flora, and even the playfields of local parks may represent an exotic ecological community, held together by repeated fertilizing, reseeding, and artificial watering. Plant stores and pet shops reach many city dwellers, marketing nonlocal nature for private use.

There are distinctive patterns that guide the use of urban natural areas, especially parks. A variety of authors have attempted to discern the unique characteristics of urban recreation (for a review, see Dunn 1980). These characteristics include distinct cycles of park use, norms for social interaction, and territorial boundaries that separate park users by age, class, or ethnic group (Lee 1972). The city park may be a source of social integration allowing friends to meet, couples to court, and gangs to assemble (Machlis et al. 1981).

Of these variables, it is social integration that is most distinctly cosmopolitan. The sociologist Durkheim (1947) saw the high densities of urban life as leading to a division of labor that allowed

Table 1. Social change in a metropolitan community (informal social participation).

Frequency of getting together with—	Percentage distribution	
	1959	1971
Relatives (other than those living at home with you):		
Every day, or almost every day	7	6
Once or twice a week	35	31
A few times a month	21	20
Once a month	12	14
A few times a year	14	20
Less often	4	5
Never	7	4
	100	100
Neighbors:		
Every day, or almost every day	13	12
Once or twice a week	19	17
A few times a month, or once a month	23	20
A few times a year, or less often	22	23
Never	23	28
	100	100
People you or your spouse work with:		
Once or twice a week, or more often	15	14
A few times a month, or once a month	22	24
A few times a year, or less often	36	34
Never	27	28
	100	100
Friends who are not neighbors or fellow workers:		
Once or twice a week, or more often	25	19
A few times a month, or once a month	37	36
A few times a year, or less often	29	28
Never	9	7
	100	100

Source: Duncan, Schuman, and Duncan (1973:46).

for high personal freedom; in return, mechanisms for integrating the urban population were required. Table 1 shows the stability of such behaviors. A study of the Detroit metropolitan area in 1959 and 1971 suggests remarkable regularities in the frequency of interactions between relatives, neighbors, and others. Little variation was apparent over a decade marked by urban riots, student rebellions, assassinations, and moon walks (Cheek and Burch 1976). Social integration, it seems, remains an urban imperative.

The city's natural areas have traditionally provided an arena for this social phenomenon. Lovers' lanes, plazas, gardens, and parks provide locales for necessary social bonding. Nature in the city often serves as a backdrop for courtship, political gatherings, criminal activity, family outings, athletic competition, and other forms of critical urban interaction. A study of fifty cemeteries in greater Boston found a variety of uses (Table 2), with 45 percent of cemetery visitors not involved in gravesite visits (Thomas and Dixon 1974).

There is a mixed pattern of ownership and access. As Table 3 (Burch et al. 1978) suggests, there are several alternatives as to who owns natural areas within the city and who has access to them. The answers depend on cultural, political, economic, and historical circumstances.

In feudal times, natural areas such as urban gardens and nearby hunting grounds were owned and managed by the lord, and the general population was barred from their use (Mumford 1956). The emergence of capitalism brought with it a redistribution of owner-ship and an increase in public access—the museum, amusement park, zoo, and aquarium took on the form of private property with regular public access. Contemporary parks, with public ownership and access, are more recent inventions; for example, New York's Central Park was developed in the 1850s.

The modern city shows a mixed pattern of ownership and access. Socioeconomic status tends to segregate neighborhoods and their residents, as Berry and Kasarda note:

> High-status neighborhoods typically are found in zones of superior residential amenity near water, trees, and higher ground, free from the risk of floods and away from smoke and factories, and increasingly

Table 2. Activities found in fifty greater Boston cemeteries during 200 hours of study.

	Total number of people
Family gravesite visits	726
Historic gravesite visits	657
Car drivers passing through	323
Pleasure walking	256
Relaxing or sleeping	218
Bicycling	104
Dog walking	40
Athletics, including baseball, football, golf, jogging, and Frisbee playing	35
Games, including tag, hide-and-seek, hopscotch, card playing, and setting off firecrackers	21
Drug or alcohol consumption, including glue sniffing and marijuana smoking	18
Feeding wildlife	18
Fishing	16
Berry picking	15
Chipmunk trapping	9
Stone rubbing	8
Gardening	6
Model plane flying	6
Photography	2
Drivers' education	2
Eating lunch	1
Car washing	1
Peeping Tom	1

Source: Thomas and Dixon (1974:108).

Table 3. A typology of urban ownership and access; some examples.

	Private access	Public access
Private ownership	a person's residence	cemetery
Public ownership	mayor's residence	public park

in the furthest accessible peripheries. Middle-status neighborhoods press as close to the high-status ones as is feasible. To the low-status resident, least able to afford costs of commuting, are relinquished the least desirable areas adjacent to industrial zones radiating from the center of the city along railroads and rivers, the zones of highest pollution and the oldest, most deteriorated homes (1977:32).

Hence, access to urban nature may be related to a host of sociological and economic factors.

The most obvious natural areas are public owned with public access (parks), but the amount of privately owned nature in the city may be surprisingly high. In the previously mentioned study of Boston cemeteries, 42 percent were privately owned, and 91 percent had public access. This is significant acreage, as over a third of Boston's open space is within its cemeteries (Thomas and Dixon 1974). Country clubs, yacht clubs, golf courses, and exclusive residential districts often include natural features. Ownership of urban nature may even be fashionable for corporations—the fringes of New York and its satellite cities are interspersed with company headquarters, each with acreage left in woodlot, glen, or open field.

Implications for Interpretation

It has been suggested that there are at least four characteristic patterns concerning nature in the city: minimal interdependence between the city and local nature, a tendency to collect and display exotica, the importance of nature as a backdrop for social integration, and mixed patterns of ownership and access. Each has implications for urban interpretation.

The minimal interdependence with local nature makes urban interpretation more difficult. Very few natural ecosystems exist in our large cities. While the Jamaica Bay Wildlife Refuge near New York's JFK Airport is an exception, Central Park's manicured setting is more typical. Most urban parks and preserves are in what ecologists call "anthropomorphic climax"; i.e., the community of plants and animals is dependent upon man's activities. Hence, local ecosystems are often altered, and it is difficult to find significant acreages that include native species in natural communities. Interpreting local nature may require extra effort to find, protect, and manage these places.

Further, the interdependence between an urban population and its "ghost acreage" is often disguised. Supermarkets serve as continuously stocked cornucopias, water is always on tap, and garbage is predictably carted off elsewhere (most of the time). In fact, it is not until natural disasters or social unrest (such as labor strikes) occur that these interdependencies are apparent to the urbanite. Interpreting a city's ghost acreage and its fragile ties to distant ecosystems could be an important revelation to urban populations.

The city's role in collecting and displaying exotic nature is an opportunity and challenge. As described earlier, the urban center is the locale for major botanical and zoological collections, both deliberate (zoos, arboretums, and aquariums) and circumstantial (residential landscaping, maintained ball fields, vacant lots, and so forth). Such exotic flora and fauna play important roles in the anthropomorphic climax communities of most urban open space. Interpretive efforts could focus on the utilitarian values of nature in the city—the approach largely taken by those involved in urban forestry programs (Driver et al. 1979).

Nature interpretation in an urban society competes with the other attractions of the city. Art museums, theaters, movie houses, concert halls, and sport stadiums are all examples of the urban center's ability to concentrate and mix the human and economic resources of a region. While several studies have found environmental concerns and park going associated with high levels of education and income (Cheek and Burch 1976), other cultural institutions draw similar audiences. An opportunity lies in creatively linking interpretive programs with special exhibits in art galleries, with concert series, and even with sporting events.

Urban exhibits of nature attract a nonlocal audience, and this·· special population may present special challenges. For example, visitors to zoos and aquariums may include a substantial number of vacationing families, suburbanites and foreign tourists (Cheek 1976). Research by Berry and Kasarda (1977) documents that suburban populations in general, and the commuting population in particular, have large impacts on urban recreational services already strained by lack of financial resources. They note:

Exacerbating the service-resource problem facing the central cities has been the fact that suburban population growth has not been matched by a proportional growth of suburban public services . . . Evidently, it is not economically rational for suburban-area residents to build and operate their own libraries, large parks, zoos, museums, or other public facilities if they have ready and free access to those in the central city (1977:226).

A key challenge to urban interpretation is to increase the role of suburbs in providing interpretive opportunities or contributing to the cities' efforts.

Further, nonlocal audiences may require special interpretive programming. Interpretive planning for distinct populations is important (Machlis and Field 1974), and nonlocal visitors are no exception. They may require more information concerning visitor services and regulations and an interpretive introduction to the city as a whole. The opportunity is to reach a regional, national, and international audience with introductory programs that may also prove popular with locals.

Because urban nature is a setting for critical forms of social integration, interpreters should plan for each activity. The gardens, riverfronts, parks, and zoos of our major cities also are settings for strengthening the social bonds of kinship, friendship and neighborhood. Urban interpretive programs can offer these social values at the same time they inform and inspire visitors. In a study of an urban park in China, Machlis et al. found this multipurpose use of urban nature to be widespread:

Just as a particular location in the park can be used for many purposes at the same time, a particular activity can serve several park functions. An example is the raising of lotus *(Nelumbo nucifera).* The flower is enjoyed for its aesthetic value during the Lotus Blossom festival which brings together people from throughout the region. The petals are a culinary delicacy. Leaves of the plant are used in cooking to wrap food stuffs. The young root of the lotus is slivered and eaten; older roots of the plant are milled into flour. Thus, one activity within the park serves many purposes (1981b:10).

Natural areas may be important locales for holding festivals, craft fairs, exhibitions, and other large-group activities. Natural history programs may be organized to maximize the social bonding of smaller groups, e.g., interpretation that encourages parent-child interaction.

The social processes that characterize urban open space may also have negative consequences. Competition between interpretive programs and other uses may range from the commonplace (joggers versus birdwatchers) to extreme cases of conflict and displacement, such as juvenile gangs coopting territory for their operations. These managerial realities will affect urban interpretation.

The mixed pattern of public and private property ownership will require cooperation between the public and private sectors. In the previous section, I described how postfeudal economies led to a mixed pattern of public and private property ownership and access, and how speculation and development acted to reduce the amount of urban open space.

What is preserved are likely to be fragments of ecosystems, though certain city parks closely resemble whole ecological units (e.g., Rock Creek Park is an important watershed in Washington, D.C.). Interpretive programs that effectively deal with the levels of community and ecosystem must usually cross boundaries between public and private rights. For example, few urban waterfronts could be interpreted well without encountering almost every type of ownership/access pattern described in Table 3.

Hence, cooperation between the public and private sectors may be a necessity for effective urban interpretation. Opportunities for such cooperation exist; the recently completed National Urban Recreation Study found that 70 percent of the neighborhoods surveyed had private nonprofit recreational services, and 44 percent had private for-profit services. Further, Table 4 shows these services are often located in residential districts away from large urban parks. Interpretive programs could be integrated into these agencies' and businesses' traditional programming.

Table 4. Percentage of urban neighborhoods with private nonprofit recreation services.

Neighborhood income level	Percentage
High	50
Medium	67
Low	80

Source: Heritage, Conservation and Recreation Service (1980).

Interpretation in an Urban Society

Clearly, the possibilities for urban nature interpretation are as varied as the potential sources of environmental knowledge in the city. In addition to the traditional interpretive efforts at large parks, zoos, and aquariums, many other types of institutions are involved: factories and light industries give tours; breweries are open to beer-tasting visitors; travel companies offer ferry rides, bus rides, and walking tours; and so forth. *All have potential as part of an urban interpretation program.*

Further support comes from the study of tourism. In his book *The Tourist: A New Theory of the Leisure Class,* Dean MacCannell (1976) suggests that much of the way we interpret new environments is structurally similar to the processes used by tourists. His analysis of urban touristic activity argues for a wider view of urban interpretation. MacCannell suggests that, for tourists, urban areas are composed of tourist districts: Paris is made up of the Latin Quarter, Pigalle, and Montparnasse; San Francisco is made up of Haight-Ashbury, the Barbary Coast, and Chinatown. Tour guides and travel literature suggest or recommend certain regions, communities and neighborhoods, and the tourist then "discovers" such features as markets, restaurants, people, and importantly, nature.

Several features seem to be especially attractive as objects of tourist interpretation: commercial establishments, special residential districts, unique occupations and public works (including parks). A striking example is the famous tour of the Paris sewer system. A guidebook published in 1900 describes the tour:

In the Place du Chatelet is one of the novel entrances to the vast network of sewers by which Paris is undermined. They are generally shown to the public on the second and fourth Wednesday of each month in the summer . . . The visit, in which ladies need have no hesitation in taking part, lasts about 1 hour, and ends at the Place de la Madeleine. Visitors are conveyed partly on comfortable electric cars, partly in boats, so that no fatigue is involved (Baedeker 1900:64).

What is arresting about this example is its potential for interpreting the urban environment. All components of the city, no matter how unrelated they are on the surface, are interconnected underground. This is interpretation at its ecological best, and it is fascinating for the urban dweller and visitor alike. We interpreters need to develop similar activities; I believe this to be the challenge of interpretation in an urban society.

Thoughts on a New Interpretation
(1985)

Donald R. Field

Gary E. Machlis

Introduction

The literary motifs of a culture are indicators of deeply held paradigms about the world. In the Occidental literature devoted to humanity and Nature, two central themes emerge. The first is people against Nature: the conquest or taming of wilderness for human settlement and occupation, and the exploitation of natural resources. The second is people defending Nature: preserving wilderness, parks, endangered species, and excluding human activity from special enclaves. The dialectic arguments which emerge are framed rather simply: resource development vs. preservation, with Truth being found in the temporary, political victory of one world view over another.

Paradoxically, both views share a common dimension: *Homo sapiens* is treated as separate from the natural world. The dialectic arguments have carried over into debates about national parks in America. They are enhanced in part by the enabling legislation establishing the National Park System, which draws attention to the dual responsibility of preservation and use.

Regardless of its rhetorical power, the debate between preservation and use may be artificial, and actually obscure the fundamental problems between humanity and Nature. It may detour our analysis from the critical issues associated with human behavior, natural resources, and parks, and fool us all—managers, planners, rangers, ranger interpreters, scientists, politicians, and citizens—into seeking and accepting simple and incomplete solutions to complex problems.

This chapter builds on the premise that humankind must be considered as part of the ecosystem whether we seek to become observers of the human scene or problem solvers. In this context, a human ecological perspective is discussed. We suggest that interpretation might be viewed as an ecological function and that an emerging exchange relationship between people and the interpretive specialist forms the basis for a "new interpretation." Next, we identify a set of tasks for the new interpretation, although they are more suggestive than definitive. We conclude the chapter with a call for a human resource management plan. Such a plan will add legitimacy to and authority for a new interpretation.

Human Ecology and Parks

Human ecology focuses upon the environmental basis of social organization (Hawley 1950). Central to social organization is each society's definition of its resources. Simply stated, natural resources are a product of society, not solely of the earth, and the very definition of a resource may vary from time to time, place to place, or group to group. One culture's precious metals may be another's junk trash (Alexander Spoehr said this more eloquently in 1956).

The reason that social definitions are so important to understanding interactions between people and Nature is that social systems—values, norms, institutional structures, sociopolitical arrangements, all this cultural "baggage"—influence how resources are defined and treated, and these definitions are changing all the time. Social change permeates society, requiring adaptation of people and human institutions to new environmental conditions. The static truth sought by the dialectic argument is illusory, as Firey realistically notes:

> Plato's ideal of a government by philosopher kings could never work for reasons which lie in the very nature of a social order. So too, there are ideals of resource development and conservation which can never be built into any social order. . . There are mechanisms operating that forever sift and sort the resource processes which are possible in a given habitat or which are conceivable in a given culture (1960:2).

In contrast to the dialectic approach is the ecological, which assumes a connectedness between human values, human behavior, and the environment. This is not a new paradigm, though it is gaining renewed support as the complexity of humanity's role on earth becomes more apparent. René Dubos in his book *The Wooing of Earth* states:

> The ecological image of human life that is now emerging is in part a consequence of concern for environmental degradation. It has also been influenced by the development of new scientific disciplines such as cybernetics, information sciences, general systems theory, and hierarchy theory. Its more profound origin, however, is the increased awareness of the intimate interdependence between human beings and their total environment (1980:146).

The relevancy of the human ecological perspective for park management is apparent. Parks are a product of human society. As such, they reflect a social definition of what such places are and should be. Like other resources, the descriptions of parks and the justification for them have changed over time. In the more than a century since the establishment of Yellowstone National Park, we have witnessed a complex set of human values assigned to national parks by people who argue for them, establish them, manage them, use them, and live in and around them. In his book entitled *National Parks: The American Experience,* Alfred Runte (1979) reminds us that parks reflect the social values and cultural traditions of the society creating them. Images of national parks have included such phrases as "worthless lands," "scenic landscapes," "economic benefit," and "self-regulating plant and animal communities," to name a few.

Definitions or cultural meanings of national parks—what a park is—are many and diverse. Perhaps a thread of stability or consistency can be found with regard to the "natural environment" (i.e., the plant and animal community) of a park, but because we have excluded people from the park equation, our understanding of human behavior within the park environment is underdeveloped. George Wright, Joseph Dixon, and Ben Thompson noted in 1933 the importance of understanding our place within the park ecosystem. They note that:

> Since he [sic] is in the parks permanently both as a resident and a seasonal visitor, man must henceforth be considered an integral part of those macrocosms. The significant difference between himself and all other ecological factors is that he is conscious of his relationship to the other elements of the park world and hence can regulate, or at least modify, his own purpose. It happens that in the parks the purpose dominating man's relations to his environment is the maintenance of all the animal and plant life in an unmodified wilderness state. In order not to defeat his own ends, he contrives that his presence shall disturb the wildlife to the very smallest degree that his ingenuity can manage (1933:53).

As professional park managers, we might be wise to heed this advice. We have recognized the dynamic nature of plant and animal populations in parks, but attempt to retain the human animal in a static state. Yet the conditions under which people enter park ecosystems in 1980 are not the same as in 1872, 1916, or 1966. We recognize the adaptation of plant and animal species in parks as a natural process, but treat the adaptation of people to changing management policies, concession facilities, transportation systems, trail systems, etc., as problematic. We view succession of plant and animal communities as natural and attempt not to interfere with the process, but often resist human adaptation. We anticipate a biological response to management, but often strive to prevent a human response to such manipulation.

Professional management of parklands often involves manipulation of the ecosystem, which may have consequences for the people who use them. The closure of zones within a park to human access, the removal of campgrounds, use of backcountry permits, alteration of transportation systems, and construction of hotel accommodations are each examples of management actions which may alter the ecosystem and the behavior of people within the system.

The relevancy of human ecology for interpretation should likewise be apparent. Interpretation is a park management function and as such is a component of the park ecosystem (Machlis et al. 1981a, Machlis and Field 1984.). Interpretation has the capacity to manipulate or influence the movement of people through the ecosystem both in time and space by the location of visitor contact points within the system, including visitor centers, the timing and location of walks and talks, etc. In addition, interpretation has as a central goal the exchange of information on flora, fauna, or cultural objects of a park to people. The product of interpretation is the successful dissemination of information resulting in improved knowledge about the ecosystem. The content of maps, slide programs, brochures, oral history demonstrations, etc. is a form of exchange within the system which has potential for behavior modification.

The interrelationship of diverse visitor groups in such a complex setting as a park requires substantial adaptation. An interpretive program that describes local flora and fauna, informs visitors as to hiking and sightseeing opportunities, and explains park regulations is part of this process. Seen in this light, interpretation is the exchange of information critical to adaptation within a park ecosystem, and the interpreter fulfills a specific ecological function. But the interplay of people and interpretation is proving to be even more than this.

Traditionally, interpretation has been responsible for the transmission of information about the park to the visitor (Sharpe 1982), as shown in Figure 1. Most interpretive activity has been perceived as a one-way flow of communication, except for the well-established need for audience feedback (Ham 1982).

A "new interpretation" would have a greatly broadened scope. Its function would include traditional interpretive activities, but also involve the transmission, receipt, and interpretation of information from the social environment of the park to park management, as shown in Figure 2. A critical component of a new interpretation is the social environment of a park. As articulated in the ecological model, this social environment implies a constant interaction among all groups of people comprising the ecological system. There are natural communication links between and among concession personnel, park rangers, and maintenance staff, as well as the various publics who use the park. Each communication link provides insight and perspective about these groups' definition of the resource and clues about how they are interacting with the resource and each other.

A new interpretation becomes a catalyst in this interaction process, and rightly so. Interpretation has as much to offer other divisions within park operations as it does the public. Interpretation is interdependent with resource management, ranger activities, and maintenance. The communication skills the interpreter has—the special ability to understand and interact with people, the knowledge

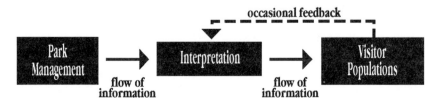

Figure 1. Traditional interpretation.

THE SOCIAL ENVIRONMENT OF A PARK

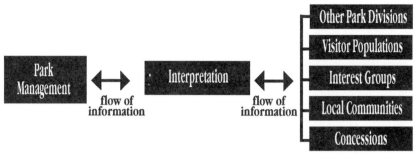

Figure 2. A new interpretation.

of how to package and disseminate information—are professional assets of inestimable value to park management functions. This new interpretation would, in essence, become the organizational focus of human services within the park.

In the next section we suggest a series of tasks that a new interpretation might address.

Tasks for a "New Interpretation"

Human Resources Basic Inventory

Considerable attention has been given to completing a basic inventory of natural and cultural resources—the objects for which an area is set aside. Yet it is the human species which is the key actor in system change and impacts upon those natural and cultural resources. Careful management requires a basic inventory of human populations in parks, their distribution, concentration, and succession, such that change and impact can be assessed. Monitoring of visitor use is not only essential for changing interpretive exhibits, talks, and walks, but also for assigning maintenance activities and law-enforcement patrols. Once completed, a human resource inventory becomes the data base by which a new interpretation monitors the human system over time and generates information about people in parks and human adaptation to the system.

Park Strategic Planning

A basic inventory of human resources associated with a park ecosystem allows the development of a few key social indicators to follow over time. These social indicators can be essential descriptive measures of a strategic plan for the park. What will visitation issues be in the year 2000? What changes should management consider in its operational style to protect resources and serve visitors in the year 2000? What about new transportation systems for parks? How will regional population growth influence park policy? For example, the Rocky Mountain region west from Ft. Collins to Colorado Springs is predicted to double in population by the year 2000. What does this mean for those who manage Rocky Mountain National Park? The new interpretive division, with its data in place, can chart alternative futures for park visitation and alternative management strategies and interpret them for park management.

Liaison with Park Constituencies

Because parks are interdependent with local communities, imbedded in regional social systems, and responsive to national politics, each park has a wide range of constituencies that have an interest in influencing park policy. Examples include local chambers of commerce, environmental groups, farmers, developers, the transportation industry, county, state, and regional governments. Managers need to have park policies interpreted for these groups, and to receive feedback from them. Examples include public hearings, "state of the park" reports, public relations work, and so forth. A "new interpretation" could serve as an important liaison between park management and these organized publics.

In-Service Training

Because of the heavy need for in-service training, and the difficulties of funding such activities on a broad scale, park management will necessarily need to develop ways to train itself. Park-level courses in everything from supervision to computer skills are needed. A "new interpretation" could become the focal point for such activities, organizing park-level seminars, training professionals, and coordinating self-teaching programs for the entire park staff.

Traditional Objectives

We do not suggest that interpretation should reduce, weaken, or abandon its traditional function of educating and entertaining visitors. This is its primary mission, and continued emphasis on these traditional objectives is required. Yet the visiting public is slowly shifting, and interpretive programming may need to likewise shift its priorities. More seniors are going to visit parks as the population ages; the baby boom population will soon be raising their families and bringing them to the parks, foreign tourism will increase in predictable cycles determined by the value of the American dollar, international economy, and private sector marketing. A "new interpretation" must contrive to serve these visitors, even as it expands its other functions.

Conclusion

Interpretation divisions are seeking ways to expand their role and function within the management system. Some interpretive divisions have been given responsibility for data collection and storage of human-use data in parks including visitor and campground statistics. Others have been given the responsibility for public involvement activities on a wide range of management issues. Some have been asked to provide strategic planning activities where forecasting of future use is desired, while others have been asked to simply project recreation use trends based on current use levels, and still others have been asked to monitor visitor response to management programs, most notably human safety and health programs. These duties and responsibilities are examples of the "new interpretation" and additional tasks could well be noted.

Tasks which have been suggested for the new interpretation need to be addressed in a planned way. They imply a more specific statement of agency relationship to people, and an importance attached to people in agency activities heretofore not stated. A human resource management plan is suggested.

Resource management agencies such as the National Park Service must decide what their responsibilities to their clients are and what the relationship of people to agency goals and objectives ought to be. Within the Service considerable rhetoric prevails about the

the dual mission of preservation and conservation of natural and cultural resources for future generations and the public enjoyment of these resources, but attention given to natural and cultural resources and to human resources is unequal. Contrary to popular myth, the human resource receives less management attention, so far as studies and accumulation of data are concerned.

The myth arises from the amount of time and money spent on buildings, roads, and other facilities, purportedly to "serve people" but most often without a clear idea of how these services actually meet human needs in parks. Concerted effort is in fact being given to both natural and cultural resource management. Policies and guidelines are in force which direct park superintendents and their staffs to inventory resources and prepare a plan for conserving those resources and initiating mitigating efforts to resolve problems potentially affecting them. But there is no human resource management plan. There are few national policies that define the responsibilities of the park superintendent to the client, and those that do exist refer mainly to physical health and safety. There are few evaluation standards to assess how management actions interfere with or unduly alter human use patterns in parks. There is no policy which integrates natural and cultural management plans with human resource management plans. Until there is a human resource management plan, management functions cannot be evaluated in any meaningful way.

Interpretation is perhaps the dominant human services function of all divisions. Interpretation interacts with the public not as a problem, or an impact, but as people adapting to a variety of park environments. Responsibility for a human resource management plan would be consistent with interpreters' other emerging duties and would provide the quantitative indicators sought by interpreters to document the services they provide to park management and the American public. A human resource management plan might well be the process whereby a new interpretation emerges within park management; but more importantly the preservation of a park ecosystem and the place of humankind within that system depends upon the kind of knowledge a new interpretation can provide.

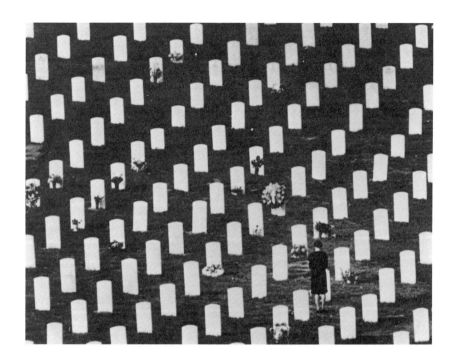

Interpreting War and Peace
(1985)

Gary E. Machlis

$\mathbf{T}$wo of the most important and common topics that rangers in the National Park Service must interpret are those of peace and war.

The National Park Service now manages over fifty war-related sites, one of the largest such inventories in the world, and interpreters at these areas communicate to large numbers of visitors—1.29 million at Gettysburg in 1984 alone. In addition to this historical focus, the issues of peace and war have a larger relevance as two of the most crucial issues of our age. We need only think of the two world wars in this century, the terrifying arms race between the superpowers, and the struggles in Central America, Afghanistan, Lebanon, the Persian Gulf and elsewhere for confirmation.

What is the relationship among interpreters, interpretation, and the issues of peace and war? What are interpreters doing in the Service and elsewhere, and what are the implications of their efforts? This chapter will examine the bases for interpretation of these issues and some current efforts and trends, and suggest some alternatives for the future.

Overview

War has always been a part of human history, though the scale of such conflict has steadily risen. Norman Cousins has estimated that between 3600 B.C. and the present—5,600 years—there have only been 292 years of world-wide peace. His guess is that there have been at least 3.5 billion war dead, a number equal to approximately 80 percent of the current world population (Beer 1981).

War has many impacts beyond the immediate deaths of soldiers and civilians. These include increased disease, general malnutrition, destruction of habitat, increased pollution, higher prices, and demographic change. Yet war also has been shown to enhance national solidarity and community spirit, improve technology, medicine, and some forms of trade, and stimulate social change. In addition, many nations fight the *bellum justum* or "just war" to protect cherished values—the very underpinnings of a society. In the 1967 Mideast War, Israeli soldiers liberated the Wailing Wall in Old Jerusalem with prayers and thanks to God; similarly, Egyptian soldiers liberated parts of the Sinai in 1973 with cries of "Allah is Great!" and prayers.

How Important Is Interpreting Peace and War?

With the documented history of wars and the immensity of their destruction, most would agree that, given the protection of cherished values, war is generally bad and peace is good. Why then, should interpreters interpret peace and war to the public?

Interpreting war has several benefits. First, it helps us understand the origins of wars. At the outbreak of World War I, the ex-chancellor of Germany, Prince Von Builow, asked his successor, "How did it all happen?" The new ex-chancellor replied, "Ah, if we only knew." Interpretation can help us know.

Interpreting war also commemorates the sacrifice of those who gave their lives in combat. The major battlefields of the Civil War were preserved largely for this purpose. Foresta, in *America's National Parks and Their Keepers*, writes:

> These preserved battlefields carried great emotional and symbolic weight in late 19th-century America, commemorating as they did the deaths and personal sacrifices of the nation's most traumatic military conflict. Veterans from every state returned to them by the thousands for massive reunion encampments on the anniversaries of the battles fought there (1984:129).

Modern sites, like the Viet Nam Veterans Memorial in Washington, D.C., have similar, dramatic impacts upon visitors, especially veterans.

Interpreting war can help us in preparing for future wars. Originally, many of the battlefield sites now managed by the National Park Service were established by the War Department, and one of their intended uses was for the study of strategy by young officers. Some sites are still used this way, serving a research function not unlike that served by wilderness areas in the study of ecosystems.

Finally, interpreting war can help communicate its consequences. The personal horrors of war require interpretation for citizens who have little or no experience of military violence and invasion. A new generation of Americans, to whom Viet Nam is history and World War II is ancient history, cannot be reminded, for they do not remember. They must be enlightened as to the impacts of war. Effective interpretation, as Freeman Tilden described it, can help the public acknowledge the civilian suffering and sacrifice associated with war.

Interpreting peace also has several benefits. Of principal consequence is that interpreting peace illustrates its possibility. The Rush-Bagot Treaty of 1817, which demilitarized the Great Lakes, has been successful for 167 years, and several Canadian and American communities periodically celebrate its signing. Interpreting peace also illustrates its difficulty, such as the struggles of the League of Nations after World War I. These efforts for peace offer interpretive opportunities—the European home of the League, for example, even now remains unrestored and largely unvisited. And, of course, interpreting peace may remind the public of its value, benefits, and pleasures.

What Are Interpreters Doing?

Examples (not all from the National Park system) can illustrate the diversity of interpreters' approaches to war and peace. At Auschwitz, the Nazi concentration camp in Poland, the barracks and crematoria are starkly preserved, and photographs are used to communicate what happened there. At the *Arizona* Memorial, visitors, many of them Japanese, take a short but moving boat trip out to the sunken battleship. At Blaine, Washington, a peace arch commemorates the long, open border between the United States and Canada, yet is mostly visited for its beautiful gardens and picnic areas.

Sometimes visits to such areas can be especially poignant and revealing. The American newspaper columnist Richard Reeves (1984) visited France's Fort 35/3, a monument to soldiers who fought on both sides of the Maginot line. He wrote:

> I stopped, too, at the American cemetery . . . where 6,012 Americans killed in World War I are buried. The cemetery, beautiful in its setting and symmetry as the last resting place of men like Carey and Cohen, receives almost no visitors anymore.
>
> "I wonder why," I said. "You'd think their grandchildren would come now."
>
> "They never had grandchildren," said my wife. "That's what war is about."

Other examples reflect different priorities. At Gettysburg, many visitors are attracted to the large electric map, and never visit the actual battlefield. Several years ago, the Air and Space Museum in Washington, D.C., had an interactive exhibit on the then-unfinished cruise missile; the visitor could push a button, send a missile on its way to a target, and presumably walk away supporting the Administration's position on its importance in the country's defense. In Viet Nam, the North Vietnamese quickly developed a war museum in Ho Chi Minh City (formerly Saigon), complete with G.I.s' dog tags, interpretive displays on shooting down American helicopters, and a bean-bag toss where schoolchildren can win candy for hitting Uncle Sam.

And in some cases interpretation (or the lack of it) reflects the powerful cultural politics of war and peace. Some Park Service areas, such as Fort Laramie and Fort Bowie, served as centers of operation against Native Americans; others reflect direct military engagement, such as Big Hole National Battlefield. Joseph Meeker, in his essay reprinted in this volume, offers this criticism:

> Many of the parks specifically glorify the white conquest over Indians or commemorate the white appropriation of Indian lands. Even the few preserved Indian victories are monuments to white dominance, as at Custer Battlefield, where it is shown how the Indians won the battle while losing the war.

At Tulelake, California, site of one of the camps where Japanese-Americans were interned during World War II, there has been in the past little effort to restore and preserve an unpleasant part of American history. Only recently, Congress requested that the Park Service study sites related to the War in the Pacific and, this year, the Manzanar War Relocation Center near Lone Pine, California, was made a historic landmark.

Hence, exceptions exist. Roger Starr of the *New York Times* has written about one such exception:

> Nations usually erect battlefield monuments to celebrate glorious victories. It is with no small pride that the visitor discovers a very different and much more credible motive for a national monument near the small Montana town of Wisdom. The government has

erected a monument here to acknowledge its own misunderstanding of what settlers really needed . . . It's a rare thing in the history of the white man's [sic] dealings with the red man, this willingness to admit error that is not far from wisdom (1983).

And, of course, there are the many other battlesites, the state and local battle re-creations that are popular tourist attractions, black powder demonstrations, living history programs, and so forth.

Four Themes for Interpreting War and Peace

There seem to be four major themes that commonly appear in the interpretation of war. The first concerns the underlying causes of a particular struggle, such as the westward expansion of whites into the Indian territories in the 1800s. The second deals with the events of a battle, campaign, or war—troop movements, chronology of combat, and so forth. An example would be a description of the campaign for Vicksburg during the Civil War. The third theme focuses on the techniques of war. These include weaponry, encampments, defensive equipment, and fort architecture, as well as the interpretation of combat conditions, daily life on the home front, and so forth. The fourth examines the wider impacts of the confrontation—social, political, economic, and environmental.

The interpretive program at a war-related site may need to be balanced, and deal with causes, events, techniques, and impacts, as well as their relationships. To learn about the complex causes of the Civil War without understanding specific battlefield events is an abstraction of minimal interest to the visitor. But a focus on the techniques of war (such as how to fire a cannon) without a complementing interpretation of its impacts can reduce the importance of a historic site visit to an engineering lesson. Balancing interpretive themes may be the best assurance of having a balanced interpretive message.

How are sites in the National Park system interpreted? Other than the 1972 *Part One of the National Park System Plan: History*, there are few systematic data. To gain a general overview, the official park brochures for fifty military sites, battlefields, and monuments were examined. The brochures vary in age and detail, but give a reasonable indication of the major themes addressed at each site.

Table 1 is based on a careful reading of each brochure. The table shows that almost all (94 percent) the brochures for war-related sites deal with events, and a large number (40 percent) deal with techniques. Fewer treat causes and impacts as major themes. While brochures certainly do not reflect the full range of interpretive messages offered visitors, the table illustrates how difficult it can be to interpret certain facets of war.

What Are the Consequences of Current Efforts?

First, a deep understanding of patriotic sacrifice can be gained by the visitor at places like Morristown and Valley Forge. As Freeman Tilden tells the visitor in the Colonial National Historic Park brochure, ". . . it is your history." Second, the brutality of war can be communicated, sensitively and realistically, as at Andersonville National Historic Site. There are numerous examples throughout the National Park system of war being interpreted with such care and thoughtfulness. And, clearly, military events and strategies can be studied with special insight at the actual sites of such battles.

Yet other consequences exist. Warfare can often be romanticized. Bloodless recreations of battles (either performed or displayed) can distort the verity of war and make it difficult for visitors to have a realistic view of history. Emphasis on soldiers and battle scenes often slights the role of home life and women. The manicured and serene environments of most sites disguise the ecological damage that was a consequence of struggles which took place there.

Table 1. Distribution of sites by brochure themes.

Themes	Number of sites	%[1]
Causes	14	28
Events	47	94
Techniques	20	40
Impacts	12	24

[1]Totals are greater than 100 because many brochures deal with more than one theme.

Interpretation can also further the militarization of public life. Interpretation can be used, as in the Air and Space Museum, to alter public opinion regarding the military, warfare, and other peoples (whether this is good or bad is a different issue). In some cases it can glorify conquest and combat. The very effectiveness of some programs may make war intriguing or attractive.

What We Might Do

I have suggested that interpreters are sometimes negligent in the care with which they interpret peace and war. The harder, more difficult issue is what to do about it.

Self-reflection is needed on these issues. There are difficulties in interpreting peace; it is often perceived by interpreters as vague, complex, and having little entertainment appeal. Interpretive sites appropriate for interpreting peace (such as Perry's Victory and the International Peace Memorial) are harder to find than those focusing on war. Legal mandates, legislative intent, local politics, and a manager's own political views may also make such interpretation hard to establish.

The four themes previously described for interpreting war may also prove useful to the interpretation of peace. The events of peace (say the ending of World War II) can be interpreted along with the techniques of peace (the drawing up of peace treaties, enforcement of conditions, and so forth). Similar arguments can be made for the causes and impacts of peace.

There are also difficulties in interpreting war, precisely because it is so emotionally powerful, exciting, and politically charged. There continues a tradition of interpreting war from the "great man" or "battle scene" point of view. The techniques of war hold our fascination. Some interpreters have personal, vested interests in interpreting the glory, color, and pageantry of war. Governments and sponsoring agencies, as well as the public, sometimes have strong opinions and may control the treatment of historic sites by interpreters. Hence, interpreters must seriously reflect on what they intend to accomplish when they interpret war or peace. As a profession, we must address the dilemmas of enlightening the public without romanticizing the subject. We can expect some controversy as this is done.

What else might we do? There is a good deal of scholarly literature on peace and war, and this literature can help interpreters put their site-specific efforts in a broader context. The classic study of war is Quincy Wright's (1942) *A Study of War*. It contains detailed statistics and outlines of historical, economic, social, and political approaches to understanding how and why war occurs. A more modern volume is Beer's 1981 *Peace Against War: The Ecology of International Violence*. An introductory text on many college campuses, it takes the approach that international violence can best be understood by a systematic study of its causes, similar to the way epidemiologists study disease. It is balanced, full of facts and figures, deals extensively with peace and peace treaties, and has an exhaustive bibliography. A third recommendation is William Cottrell's unique (1972) essay "Men Cry Peace." Cottrell outlines a science of peace, and suggests its value to modern societies. Park libraries may want to purchase or borrow these books, and interpreters ought to read them carefully.

Interpreters need to openly discuss and debate the issue of how to interpret peace and war. Perhaps a national conference or regional meetings on these themes would help to sensitize interpreters and air the wide range of opinions, some strongly held, on interpreting war and peace. The National Park Service (or its interpreters) should help organize such efforts by virtue of its leadership in managing military sites. Training programs at the university and agency level could include material on the topic.

Some research may be needed. For example, studies of interpretation's impact upon environmental values are common, yet we know surprisingly little about the impact of historical interpretation upon visitors' values and attitudes toward war. What if it can be found that a visit to a battlefield changes a visitor's attitude toward war, one way or another? What if the interpretation had no impact at all? Either finding has implications for interpreting war and peace. Interpreters can encourage such studies by cooperating with local and regional universities, whose graduate students continually search for important topics for their thesis work.

Conclusion

John F. Kennedy's 1963 summer speech at American University is largely ignored now in this era of Cold War rhetoric and military build-up. His speech called for an American Academy of Peace, where young Americans could study the skills of peace making. He said:

> I realize that the pursuit of peace is not as dramatic as the pursuit of war, and frequently the words of the pursuer fall on deaf ears. But we have no more urgent task.

In this hopeful yet dangerous age, Kennedy's plea underscores the need for interpreters to reconsider how they interpret peace and war.

The Devil's Work in God's Country
Politics and Interpretation in the 1990s
(1989)

Gary E. Machlis

Freeman Tilden (1977) called interpretation a public service "recently come in to our cultural world." Perhaps he hoped it would be aseptic, dignified, and humane, provoking and delighting citizens to learn about Nature and History. But in contemporary America, interpretation is a political act, and is increasingly intertwined with the chaotic democracy that is American politics.

Interpreters are increasingly asked to interpret critical resource issues and work with local communities. They are asked to organize volunteer and friends groups, cooperate with the private sector, respond to legislative inquiries and visits, and lobby for additional resources. All such activities require political savvy, skills, and success. If politics is, as the eminent political scientist Mark Twain implied, "the devil's work," the interpretive profession is now called upon to do the devil's work in God's country.

The new politics of America bears little resemblance to the efficient and polite democracy of our grade-school textbooks, Boy Scout manuals, or nostalgic (and forgetful) remembrances of grandparents. The changes have been cumulative, but two important dates, 1945 and 1974, reflect major shifts. Samuel Hays (1987) argues that the end of World War II is a dividing line in American politics and environmental history. The war is the historical boundary between old and new values, marked by several trends. First, the population became more educated, due in part to the G.I. Bill, and second, the general public became more concerned with quality of life as an idea or value. Third, discretionary income rose—from necessities during the Depression to amenities during the 1960s. Wants became needs and consumption rather than production increasingly guided American economic and political decisions. Fourth, a new class of experts emerged which included managers, bureaucrats, lobbyists, advocates, designers, planners, and fundraisers. Fifth was the formation of "iron triangles" composed of agency, legislative, and interest groups aligned together.

The second date, 1974, was a pivotal point in the redistribution of power in America. Hedrick Smith (1988) points out that "Richard Nixon was driven from the White House by the Watergate scandal . . . forces which had been pulling at the threads of power for several years finally ripped apart the tighter weave of the old power structure." Congress seized power through the Budget and Impoundment Control Act of 1974, which barred future presidents from refusing to spend what Congress voted. The Congressional Budget Office was established; no longer would the Administration's figures be the only ones debated. In the House of Representatives, the seniority system was overthrown; scores of subcommittees were formed, each overseeing a piece of the federal machinery. A large class of first-year House Democrats was elected, further weakening the traditional political power structure, and increasingly independent Americans split their votes, weakening the major parties. The scandals of Watergate led to a series of campaign reforms that in turn led to the creation of powerful political action committees (PACs).

One result has been the explosive growth of special-interest politics. Statistics tell the story. In 1961 there were 365 registered lobbyists in Washington; in 1987, there were 23,011. (There are now 43 lobbyists for every member of congress.) In that pivotal year 1974, PACs for various causes and interests numbered 608: in 1987 there were 4,157. These PACs raised $8.5 million in campaign money in 1974; in 1986 they raised and contributed $132.2 million.

In addition, the tools of politics have dramatically changed. Video feeds allow politicians to stage events and beam them by satellite to home-state televisions; both political parties have expensive studios in Washington dishing out these "electronic press releases." High-technology computerized mail allows the "narrowcasting" of messages aimed at specific demographic or interest groups. A machine ink that looks as if it was signed by someone (it even smudges properly) has been developed. With ever-growing staffs, contact with local constituencies has increased, involving favors from small to sleazy. And, of course, there is all that money; only the naive should be surprised at both the level and ease of corruption in our political system.

With the proliferation of focused lobbyists and PACs with specific legislative agendas, it is now virtually impossible for a single member of Congress to cover (in depth) all the issues. The net effect is the "balkanization" of power, a rise in importance of congressional staff and the increasing importance of negative power—the ability to prevent things from happening. Negative power has been adopted by the environmental movement, stopping nuclear power plants, below-cost timber sales, water diversions, and so forth. The use of negative power in modern times has provided the general public with a new avenue for political power.

This does not mean, however, that our entire public is politically active; indeed, policy formulation is largely decided by the powerful with self interests and influence. Figure 1 suggests that for each issue or interest, there are different publics, or constituencies. Some may join for alternate reasons (pro-gun groups include both hunters and constitutionalists, tourism associations include ORV groups and wilderness users). The contemporary political strategy involves expanding the interested and attentive publics. In addition, there are increasing linkages between policy leaders and organizations called "interorganizational connections." These shifting coalitions with different causes and power bases may coalesce on a specific issue, only to disband when the issue is closed.

Interpretive politics is derivative of the national political scene. There has been a proliferation of national park "friends" groups; in 1987 there were 150, each a constituency capable of organizing its positive support and exercising its negative power. There are 65 cooperating associations serving 330 units of the National Park System, membership of the National Park and Conservation Association (NPCA) is now 60,000 strong, and other organizations (like National Association of Interpreters) represent important actors in interpretive affairs.

Conservationists and the National Park movement in particular have discovered the importance of interpretation as propaganda, agency boosterism, or call to action. McKendry, writing in the NPCA's planning document, *Interpretation: Key to the Park Experience,* said:

> Interpreters commonly believe that their goal is to change visitor behavior. Building from that, they are directed to expand from personal services to mass media to spread their interpretive reach and volunteer programs to build support for the parks. Not only are

interpreters' responsibilities expanding, but many of these responsibilities can be regarded as activism (1988:42).

What should interpreters be prepared for? How can they prepare? It is clear both that enmeshing of parks and politics will continue and that public distrust of experts and "iron triangles" will likely rise. We should not underestimate the linkages between symbols of technological failure such as Chernobyl, Bhopal, Three-Mile Island, Love Canal, and Challenger and the rise of fundamentalist groups, garage-front churches, anti-evolutionists, and resistance to "environmental education." Using interpretive activities as forums for environmental politics has its dangers. As one visitor commented to me after enduring several political diatribes masquerading as interpretive walks: "I wanted to learn about the park. After the second lecture, I just quit going to the visitor centers or listening to the bastards."

Parks and historic sites will increasingly be tools for economic development, with struggles appearing between states for the disposable income of baby boomers on vacation. The political and

A CONCEPTUAL FRAMEWORK

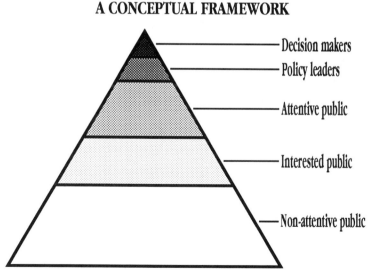

Figure 1. *A stratified model of policy formation.*

economic importance of gateway communities and tourism, and the contribution of parks to this scheme will make interpretation an important player in the marketing of tourist regions. County commissioners, governors, and state legislators will be interested in the content and delivery of interpretive programs, and their agendas may clash with the agencies involved. Interpreters will be caught in the crossfire.

The result is that, to be effective, interpreters may need to borrow from the politician's bag of technological tricks and political strategies. Local members of congress must be counted, and convinced to take on a park's agenda as his or her special interest. Electronic news releases, video feeds, and targeted messages for the general public will likely become standard interpretive tools. Friends groups may be recast as political constituency groups or even park-oriented PACs, and such groups will increase their membership (and hence political power) by reaching out to casual visitors, in addition to locals and committed enthusiasts. Coalitions will form and conservation organizations will "capture" themes and prey on each other for resources and media exposure.

Interpreters have both the potential and responsibility to play a crucial role in the functioning of park ecosystems. But to do so will require new skills and a willingness to grapple with difficult issues. To be effective in the 1990s, I feel (perhaps fear) that interpreters will have to do the devil's work in God's country.

Crossing Borders
and Rethinking a Craft
Interpretation in Developing Countries
(1991)

Sam H. Ham

David S. Sutherland

Introduction

Growing international awareness of the global environment has focused worldwide attention on the loss or degradation of natural resources and on the notion that some resources, such as biodiversity, the atmosphere, the ozone layer, and marine ecosystems, are world resources regardless of where they occur geographically. We have seen renewed interest in and government support for the creation of public environmental awareness programs, not only in developed countries like the U.S., but in developing countries across the world. Government foreign assistance agencies and international conservation nongovernment organizations are earmarking unprecedented amounts of financial and human resources to assist developing countries in their efforts to heighten public awareness about relationships between the environment and quality of life.

A major emphasis in environmental awareness strategies has been the development of interpretive programs based in parks and protected areas. In developed countries, these efforts typically represent the continuation of a historical tradition of interpretation, and are carried out by trained specialists working for organizations with an established interpretive function. By contrast, most developing countries lack this tradition, as well as the financial and human resources necessary to establish one. Increasingly they look to developed countries, not only as sources of economic and technical assistance, but as a model for how to develop their own interpretive programs.

It seems clear that a U.S. model of on-site interpretation—one emphasizing our media, type of content, and the assumption of a literate, ethnic-majority, middle-class, pleasure-seeking audience—is taking hold in some developing countries. There is nothing inherently wrong with this, just as there was nothing inherently wrong with worldwide experimentation with the U.S. national park model. But if experience has taught us anything about national parks, it is that our model has not always worked elsewhere quite as well as some think it has worked here. (Some might argue that it has not worked perfectly here, either, but that is beyond the scope of this essay.) Differences in culture, customs, socioeconomic conditions, and other factors have led many developing countries to evolve their own tradition for protecting natural resources, and the international community has responded by advancing the notion that each country must find its own tradition—one that will work best there. Simply put, that is the point we wish to make about interpretation in this essay.

It is natural that interpreters in developed countries want to augment the efforts of their counterparts elsewhere. Driven by deep convictions about the global environment and the suspicion that time is short, many of us have turned our attention to helping countries where cadres of professional interpreters are only now beginning to appear. Our success in doing this, however, may depend less on how well we understand interpretation in our own country than on how well we understand its application in the countries we are trying to assist. Understanding that the form and ·character of interpretation must be adapted to the situations in which it will be practiced seems fundamental; but we do not always put this understanding to use in the training and technical assistance we offer to our colleagues in developing countries. Although the U.S. concept of interpretation as an on-site educational effort geared to visitor populations seems to enjoy widespread acceptance in the developing world, the audiences that might be targeted and the communication approaches that might be used to reach them seem less clear when differences between countries are examined. The main purposes of this essay are to present some of these differences and to consider their possible implications for interpretation in developing countries. Interpreters need to "cross borders" and rethink their craft.

The Premise

Our premise is that interpretive efforts should be adapted to the audiences, social settings, and biophysical environments in which they take place. Though theoretically intuitive, in practice such a view may not be embraced by all U.S. interpreters because it reveals a new layer of complexity in what, to some, is already a complicated task. Yet, in the U.S., a growing body of evidence paints a picture of a diversifying visitor population, one which consists of many subpopulations who may see parks, interpretation, and the very idea of a "park experience" in dramatically different ways. From a communication standpoint, these visitor subgroups constitute different audiences for interpretation, and taking their differences into account allows a more directed, and conceivably more successful, approach to interpretation.

In the discussion which follows, we will suggest ways in which protected areas in developing countries might be expected to differ from those in developed countries. Included in this discussion are differences in geography and socioeconomic conditions which may influence the form and content of on-site interpretive programs, and thereby suggest strategic audiences. We then describe four of these audiences and consider implications for interpretive programs designed to reach them. We conclude by raising some questions about the role that U.S. interpreters might assume in training and technical assistance programs in developing countries, and by offering some suggestions on how we might strengthen our contributions to these important efforts.

Good Guys and Bad Guys: Rethinking Some Familiar Ideas

"Protected" areas, by definition, are lands we presume would be threatened by development or ecological damage were it not for their special legal status. Typically, the underlying goal of management is to preserve the qualities and features contained in these areas in such a way that the benefits they provide (whether ecological, scenic, or cultural) can be perpetuated indefinitely. Protecting such areas against encroachment is therefore a primary management concern and a common topic of interpretive programs.

In developed countries, we can readily identify potential encroachers: timber interests, oil and gas interests, mining interests, commercial developers, industrial polluters, poachers, and others who might exploit protected lands for commercial or personal gain. But ours is a system of checks and balances—although our free enterprise system encourages growth and expansion, our protected area systems attempt to prevent them from occurring inside our parks and preserves. To the extent this model works, it is partly because of the vast amount of land outside our protected areas—lands which contain raw materials to support industry and economic development, thereby reducing pressure on protected lands. It has been said, for example, that Yellowstone is possible because of Iowa and Nebraska (Machlis 1991). In this purely economic sense, protecting land is possible because we can afford to protect it, and our negative view of "encroachers" may stem from an assumption that there is plenty of outside land for them to exploit. From the environmentalist's point of view, the good guys and bad guys are easily distinguishable on this basis. Recent experiences, however, suggest that as scarce resources (e.g., old growth forests, threatened species, potable water, salmon, fossil fuels, etc.) dwindle in supply outside of protected areas, unprecedented pressures to exploit protected lands can be expected, and the lines of distinction between the good guys and bad guys will blur.

In many respects, this is the scenario found in developing countries today. Generally, they are poor, small, crowded, and possess only limited arable and undeveloped land when compared to developed countries like the U.S. and Canada. The figures in Table 1 (excerpted from worldwide data compiled by the World Resources Institute 1990) provide a representative comparison of developed and developing countries. Although variation exists, a clear pattern emerges: most developing countries do not have, and probably will not have, the large protected area systems we are accustomed to in our country. In the face of rapidly growing populations and a declining base of undeveloped land, they simply may be unable to afford them. Unlike the U.S., which began setting aside large tracts of protected lands early in its history, some developing countries do not have protected area systems, and most of those that do have embarked on the idea only during the past thirty or forty years. The results are that vast areas of uninhabited lands are scarce or absent in many developing countries, and pressures are mounting to exploit those that remain (MacKinnon et al. 1986, McNeely et al. 1990).

Most developing countries lack "outside" land to support human populations and economic growth. Unlike in the U.S., encroachment on protected lands occurs not only from inadequate management

Table 1. Comparisons between selected developed and developing countries.

	Population density per 1000 ha (1989)	Cropland ha per person (1989)	Undeveloped lands (1000 ha)	Per capita income in U.S. $ (1987)	Population growth % (1985-90)	Life expectancy at birth
United States	270	0.77	44,058	18,529	0.82	75.0
Canada	29	1.75	640,587	15,160	0.88	76.3
Syria	655	0.47	—	1,645	3.57	65.0
Egypt	530	0.05	42,540	678	2.55	60.6
Liberia	257	0.15	1,420	451	3.18	51.0
Tanzania	297	0.20	7,053	180	3.67	53.0
Zambia	110	0.64	15,075	248	3.76	53.5
Honduras	445	0.36	1,126	808	3.18	62.6
El Salvador	2,478	0.14	—	842	1.93	67.1
Trinidad/Tobago	2,462	0.10	—	4,199	1.59	70.2
Colombia	300	0.17	15,156	1,238	2.05	64.8
Peru	170	0.17	36,660	1,467	2.51	61.4
Malaysia	516	0.26	2,844	1,820	2.31	68.6
India	2,811	0.20	1,161	311	2.08	57.9
Thailand	1,075	0.37	2,809	850	1.53	64.2
Pakistan	1,541	0.17	2,737	353	3.45	52.1
Bangladesh	8,404	0.08	—	164	2.67	49.6
Nepal	1,366	0.13	—	161	2.48	47.9

— Data not available

Source: World Resources Institute (1990).

and commercial exploitation (both legal and illegal), but also from local people who inhabit, and whose families may have traditionally inhabited, lands adjacent to or even within the boundaries of protected areas. Often, the boundaries of protected areas were drawn around existing populations, instantly converting what were once traditional lifestyles into "illegal activities." These people have few alternatives to their present lifestyles and nowhere else to go.

An example are the countries of Central America. Although they are predominantly rural, their small size contributes to dense populations. Unable to obtain credit or title to private lands, most of the rural population resorts to migratory (slash and burn) agriculture as its main sustenance activity. These migrations routinely lead to arable lands in protected areas and buffer zones because they are all that are available to these people (e.g., see Nations and Leonard 1986, Daugherty 1989, Barborak and Ham 1989). With few exceptions, large tracts of undeveloped land, as in U.S. protected area systems, simply do not exist in the region. Yellowstone National Park is, itself, one half the size of El Salvador; and the classified wilderness lands in just the state of Alaska comprise a land area almost half the size of all of Central America (U.S. Geological Survey 1987, Leonard 1986). The U.S. model of vast pristine wilderness areas, national parks, and wildlife refuges may not fit Central America nor, for that matter, much of the developing world. The very poor are forced to live on two margins: the margin of protected land and the margin of survival. When they move into protected areas, they are labeled *invasores* (invaders). It will be extremely difficult to win their support for and compliance with conservation objectives, since these objectives often appear to conflict with their right to survive. Yet because of the potential threat they pose their compliance is crucial, and interpretive programs may represent an important strategy for bringing it about.

U.S. advocates for international parks and protected areas have not always been sensitive to this difference between their country and the developing world. An example is the "Just Say No to Development" philosophy which was espoused by a leading U.S. authority to delegates from sixty countries attending the Fourth World Wilderness Congress (see Nash 1988). According to this philosophy, human economic or exploitive uses of protected lands are wholly unacceptable if protection of those lands is to be possible. Although the argument may make some sense in large developed countries like the U.S., it is rejected by experts from developing countries (e.g., Kakabadse 1988). In their view, human use of protected areas is not only necessary, but inevitable. Just saying "no" may be impractical, if not impossible, in countries where protected areas must somehow benefit the *invasores* or perish. If this is true, interpretive programs which attract such people make more sense than ones which condemn them.

In developing countries, human habitations within or adjacent to protected areas can, and inevitably do, constitute part of what is being managed and preserved (Arboleda et al. 1989). The goal is a sustainable interaction between *Homo sapiens* and the natural environment. Although engendering difficult management questions, this outcome, which international conservationists call "sustainable development," seems a more appropriate and realistic management goal than a "just say no" or "good guys versus bad guys" stance. As we discuss later, it may also represent an important topic for interpretive programs.

Benefits of Interpretive Programs

In many respects, the visitors one might expect in a park or protected area in Guatemala, Sri Lanka, or Pakistan are similar to the middle-class pleasure seekers we find in U.S. parks. They have both the discretionary time and income to visit parks, and for some, park going is a preferred use of leisure time and the benefits of interpretive programs usually cited in the U.S. (e.g., enhancing recreation experiences, fostering appreciation for natural settings, resource protection, and public relations) seem to apply.

As in the U.S. (see Cordell et al. 1990 and Meeker 1973), outdoor recreation participation by domestic populations in developing countries seems dominated by the middle-class ethnic majority. Although site-specific data are lacking, it seems reasonable to assume an even more pronounced bias toward upper income brackets because of the absence of a well-defined middle class in many developing countries. By most accounts, two classes (the poor and the rich) are the norm in the developing world (e.g., see Kissinger 1984, Torres-Rivas 1983, World Resources Institute 1990). In Central America, for example, half the population in 1970 was earning less than U.S.$75 per year, while 5 percent made over $18,000 (Torres-

Rivas 1983). It seems probable that the main beneficiaries of conventional on-site interpretive programs in developing countries constitute a small but comparatively wealthy minority. Putting aside any judgments about this unequal distribution of wealth, an important implication of these data is that interpretive programs in these countries stand to reach an important and influential population segment, possibly much more influential than the typical U.S. interpreter usually encounters.

Besides the political clout they might possess, these visitors (coupled with a growing number of foreign tourists in many countries) help stimulate local and national economies through purchases of food, gasoline, souvenirs, lodging, and other services (Budowski 1990, Foster 1989, Ingram and Durst 1987). Interpretive programs which enhance tourists' experiences may serve an important marketing function, thereby augmenting economic development.

Beyond serving these traditional leisure audiences, interpretive programs in developing countries can directly benefit local populations in other ways. If, as Tilden (1957) argued, interpretation should address itself to the priorities and experiences of the audience, we might expect the topics of programs aimed at these poor local people to be very different from the topics U.S. interpreters typically treat in their programs. Programs on sanitation, hygiene, and food preparation and storage might be popular with such audiences, not just because they are intellectually stimulating, but because they address the priorities of their audiences: health, quality of daily life, and survival. Conceivably, what an illiterate farmer and his family learn from a skilled interpreter could save, extend, or substantially improve their lives, at the same time contributing to the protection of the area. Such a possibility becomes clearer when one considers that in many developing countries infectious diseases and intestinal parasites, both due to inadequate knowledge about sanitation, are among the leading causes of death (e.g., see Hammond 1990 and Leonard 1986). Programs addressing these issues would be dramatically different from U.S. notions about park and forest interpretation.

Management programs might also benefit from interpretation aimed at local populations. In the U.S., recreational visitors are usually the major management concern. In developing countries, the predominant problems often stem from human populations living adjacent to and within protected areas—people who probably will never "visit" the areas in a recreational sense. Migratory farmers move into protected areas or sensitive buffer zones in search of arable land, game, pasture, or fuelwood. As we earlier suggested, when sustenance for these people disappears outside of protected areas, their search for land will inevitably push them into conflict with protection efforts.

In the Latin American tropics, the situation is exacerbated by poor soils. Local peasants (*campesinos*) burn and clear a section of tropical forest in order to graze their animals and plant their crops (usually beans and corn). They typically remain on the site until the soil is depleted of nutrients, at which time they migrate to a new section of forest where the cycle repeats itself; in most cases the cycle takes only ten years or less (Nations and Leonard 1986). Without active reforestation efforts, these areas do not regenerate easily. Given the rates of population growth in these countries, this traditional cycle virtually ensures the eventual deforestation of vast regions of Latin America. In the meantime, critical upstream watersheds are choked, threatened species are pushed to the brink of extinction, and the nature of both humid and dry tropical forest ecosystems is being altered rapidly. In some of the small countries of Central America national deforestation is possible within the next generation.

Two nonregulatory management approaches are being used to combat these trends, one aimed at keeping the *invasores* out of protected areas and buffer zones, and the other at managing the impacts of human habitations already inside them. In both cases, the emphasis of these nonregulatory efforts is communication. Extension programs for populations living within protected areas and buffer zones are a common management activity in developing countries. They demonstrate tilling, soil management (terracing, catch-basins, etc.), planting, nutrient cycling, and multiple-crop agroforestry techniques which significantly reduce impact on soils, increase crops and income, and, in some cases, greatly prolong the productive life of tropical soils. Sanitation, hygiene, health, and nutrition are often stressed as well (see, for example, Ham 1990 and Ham and Valencia 1990).

In the U.S., extension programs are not generally considered interpretation because they usually do not address the management objectives of our parks and protected areas or the interests of our on-site audiences. In developing countries, however, these topics may be of great interest to local populations and might be considered integral to the objectives of interpretive programs. Discussing what he termed the "visitor's chief interest," Freeman Tilden reminded us that:

> Any interpretation that does not somehow relate what is being displayed or described to something within the personality or experience of the visitor [audience] will be sterile (1957:11).

Clearly, applying Tilden's often-cited principle requires an understanding of the audience's interests and experiences. In the U.S. we have developed a tradition (or model) of interpretation based, in part, on what we know about our visitors, and what we think they want and expect in our parks and protected areas. It is natural that we have developed our craft in terms of this model, including the communication settings we have created, the media we utilize, the topics we interpret, and the communication strategies we employ. And in our own culture this model seems to work and make sense. But when we step into someone else's culture, much of what we assume about our audiences back home may no longer apply. Our customary ways of doing things—our traditional topics and communication approaches—may fall short of the mark if their use is based on assumptions about the audience which do not hold. In developing countries, interpretive programs aimed at local people may not always lend themselves to our tradition, and our customary distinction between natural resources extension and park interpretation may even be counterproductive. Clinging too tenaciously to a model which separates them may severely limit the contributions we might otherwise make.

Interpretation—Service or Strategy?

If not through a U.S. model, how then should we view on-site interpretation in developing countries? Interpretive programs in developing countries may serve a more strategic environmental education function than do their counterparts in U.S. parks and protected areas, the latter often emphasizing service to visitors. This is not to say that U.S. interpretive programs do not serve both purposes; interpretation's role both as a visitor service and as an environmental education activity is well established in U.S. parks (Brown 1973). In addition, serving national and foreign visitors is certainly an accepted goal of interpretive programs in many developing countries (Morales 1987, Ham and Enrìquez 1987). The difference is one of relative emphasis.

In developing countries, informal environmental education programs, such as on-site interpretation in protected areas, zoos, museums, botanical gardens, and other leisure settings, are often included as key components of national environmental education master plans. These plans (or "strategies" as they are often called) detail the complementary roles not only of park-based interpretive programs, but of formal school-based programs, the national mass media, community and adult-education programs, and even activities aimed at civic groups like Rotary International and Boy Scouts. What they represent is a coordinated effort which assigns communication roles and responsibilities to different institutions based upon the kinds of education they are designed to conduct, and the kinds of audiences they are positioned to reach (see, for example, Guier 1989, Daugherty 1989 and CONAMA 1990). Typically, these strategies describe who the audiences of on-site and off-site interpretive programs will be, the specific educational objectives they should be designed to achieve, and the time period in which intended results should materialize (e.g., CONAMA 1990, Ham and Valencia 1990, Guier 1989). Rarely is interpretive planning in U.S. protected areas so thoroughly integrated into this wider environmental education context.

Although not all countries approach interpretive planning quite so systematically, the notion that it fills a strategic role in a larger environmental education effort seems more widespread in developing countries than in developed ones. Published examples are found in Guatemala (CONAMA 1990), Costa Rica (Guier 1989), Tunisia (UNESCO 1987b) and elsewhere (see, for example, UNESCO 1991 and UNESCO 1987a). Many factors could contribute to the acceptability of this model in the developing world:

1. The relatively small size of most developing countries facilitates a national education policy and integrative planning.

2. The lack of financial and human resources encourages coordination.

3. The simultaneous birth of interpretation and environmental education in many of these countries gave them common roots and logically brought them together from the outset.

4. Because conspicuous human suffering creates a sense of urgency about slowing environmental degradation and increasing the quality of life, many developing countries have simply concluded that environmental education should be interpretation's primary aim.

Thus, an emerging model for on-site interpretation in many developing countries treats interpretive programs more as a communication strategy than as a service for visitors, though both are certainly included. In this context, "strategy" refers to purposeful communication aimed at audiences who are singled out because their behavior or social position influences conservation. Who these audiences might be, and how interpretive programs in developing countries might be structured to reach them, are the subjects we take up next.

Key Audiences for Interpretation in Developing Countries

Although many potential audiences exist for on-site interpretive programs in developing countries, four (Table 2) have emerged repeatedly as being most important because of the direct relationship between their actions and the condition of parks and protected areas, and/or their capacity to influence other people and thus accelerate the diffusion of environmental ideology (see, for example, Wood and Wood 1987, Medina 1989, Ham et al. 1989).

Table 2. Typology of audiences for interpretation in developing countries.

Audience	Primary mechanism for communication opportunity	Sphere of influence
Local people	Staged events or organized tours	Direct daily impact on condition of protected resources and on adjacent lands; significant political potential.
National tourists	Outings or visits to protected area	Intermittent impact on protected resource; direct political influence; economic impact.
Influential groups & citizens	Staged events or organized tours	Direct influence on policy and public opinion.
Foreign tourists	Visits to protected area (private or organized groups)	Intermittent impact on protected resource; indirect influence on policy; economic impact.

First, subsistence-level locals living either within or adjacent to park boundaries may have negative impacts on environmental quality; interpretive programs may encourage them to explore and gradually adopt more sustainable land uses. Second, upper- and middle-class nationals who visit protected areas can be exposed to information about biodiversity and sustainable development. Third, interpretive programs may target groups of nationals (such as village leaders, religious figures, politicians, or celebrities) who have great potential to influence how others think. Fourth, foreign tourists visiting the region's protected areas can receive these same messages while also learning to appreciate differences between the countries they are visiting and their own. Interpretive programs can expose these foreign visitors to the necessity for and models of sustainable development. As Table 2 suggests, these audiences differ from one another not only in the ways they may influence conservation efforts, but in the kinds of opportunities available for reaching them.

Local People

It seems clear that people who live near or within the borders of protected areas constitute an important audience for interpreters. As many have argued (e.g., Galeano 1973, Nations and Leonard 1986, Wood and Wood 1987, McNeely et al. 1990, Hammond 1990), it is easy to blame such people for the ecological damage their activities produce, but they usually are not aware of economically viable alternatives to their current lifestyles, nor of the environmental consequences they engender. Interpretive programs in local protected areas may help to raise their awareness about such things, at the same time showing them how to make immediate improvements in their living conditions and reduce their impacts on protected natural resources.

As we suggested earlier, on-site interpretive programs for this audience may take the form of extension programs in agriculture, natural resources, and health to show these people what alternatives exist and how to incorporate them into their lives. Alternatives which are perceived to be advantageous to budgets or health will be embraced by this audience. Designed at the appropriate scale and delivered with the sensitivity and clarity that exemplify effective extension efforts (e.g., see Bunch 1982, Rogers and Shoemaker 1971), successful interpretive programs may produce relatively quick and enduring improvements in the environment-related behaviors of their audiences, improve relations between local people and protected-area personnel, and diminish management problems such as encroachment, illegal tree felling, and theft or destruction of archaeological resources.

Since subsistence-level audiences are often concerned with day-to-day survival and have little economic flexibility to accept risks, effective programs for this audience should not utilize highly conceptual, affective, or romantic appeals or promise only intangible future benefits (Jones 1989). Rather, they should stress immediate improvements in the farmer's economic and physical well-being, such as the direct benefits of a local protected area for the inhabitants who live around it. As Richard Donovan, manager of a U.S. AID forest conservation project, observed of Costa Rican *campesinos*:

> If we want the forest to be preserved, the bottom line is we have to produce cold, hard cash for the *campesino*... The *campesino* cannot find what he's looking for in a conversation about global warming; he's looking for sustenance (Jones 1989:10).

In Donovan's view, people at the subsistence level respect results, not theory, abstract concepts, or philosophy. Interpreters could therefore educate local residents about a park's practical function to protect critical watersheds for drinking water, serve as a refuge for important game species and medicinal plants, or to generate income from tourism. Besides underscoring the value of protected areas, interpreters could incorporate environmental education and sustainable development messages into their programs for local people, drawing examples from local protected areas.

Interpreters who target this audience face several challenges. In Latin America, for example, Galeano (1973) has forcefully argued that the attitudes, world views, and ways of life of the rural poor have been forged by centuries of hardship and oppression at the hands of outsiders. Today these attitudes and ways of seeing things cannot be changed easily. An interpretive program which suggests changes may be perceived by local people as an indictment of their way of life. With little to call their own, they may cling proudly and defensively to their culture, and may justifiably respond with hostility or loss of face to what they perceive as criticism, regardless of the interpreter's desire to help. Successful programs, therefore, will stress practical relevance and sensitivity to the local peoples' way of life while offering demonstrable improvements in their living conditions. Effective interpreters will not claim, or appear to claim, a monopoly on knowledge because of their social status and formal education; rather they will be open to learning from local people and be willing to explore options with them, not for them.

Because they may lack formal education, and are frequently reluctant to trust strangers, local people are sometimes perceived as being unintelligent by outsiders. This may lead well-intentioned interpreters to condescend or talk down to local audiences. Interpreters working with local people would do well to recall Tilden's (1957) first and sixth principles. Watered-down interpretive programs designed for other audiences will not work as well as programs which address the realities of these people's day-to-day life. Abstract concepts and theoretical science will likely be rejected or ignored, while information which provides an economic advantage or edge on survival will be embraced. Demonstrating rather than merely describing these advantages will almost always be required if communication aimed at these audiences is to produce intended results.

It is also important for interpreters to remember that local people may feel hostility to protected areas because they restrict access to important resources. Local people may also feel excluded from protected areas, and perceive them as reserves for the national elite and rich foreigners (see Mishra 1984). Interpreters can counter this tension by making local people feel welcome. There are many ways to build such bridges of good will, such as distributing free admission passes in local villages, providing a weekend free bus service, helping local schools to arrange field trips, and sponsoring receptions and organized events to which local people are specifically invited.

Since the rural poor often have very limited access to transportation, interpreters may need to organize field trips and bring groups of local people on-site to receive interpretive programs. Ecuador's Ministry of Agriculture and Livestock annually conducts such programs for hundreds of indigenous people living near national parks. The *campesinos* seem to enjoy the experience, as well as the attention they receive, and park managers claim that the program has helped mitigate certain problems, especially fuelwood cutting in buffer zones.

In cases where this approach is not practical, interpreters may need to develop outreach activities in communities adjacent to park borders as an extension of on-site interpretation, essentially taking the park to local people who are not able to visit. Not only might outreach programs include presentations for local schools, community groups, and clubs, they might also capitalize on the timing of traditional community celebrations and festivals, and make use of traditional educational approaches. For example, presentations which involve drama and role playing have proven effective in health education programs in many developing countries, especially when community members, themselves, do the acting (Werner 1980, Werner and Bower 1982, UNESCO 1991).

Local mass media may also be used to reach this audience. In particular, radio offers several advantages:

1. It is a common source of information in rural areas where print and other broadcast media are either inaccessible or cost prohibitive to rural families.

2. It does not require literacy, allowing children and illiterate adults to easily comprehend its messages.

3. Because it does not require electrical current and lends itself to group listening, it reaches many people.

4. Listening to radio is a popular form of recreation in many remote rural areas.

Because of these advantages, radio is emerging as a common interpretive media for rural audiences in many developing countries (see Bajimaya and Fazio 1989, AED 1989, 1990, Ham and Castillo 1988, 1990 and Dodd 1987).

National Tourists

Members of this middle- and upper-class audience have the leisure time, discretionary income, and means of self-transport to visit protected areas. In contrast to subsistence-level nationals, the middle and upper classes enjoy greater social status, education, and political leverage to lobby for environmental reforms. Their social position gives them a degree of opinion-leader status and makes them frequent trend setters. On-site interpretive programs at protected areas may create in these people a greater sense of urgency about the environment than currently exists. In addition, park visitors from these classes may be willing to donate time, money, materials, and talent to improve protected area management, or to support interpretive efforts.

An understandable phenomenon among middle- and upper-class nationals is that they sometimes reject environmental reasoning because it is assumed to be a foreign ideology in sovereign territory—outside interference in their domestic affairs. It is not the notion of environmental quality that they resist, but the meddling of foreigners in their homeland. To the extent these people come to see conservation as their own national priority, they will be more inclined to support or even participate in their country's environmental movement.

In this context, sustainable development, rather than uncompromising protectionism, emerges as an important theme for interpretive programs aimed at middle- and upper-class tourists. Messages might emphasize how and why protected lands can pay for themselves, and counter the attitude that protection or restrictive management only "locks up" needed resources (see, for example, Peters et al. 1989). Other important topics include the irreplaceability of some resources (including water, soil, wildlife, and plants), the tangible values of national biodiversity, how the selfish actions of some people can deprive others of their right to a healthy environment, and preservation of historical resources and traditional cultures. Especially important is to give this audience (which may have political influence) clear suggestions for where and how to act on its new knowledge.

Where feasible, these ideas can be communicated through conventional interpretive media (talks, exhibits, living history, audiovisual programs, etc.). Middle- and upper-class audiences may respond more favorably than subsistence-level audiences to patriotic or romantic appeals, e.g., that preservation protects an important part of national culture and identity. Experience has shown that linking environmental ideology to a loveable yet knowledgeable animal personality makes it more interesting and acceptable to the lay public. In some countries, charismatic local wildlife have been used as mascots (such as "Mack the Macaw" in Trinidad and Tobago, "Puhl the Armadillo" in Costa Rica, "Vincie the Parrot" in St. Vincent, and "Smokey the Bear" in the U.S.).

Influential Groups and Citizens

Influential groups and citizens are a diverse and complex audience for interpreters, yet possess enormous potential as agents of change. As informed recipients of interpretation, they may serve as convincing spokespersons and powerful activists to advance the creation 'and sound management of protected areas.

Influential people occur at all socioeconomic levels of a society, and may be identified within both of the aforementioned audiences. In a town or local setting, they may be individuals such as village elders, leaders of indigenous groups, priests or monks, teachers and extension agents, or high-profile innovators (such as farmers who are perceived to always be at the forefront of new technology). Alternatively, they may be members (often leaders) of organized groups such as Rotary International, Lions Club, Boy Scouts, housewives' groups, and parents' associations. At the national level, influential individuals may include military officers, politicians, high-level clergy, members of the print and broadcast media, environmental activists, entertainment and sports celebrities, artists, writers, and leaders of labor organizations and other private institutions.

These different groups may exert influence in various ways. For example, local religious and opinion leaders may use informal communication channels, capitalizing on their position as respected community role models (Calavan 1986); religious leaders may also appeal to the population's spirituality. Politicians may use more formal channels to alter legal and political structures; and military and police forces may enforce regulations supporting wise, sustainable use of natural resources. Indeed, military organizations may represent a strategic audience for interpreters since they often possess enormous de facto power within governments, making them (like politicians) potentially key architects of environmental policy. As McNeely et al. argue, there are obvious links between national security and a sustainable natural resource base:

> In most parts of the world the defense services are a dominant force politically, socially and economically. While their primary task is to defend the nation's political viability, the defense services are

increasingly coming to recognize that political, economic and ecological viability are closely interrelated. Yet they have seldom been systematically approached to provide their support for positive action in conservation of biological resources (1990:131).

Interpretive efforts directed at influential groups and citizens might take the form of organized field trips to protected areas, informal workshops, and leadership seminars. In Ecuador, for example, special seminars for local, national, and indigenous opinion leaders have been successful in generating political support for conservation in communities adjacent to protected areas (Dickinson 1990, Kernan and Ramos 1990). Some influential middle- and upper-class people may live or own property close to parks, and may control access to local resources. Interpreters could develop activities especially for these people in order to create interest and to win their cooperation and support for management programs. In St. Kitts, for example, planned interpretive programs at the Southeast Peninsula National Park include not only on-site interpretive activities for Kittian tourists, but also a series of environmental workshops for local landowners, tour companies, guide services, and other local businesses stressing the values of protected areas, native vegetation, and wildlife (Brown and Norton 1989).

Foreign Tourists

Although they are not directly involved in the daily decisions affecting protected areas in developing countries, foreign tourists may be a strategic audience for on-site interpretive efforts. There are many similarities between this audience and national visitors to protected areas—people with leisure time who arrive on their own initiative and who impact protected area resources in virtually the same way.

International ecotourists are emerging as an important market segment with considerable revenue-generating potential for developing countries (see Budowski 1990, Mudge 1989, Ingram and Durst 1987, Wilson and Laarman 1987). For example, between 1986 and 1988 twice as many foreigners visited Costa Rican national parks as nationals, and tourism overall accounted for 13 percent of Costa Rica's exports, ranking third as a foreign exchange generator behind only coffee and bananas (Budowski 1990). Although their impacts must be carefully managed, foreign tourists represent a potentially crucial source of exchange for some developing countries.

Because foreign tourists like to receive information about the places they visit, interpretation must be seen as part of the service they pay for, and which they expect. Simply put, interpretation constitutes the intellectual part of the experience tourists seek. Interesting information presented in an entertaining way adds to the quality of the experience, which creates satisfied customers and gives the tourism entrepreneur an important competitive edge against other companies (Mudge 1989, Ham 1985).

Interpretation for foreign tourists can lead to at least three desirable outcomes. First, by enhancing visitor experiences it can help foster preservation of natural features and traditional ways of life. The revenue foreign tourists generate helps to support small and large businesses whose livelihood, in turn, depends on the protection of the natural features which attract the tourists. Such businesses include rental shops (e.g., for horses, bicycles, boats, snorkeling equipment, surf boards, cars, etc.), local artisan cooperatives, souvenir shops, restaurants, snack bars, gasoline stations, small and large-scale lodging establishments, clothing stores, guide services, travel agencies, and others (Jackson 1989, Budowski 1990). For such businesses, protecting the natural and historical quality of local attractions will be a high priority as long as tourists continue to come to see them. As Budowski observed in Costa Rica:

> It is interesting to note how some businessmen have understood that their enterprises depend directly on the natural resources surrounding their property. In many instances they have stopped cutting down the forest which attracts the ecotourists. They have also invested in lands bordering their properties so as to maintain the natural forest . . . These nature-oriented businesses actively participate in research and conservation projects (1990:29).

Second, nationals who notice increasing numbers of foreign nature-seekers and culture buffs in their country may, themselves, be stimulated to explore the country's natural and cultural attributes (Budowski 1990). And third, foreign tourists may return to their own countries as valuable spokespersons for sustainable development and the preservation of traditional cultures and natural ecosystems (Budowski 1990, Ham et al. 1989).

An important consideration for interpreters is that foreign tourists in developing countries may encounter a model of protected area management that is fundamentally different from the one they are used to. Farming, fuelwood collecting, tree cutting, and permanent human settlements around and within the boundaries of a protected area may seem inappropriate to the conservation-minded tourist who knows only the lock-it-up, just-say-no model of national park or wilderness management. Although different models more akin to those in developing countries are being tried in the U.S. (e.g., Wright 1984, Shelton 1989), most nonspecialists may need careful explanations of the rationale and values of permitting sustainable human development within or adjacent to protected areas. Multilingual exhibits or brochures with titles like "Logging in the Park?" or "How Farmers Help the Reserve" could help diffuse the surprise or even outrage that some foreign tourists might feel upon encountering such activities. With raised consciousness about different models of conservation and the concept of sustainable development, some tourists might return to their home countries with even more resolve and better information to seek solutions to international conservation problems.

Because of the growing number of foreign tourists in developing countries, multilingual interpretation is becoming commonplace. In addition to materials developed especially for foreign tourists, interpretive materials developed for middle- and upper-class nationals could be translated and adapted for them as well.

Conclusion

In this essay, we have attempted to sort out what we have learned about interpretation in the developing countries where we have worked, and what the experiences of others have shown us. What stands out, far beyond any systematic conclusions or recommendations we might offer, is the clear and simple idea that the way we view and practice interpretation in the U.S. probably makes more sense here than it would elsewhere. U.S. interpreters hoping to contribute to the growth and development of interpretation in the developing world would do well to consider this idea, more or less as a point of departure.

Host countries sometimes accept the U.S. model too readily, often because the only available training materials are translated from U.S. sources. When application falls short of expectations, in-country interpreters usually blame themselves or conclude that interpretation itself is inappropriate, rather than questioning the model they have been handed. Universities are also to blame. International students studying at U.S. institutions sometimes return to their countries better prepared to work as interpreters in U.S. protected areas than in those in their own countries. Trainers and professors, whether working here or in-country, need to do a better job of listening to their students. They need to learn what it is like to be an interpreter in that country, and they need to learn what it is like to be part of the audience. Would we accept anything less of our professors and interpretive trainers in the U.S.?

Clearly, a superior strategy to exporting our model of interpretation is to assist developing countries in arriving at their own. Over many decades, interpreters in the U.S. have developed a profound knowledge about their craft. Although much of it will not apply everywhere, some of our ideas may have widespread application. The key will be to determine which ones they are. Working with our colleagues in developed countries, learning with them and through them, we can together explore a range of possibilities that neither of us is able to envision alone. Filtered through our cultures and individual realities, the ideas which have merit will be identified and put to the test. Others will be rejected. In the very best scenario, both parties will learn.

Conclusion

In this book we have tried to establish a foundation for the utilization of sociology in support of interpretation. We have done so by drawing attention to the diversity of people who utilize interpretive services. Our approach has been illustrative rather than exhaustive, in part because our knowledge about people is limited and the manner in which sociology can be applied to interpretation is still emerging. We have essentially argued that we can enhance communication of interpretive messages by understanding the behavior of specific visitor populations. Implied throughout was the principle that alternative forms of interpretation should be employed, not simply because they are unique or new but because they are appropriate to a particular visitor public.

We recognize that only a piece of the puzzle has been explored. Interpreters must expand their attention even more to the managerial realities of budgets, politics, communication technologies, and so forth. Social scientists interested in interpretation may need to consider new research perspectives that deal with the political, social, economic, and environmental contexts within which interpretation takes place. What new approaches might be useful? We offer one suggestion—the application of human ecology to interpretation.

The Roots of Human Ecology

Beginning as an offshoot of biological ecology, human ecology is an intellectual tradition long emergent in the social sciences. Examples of human ecological work can be found in anthropology, geography, economics, psychology, and political science (Young 1983). Human ecology focuses on humans' relationships with their environment and the ecological processes that influence human populations. One foundation of human ecology is natural history, which describes species interacting in their natural settings (Vayda and Rappaport 1968).

The first to attempt to apply general ecological principles to human activity were sociologists at the University of Chicago where, in the 1920s and 1930s, the field of sociology experienced rapid growth. The appeal of the ecological viewpoint lay in the wide intellectual scope it offered. Sociologists Park and Burgess drew analogies between natural and human communities, describing society's symbiotic and competitive relationships as an organic web (Faris 1967). Park and Burgess used Chicago as a "social laboratory." Their students gathered data throughout the city. The students made maps of the distribution of social phenomena such as crime, juvenile delinquency, tenant residences, and so forth.

Space and time became key descriptors of social structure. McKenzie defined human ecology as ". . . the study of the spatial and temporal relations of human beings as affected by . . . forces of the environment." In "The Neighborhood" (1922), he described the spatial structure of cities, and suggested that the distribution of businesses, industries, and population varied according to the utility and economic status of different spaces. Figure 1 shows his profile of residents' economic status in Columbus, Ohio. Hawley (1950) also used maps to learn about community structure; in addition, he

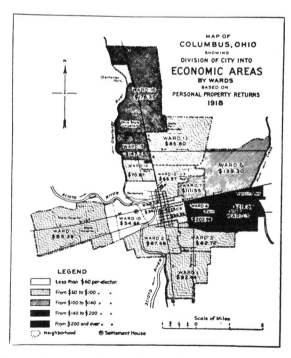

Figure 1. Economic areas of Columbus, Ohio. From Hawley 1968, p. 58.

studied humans' use of time. Figure 2 illustrates one of the many rhythms of community life he examined.

Beginning in the 1970s, this ecological perspective was applied to leisure and recreation. Cheek and Burch (1976) suggested that the physical environment is important in understanding leisure behavior, and that such behavior is characterized by peoples' recreational activities and the spaces and times in which these activities occur.

This ecological line of inquiry spawned several sustained research efforts: at the University of Washington and Yale in the 1970s and at the University of Idaho and CUNY in the 1980s. Drawing on the work of Cheek, Burch, and Field, as well as the earlier tradition of human ecology, Machlis and colleagues (Machlis et al. 1981, Machlis and Tichnell 1985, Neumann and Machlis 1989, Machlis 1989) have described parks as a special type of "human ecosystem," organized around recreation and the preservation of both natural and cultural resources.

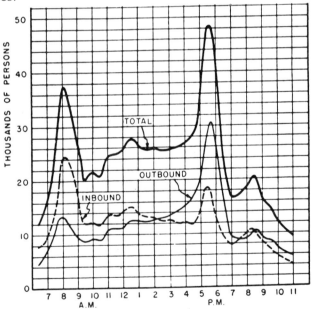

Figure 2. The volume of traffic flow into and out of the central business district, by hours of the day. From Hawley 1950, p. 303.

These programs have emphasized the gathering of data that can provide managers with "usable knowledge," i.e. information useful in decision making. The Visitor Services Project at the University of Idaho, for example, has conducted over forty separate visitor studies of sites within the National Park system, from Denali to the Everglades and the Statue of Liberty to Valley Forge and the White House. The data confirm the diversity of visitors, and reflect the spatial and temporal concerns of the earlier human ecological tradition (Littlejohn and Machlis 1990). Figures 3 and 4 show two distinct visitation patterns: Grand Teton National Park draws a national population while visitors to Glen Canyon National Recreation Area are largely from the nearby region. Such data are vital in developing a program of communicating with the public and in demonstrating the economic importance of park and historic sites. Figure 5 shows the length of time visitors waited at the White House for their tour to begin. This kind of information echoes the work of earlier human ecologists, and is useful for developing effective reservation and visitor management systems.

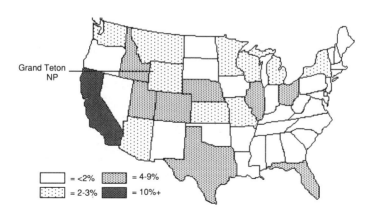

Figure 3. Visitation by state. Grand Teton National Park, 1987.

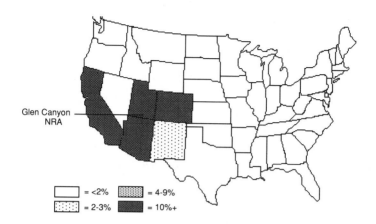

Figure 4. Lakeshore visitors by state. Glen Canyon NRA, 1988.

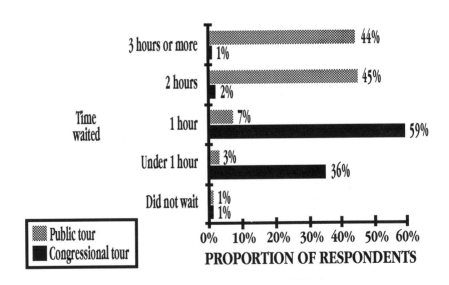

Figure 5. Length of wait for tour. White House tours, 1989.

Human Ecology and Interpretation:
A Conceptual Framework

Relative to other disciplinary orientations, the human ecological approach to interpretation emphasizes a broad set of variables and relationships. The essence of human ecology is a recognition of *Homo sapiens* as part of the ecosystem, an integral part of nature. Its central concept, the human ecosystem, is defined by the interaction of people, social organizations, and available technology in response to a set of environmental conditions. Interpretive settings such as national parks or urban historic sites can be considered as human ecosystems. Created by society, these natural and cultural entities reflect a social organization and technology for the preservation and use of unique resources. A state or regional museum, an aquarium, an art center, or a zoo can be treated as a complex system with daily flows of people, information, energy, materials, and so forth.

These human ecosystems are dynamic and adaptive. For example, moving an interpretive program to a new location or time may require visitors to change their schedules, alter density levels in a visitor center, increase impacts on one resource and lessen those on another, and force interpreters and maintenance crews to adapt their work operations and home life. "Adaptation" is a crucial term here. John Bennett, the anthropologist, writes:

> Adaptive behavior is viewed as multidimensional: what may be adaptive for one individual is maladaptive for another or for the group; what may be adaptive for humans may not be so for Nature (1976:3).

Figure 6 presents this human ecological view of interpretive settings. The biophysical environment represents those resources set aside as vignettes of natural or cultural history that support the human activity within a park or other locale. For example, a river may function as a natural area for hiking, a setting for historical interpretation, and as a source of potable water for park staff and visitors. The social environment includes the formal organizations that affect interpretive activities, such as the management agency, concessionaries, natural history associations, special interest groups, and so forth. It also includes the prevalent norms for behavior, i.e.,

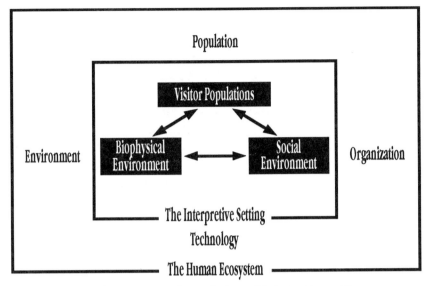

Figure 6. Human ecological view of interpretive settings.

the social definitions of which activities are appropriate within the setting.

In the human ecological perspective, visitors are a key population. Writing about national parks, Campbell notes:

> . . . Humans are the dominant species in every national park. As a result of our social evolution we have expanded into one niche after another. We have created new niches where none existed. Further, we are a highly generalized animal, capable of an immense range of behaviors. . . In short, to understand the natural systems of the park you must understand the park's most dominant species (1979:53).

Visitor publics vary in their cultural content and expression; as this volume has shown, they represent diverse subpopulations. The interrelationship of these diverse visitor groups with a complex setting like a park or historic site requires substantial adaptation. An interpretive program that describes local flora, fauna, and history, informs visitors as to hiking and sightseeing opportunities, and explains park regulations is part of this adaptive process. Seen in this light, interpretation is an exchange of information critical to adaptation within a park ecosystem, and the interpreter fulfills a very real ecological function.

Hence, the human ecological framework has several advantages. It is broad in scope and considers several variables not yet widely explored in interpretation research. It is dynamic in its concern with the ever-changing process of adaptation within the interpretive setting. Interpretation is treated as an ecological function, linked to other management activities. We think that the human ecological approach could provide both a promising framework for interpretation research, and an important link to the natural sciences and humanities that traditionally are sources of knowledge for interpreters.

The Future

The last decade of the 20th century and the first years of the next are exciting times to be an interpreter of natural and cultural history. New technologies promise to revolutionize the way people communicate. Ethnic pride and cultural pluralism are creating a world where different cultures are juxtaposed and new, hybrid cultures emerge. Environmental concern is spreading throughout the globe, and there is a growing awareness of the interdependence between preservation and development, between ecological health and quality of life.

What this affords the interpreter is the opportunity to participate in a critical societal task: the sharing of a crucial form of knowledge about our world. To do so requires that interpreters expand their world view and understanding of their clientele. We hope sociology will continue to contribute to such intellectual and professional growth. All might remember Freeman Tilden's admonition in *The Fifth Essence*:

> Interpretation is a voyage of discovery in the field of human emotions and intellectual growth and it is hard to foresee that time when the interpreter can confidently say, "Now we are wholly adequate to our task" (n.d.).

References Cited

Academy for Educational Development. 1989. "Education for social development." *Academy News* 12(2):1-3, 5-7.

Academy for Educational Development. 1990. "Nepal: teachers receive training by radio." *Academy News* 13(1):7.

Agee, J. 1960. *Let Us Now Praise Famous Men*. Boston: Houghton-Mifflin.

Anderson, N. 1923. *The Hobo*. Chicago: University of Chicago Press.

Anonymous. 1988. *Plan maestro de desarrollo conservacionista de la provincia de Galápagos. Volumen 3: Programación sectorial*. Consejo Nacional de Desarrollo, Secretaria General de Planificación, Quito, Ecuador.

Arboleda, J., Orejuela, J., Murgueitio, E., and Glick, D. (eds.). 1989. *Memorias del Taller sobre Areas Silvestres y Necesidades Humanas*. Cali, Colombia: Fundación para la Educación Superior.

Baedeker, K. 1900. *Paris and Environs*. 14th rev. ed. Leipzig: Baedeker Publishers.

Bajimaya, S., and Fazio, J. R. 1989. *Communications Manual: A Guide to Aid Park and Protected Area Managers to Communicate Effectively with Local Residents*. Kathmandu, Nepal: Department of National Parks and Wildlife Conservation/FAO-UNDP.

Barborak, J. R., and Ham, S. H. 1989. Central American Regional Environmental and Natural Resource Management Project: Environmental Awareness, Protected Areas and Biodiversity Component. Gainesville, FL: Tropical Research and Development, Inc.

Barna, L.A. 1991. "Stumbling blocks in intercultural communication." In *Intercultural Communication*, ed. L. A. Samovar and R. E. Porter, 345-352. Belmont, CA: Wadsworth.

Barr, B. B. (ed.) 1985. *Science for Everyone:* A Teacher's Guide to accompany the "My Daughter the Scientist" exhibit. Chicago, IL: Museum of Science and Industry.

Bassard, J., and Boll, E. 1950. *Ritual in Family Living: A Contemporary Study*. Philadelphia: University of Philadelphia.

Beer, F. A. 1981. *Peace Against War. The Ecology of International Violence*. San Francisco: W.H. Freeman Co.

Bennett, J. W. 1976. *The Ecological Transition: Cultural Anthropology and Human Adaptation*. New York: Pergamon Press.

Berger, P. L. 1981. *Sociology Reinterpreted: An Essay on Method and Vocation.* Garden City, NJ: Anchor Press, Doubleday.

Bernard, T. J. 1983. *The Consensus-Conflict Debate: Form and Content of Social Theories.* New York: Columbia University Press.

Berry, B., and Kasarda, J. 1977. *Contemporary Urban Ecology.* New York: MacMillan.

Blood, R. W., and Wolfe, P. M. 1971. "Resources and family task performance." In *Sociology of the Family,* ed. M. Anderson. Baltimore: Penguin Books.

Boas, F. 1888. *The Central Eskimo.* Sixth Annual Report of the Bureau of American Ethnology, 1883-1885. Washington, D.C.

Bolyard, J. E. 1981. "International travel and passenger fares, 1980." *Survey of Current Business* 61(5):29-34.

Brislin, R. W. 1991. "Prejudice in intercultural communication." In *Intercultural Communication,* ed. L. A. Samovar and R. E. Porter, 366-370. Belmont, CA: Wadsworth.

Brown, M. T., and Norton, R. 1989. "Terrestrial park and recreation plan for the southeast peninsula of St. Kitts/Nevis." In *The Southeast Peninsula Project in St. Kitts: Volume III—Parks and Recreation Plans.* Washington, D.C.: DESFIL/Development Alternatives, Inc.

Brown, W. 1973. *Islands of Hope.* Washington, D.C.: National Recreation and Parks Association.

Brown, W. S. 1989. "The business of questions and answers: An ethnographic study of the information desk at Wupatki National Monument Visitors Center." Mimeograph. Wupatki National Monument Library, Flagstaff, AZ.

Buck, R. C. 1978. "Boundary maintenance revisited: tourist experience in an old order Amish community." *Rural Sociology* 43(2):221-234.

Budowski, T. 1990. "Ecotourism." *Tecnitur* 5(27):28-30 (San José, Costa Rica).

Bultena, G., Field, D. R., and Renninger, R. 1977. "Interpretation for the elderly: a study of the interpretive interests of retired national parkgoers." *Journal of Interpretation* 3(2):29-32.

Bunch, R. 1982. *Two Ears of Corn: A Guide to People-centered Agricultural Improvement.* Oklahoma City: World Neighbors.

Burch, W. R., Jr. 1964. "Observation as a Technique for Recreation Research." Portland: U.S. Department of Agriculture, Forest Service, Pacific Northwest Forest and Range Experiment Station, Research Paper.

Burch, W. R., Jr. 1965. "The play world of camping." *American Journal of Sociology* 70(5):604-612.

Burch, W. R., Jr. 1971. *Daydreams and Nightmares: A Sociological Essay on the American Environment.* New York: Harper & Row.

Burch, W. R., Jr. 1974. "Observation as a technique for recreation research." In *Land and Leisure: Concepts and Methods in Outdoor Recreation,* ed. C. Van Doren. Chicago: Maaroufa Press.

Burch, W. R., Jr. 1986. "Ties that bind—The social benefits of recreation provision." In *A Literature Review* (Values Section). President's Commission on Americans Outdoors, 81-91. Washington, D.C.: U.S. Government Printing Office.

Burch, W. R., Jr., DeLuca, D., Machlis, G. E., Burch-Minakan, L., and Zimmerman, C. 1978. *Handbook for Assessing Energy-Society Relations.* Washington, D.C.: U.S. Department of Energy Report, Office of Inexhaustible Resources.

Burch, W. R., Jr., and Wenger, W., Jr. 1967. *The Social Characteristics of Participants in Three Styles of Family Camping.* USDA Forest Service Gen. Tech. Rep. PNW-48. Portland, OR: Pacific Northwest Forest and Range Experiment Station.

Burgess, E. W., Locke, H. J., and Thomes, M. 1971. *The Family.* New York: Van Nostrand Reinhold.

Calavan, M. M. 1986. "Community management in rural northeastern Thailand." In *Community Management: Asian Experience and Perspectives,* ed. D. C. Korten. West Hartford, CT: Kumarian Press.

Campbell, C. A. 1974. "Survival of reptiles and amphibians in urban environments." In *Symposium on Wildlife in an Urbanizing Environment,* Planning and Resources Development Series #28. Amherst, MA: Cooperative Extension Service.

Campbell, F. L. 1970. "Participant observation in outdoor recreation." *Journal of Leisure Research* 2(4):226-236.

Carr, W. H. 1976. Uncited quote In *Interpreting the Environment,* ed. G. W. Sharpe. New York: John Wiley & Sons.

Carter, D. B. (ed.) 1987. *Current Conceptions of Sex Roles and Sex Typing—Theory and Research.* New York: Praeger Publishers.

Catton, W. R., Jr. 1980. *Overshoot: The Ecological Basis of Revolutionary Change.* Chicago: University of Illinois Press.

Cha, D. 1989. "Wupatki National Monument, a place of fascination and wonders: You have got to see it." Mimeograph. Wupatki National Monument Library, Flagstaff, AZ.

Cheek, N. H., Jr. 1971a. "Intragroup social structure and social solidarity in park settings." (Paper presented at the American Association for the Advancement of Science Symposium, Philadelphia, Pennsylvania, December 26-31, 1971).

Cheek, N. H., Jr. 1971b. "Toward a sociology of non work." *Pacific Sociological Review* 14(July):245-259.

Cheek, N. H., Jr. 1972. "Variations in patterns of leisure behavior: An analysis of sociological aggregates." In *Social Behavior, Natural Resources, and the Environment,* ed. W. R. Burch, Jr., N. H. Cheek, Jr., and L. Taylor, 23-29. New York: Harper & Row.

Cheek, N. H., Jr. 1976. "Sociological perspectives on the zoological park." In *Leisure and Recreation Places,* ed. N. H. Cheek, Jr., D. R. Field, and R. J. Burdge. Ann Arbor: Ann Arbor Science Publishers, Inc.

Cheek, N. H., Jr., and Burch, W. R., Jr. 1976. *The Social Organization of Leisure in Human Society.* New York: Harper & Row.

Cheek, N. H., Jr., and Field, D. R. 1971. *North Pacific Border Study.* Seattle: University of Washington College of Forest Resources.

Clark, R. N. 1976. *How To Control Litter in Recreation Areas: The Incentive System.* USDA Forest Service Gen. Tech. Rep. Portland, OR: Pacific Northwest Forest and Range Experiment Station.

Clark, R. N., and Lucas, R. C. 1978. *The Forest Ecosystem of Southeast Alaska Outdoor Recreation and Scenic Resources.* USDA Forest Service Gen. Tech. Rep. PNW-66. Portland, OR: Pacific Northwest Forest and Range Experiment Station.

Clark, R. N., Burgess, R. L., and Hendee, J. C. 1972a. "The development of anti-litter behavior in a forest campground." *Journal of Applied Behavior Analysis* 5 (Spring): 1-5.

Clark, R. N., Hendee, J. C., and Burgess, R. L. 1972b. "The experimental control of littering." *Journal of Environmental Education* 4(2):22-28.

Clark, R. N., Hendee, J. C., and Campbell, F. L. 1971a. "Depreciative Behavior in Forest Campgrounds." USDA Forest Service Research Paper, August.

Clark, R. N., Hendee, J. C., and Campbell, F. L. 1971b. "Values, behavior, and conflict in modern camping culture." *Journal of Leisure Research* 3 (Summer):143-159.

Clawson, M., and Knetsch, J. L. 1966. *Economics of Outdoor Recreation.* Baltimore: Johns Hopkins Press.

Cleaver, E. 1970. "The land question and black liberation." In *What Country Have I? Political Writings by Black Americans,* ed. H. J. String. New York: St. Martin's Press.

Collier, J., Jr. 1967. *Visual Anthropology: Photography as a Research Method.* New York: Holt, Rinehart & Winston.

CONAMA. 1990. *Estrategia Nacional de Educación Ambiental.* Guatemala City, Guatemala: Comisión Nacional del Medio Ambiente.

Condon, J. 1991. ". . .So near the United States: Notes on communication between Mexicans and North Americans." In *Intercultural Communication,* ed L. A. Samovar and R. E. Porter, 106-111. Belmont, CA: Wadsworth.

Cone, C., and Kendall, K. 1976. "Space, time and family interaction: Visitor behavior at the Science Museum of Minnesota." *Curator* 21(3):245-258.

Cordell, H. K, Bergstrom, J. C., Hartmann, L. A., and English, D. B. K. 1990. *An Analysis of the Outdoor Recreation and Wilderness Situation in the United States: 1989-2040.* USDA Forest Service General Technical Report RM-189. Fort Collins, CO: Rocky Mountain Forest and Range Experiment Station.

Cottrell, W. F. 1972. "Men cry peace." In *Technology, Man and Progress,* 133-185. Columbus: Charles E. Merrill.

Crider, D. M., Willits, F. K.,and Bealer, F. C. 1973. "Panel studies: some practical problems." *Sociological Methods* 2(1):3-19.

D'Amore, L. J. 1988. "Tourism—the world's peace industry." *Business Quarterly.* London: School of Business Administration, the University of Western Ontario.

Darwin, C. 1860. *The Voyage of the Beagle.* Reprint. Garden City: Doubleday & Co.

Daugherty, H. E. (ed.). 1989. *Perfil ambiental de Honduras 1989.* Bethesda, MD: DESFIL/Development Alternatives, Inc.

Davis, C., Haub, C., and Willetta, J. 1983. "U.S. Hispanics: Changing the face of America." *Population Bulletin* 38:1-43.

Dean, J. P., Eichhorn, R. L., and Dean, L. R. 1969. "Limitations and advantages of unstructured methods." In *Issues in Participant Observation: A Text and Reader,* ed. G.J. McCall and J. L. Simmons, 19-24. Chicago: Addison-Wesley.

Deloria, V., Jr. 1969. *Custer Died for your Sins.* New York: MacMillan.

Deutscher, I. 1966. "Words and deeds: Social science and social policy." *Sociological Problems* 13:235-254.

DeVall, W. 1973. "The development of leisure social worlds." *Humboldt Journal of Social Relations* 1(1):53.

Diamond, J. 1980. "The ethology of teaching: A perspective from the observations of families in science centers." Ph.D. Dissertation. University of California, Berkeley.

Dickinson, J. 1990. "Conservation and development." *DESFIL Newsletter* 3(4):1,6.

Dix, L. F., ed. 1987. *Women: Their Under-representation and Career Differential in Science and Engineering.* Washington, DC: National Academy Press.

Dodd, R. E. 1987. "Mass communication campaigns for environmental education in developing countries: Honduras case study." Masters thesis, Department of Journalism and Mass Communication, San Jose State University.

Dotson, F. 1951. "Patterns of voluntary association among urban working-class families." *American Sociological Review* 16:689-693.

Driver, B. L., Rosenthal, D., and Peterson, G. 1979. "Social benefits of urban forests and related green spaces in cities." In *Proceedings of National Urban Forestry Conference*, ed. G. Hopkins. Syracuse: State University of New York, College of Environmental Science and Forestry.

Dubos, R. 1980. *The Wooing of Earth*. New York: Charles Scribner's Sons.

Dulles, F. R. 1965. *A History of Recreation: America Learns To Play*. New York: Meredith Publishers.

Duncan, O. D., Schuman, H., and Duncan, B. 1973. *Social Change in a Metropolitan Community*. New York: Russell Sage.

Dunn, D. R. 1980. "Urban recreation research: an overview." *Leisure Sciences* 3:(1):25-27.

Durkheim, E. 1947. *The Division of Labor in Society*. New York: Free Press.

Dwyer, J. F., O'Leary, J. T., and Theobald, W. F. 1979. "Putting the cart before the horse: When does the data catch up to the theory?" (Paper presented at the Tourism and the Next Decade International Symposium, George Washington University, Washington, D.C.)

Edgerton, R. B. 1985. *Rules, Exceptions and Social Order*. Berkeley, CA: University of California Press.

Eliot, T. S. 1952. *The Complete Poems and Plays, 1909-1950*. New York: Harcourt Brace.

Ellingsworth, H. W. 1983. "Adaptive intercultural communication." In *Intercultural Communication Theory*, ed. W. B. Gudykunst, 195-204. Newbury Park, CA: Sage Publications.

Erb, T. O. 1981. "Attitudes of early adolescents towards science, women in science, and science careers." In *Middle School Research: Selected Studies*. Fairborn, OH: National Middle School Association.

Evans, P. B., and Stephens, J. D. 1988. "Development and the world economy." In *Handbook of Sociology*, ed. N. J. Smelser, 739-773. Newbury Park, CA: Sage Publications.

Evans-Pritchard, E. A. 1940. *The Nuer*. New York: Oxford University Press.

Falk, J. H., and Balling, J. D. 1980. "A perspective on field trips: Environmental effects on learning." *Curator* 18:229-240.

Faris, E. L. 1967. *Chicago Sociology: 1920-1932*. Chicago: University of Chicago Press.

Field, D. R. 1971. "Interchangeability of parks with other leisure settings." (Paper presented at the AAAS Symposium, Philadelphia, Pennsylvania, December 26-31, 1971.)

Field, D. R. 1972. "Visitors to parks in the Pacific Northwest." (Paper presented at the Pacific Northwest Region Superintendents' Conference, Portland, Oregon, March 16-18, 1972.)

Field, D. R. 1973. "The telephone interview in leisure research." *Journal of Leisure Research* 5:51-59.

Field, D. R., and O'Leary, J. T. 1973. "Social groups as a basis for assessing participation in selected water activities." *Journal of Leisure Research* 5(2):16-25.

Field, D. R., and Wagar, J. A. 1973. "Visitor groups and interpretation in parks and other outdoor leisure settings." *Journal of Environmental Education* 5(1):12-17.

Firey, W. 1960. *Man, Mind and Land.* Westport, CT: Greenwood Press.

Foresta, R. A. 1984. *America's National Parks and their Keepers.* Washington, D.C.: Resources for the Future.

Foster, R. D. 1989. *The Potential Fiscal Impact from Southeast Peninsula Development 1989-1994.* Washington, D.C.: DESFIL/Development Alternatives, Inc.

Freeman, D. 1983. *Margaret Mead and Samoa: The Making and Unmaking of an Anthropological Myth.* Cambridge: Harvard University Press.

Freund, J. 1968. *The Sociology of Max Weber.* Trans. M. Ilford. New York: Pantheon Books.

Galeano, E. 1973. *Open Veins of Latin America: Five Centuries of the Pillage of a Continent.* New York: Monthly Review Press.

Geismar, L. L. 1964. "Family functioning as an index of need for welfare services." *Family Process* 3(2):99-111.

Gold, R. L. 1958. "Roles in sociological field observations." *Social Forces* 36(3):217-233.

Gottlieb, D. 1957. "The neighborhood tavern and the cocktail lounge: A study of class differences." *American Journal of Sociology* 62:559-562.

Gramann, J. H., and Floyd, M. F. 1991. *Ethnic Assimilation and Recreational Use of the Tonto National Forest.* USDA Forest Service Contract Report. Riverside, CA: Pacific Southwest Research Station.

Graves, P. F. 1972. "Summation of the forest recreation symposium." In *Summary of the Forest Recreation Symposium 12-21.* Forest Service Research Paper NE-235. Upper Darby, PA: Northeast Forest and Range Experiment Station.

Guba, E. G., and Lincoln, Y. S. 1985. *Naturalistic Inquiry.* Beverly Hills, CA: Sage Publications.

Guier, E. M. (ed.). 1989. *Plan Maestro de Educación Ambiental.* San José, Costa Rica: Fundación Neotrópica.

Ham, S. H. 1982. "Familiarity and adaptation: A study of family attendance at interpretive activities." Ph.D. diss. University of Idaho, Department of Wildland Recreation Management, May.

Ham, S. H. 1985. "Interpretation Aboard the North Star—the Role of Information Services in Enhancing the Experiences of Cruise Ship Passengers." Seattle, WA: Exploration Cruise Lines, Inc.

Ham, S. H. 1990. *Taller de Interpretación y Educación Ambiental.* Tegucigalpa, D.C., Honduras: U.S. Agency for International Development, Office of Agriculture and Natural Resources.

Ham, S. H., and Castillo, L. 1988. *Análisis de la Situación de la Educación Ambiental en las Escuelas del Àrea Rural de Honduras.* Moscow, ID: Idaho Forest, Wildlife and Range Experiment Station, College of Forestry, Wildlife and Range Sciences, University of Idaho, Publication No. 441.

Ham, S. H., and Castillo, L. 1990. "Elementary schools in rural Honduras: problems in exporting environmental education models from the United States." *Journal of Environmental Education* 21(4):27-32.

Ham, S. H., and Enríquez, J. R. 1987. *Una Metodología Propuesta Sobre Planificación de Interpretación Ambiental para los Parques Nacionales y Areas Similares del Ecuador.* Moscow, ID: Idaho Forest, Wildlife and Range Experiment Station Publication No. 310, College of Forestry, Wildlife and Range Sciences, University of Idaho.

Ham, S. H., and Valencia, L. 1990. *Bases de la Estrategia de Educación Ambiental para la Fundación del Centavo.* Guatemala City, Guatemala: U.S. Agency for International Development.

Ham, S. H., Sutherland, D. S., and Barborak, J. R. 1989. "Role of protected areas in environmental education in Central America." *Journal of Interpretation* 13(5):1-7.

Hammond, A. L. (ed.). 1990. *World Resources: A Guide to the Global Environment.* New York: Oxford University Press.

Hancock, H. K. 1973. "Recreation preference: Its relation to user behavior." *Journal of Forestry* 71(6):336-337.

Hawley, A. H. 1950. *Human Ecology: A Theory of Community Structure.* New York: The Ronald Press Company.

Hawley, A. H. (ed.) 1968. *Roderick D. McKenzie on Human Ecology.* Chicago: University of Chicago Press.

Hawley, A. H. 1971. *Urban Society. An Ecological Approach.* New York: The Ronald Press Company.

Hays, S. P. 1987. *Beauty, Health, and Permanence: Environmental Politics in the United States, 1955-1985.* Cambridge: Cambridge University Press.

Heberlein, T. A. 1971. "Moral norms, threatened sanctions, and littering behavior." Ph.D diss. University of Wisconsin, Madison.

Heberlein, T. A. 1973. "Social psychological assumptions of user attitude surveys: The case of the wilderness scale." *Journal of Leisure Research* 5(3):18-33.

Heidegger, M. 1961. *Being and Time.* Trans. J. Macquarrie and E. Robinson. New York: Harper & Row.

Hendee, J. C. 1972a. "Challenging the folklore of environmental education." *Journal of Environmental Education* 3(3):19-23.

Hendee, J. C. 1972b. "No, to attitudes to evaluate environmental education." Guest Editorial, *Journal of Environmental Education* 3(3):65.

Hendee, J. C., Gale, R. P, and Catton, W. R., Jr. 1971. "A typology of outdoor recreation activity preferences." *Journal of Leisure Research* 3(1).

Heritage, Conservation and Recreation Service. 1980. *National Urban Recreation Study.* Washington, D.C.: Government Printing Office.

Hess, R., and Handel, G. 1974. *Family Worlds: A Psychosocial Approach to Family Life.* Chicago: University of Chicago Press.

Hobbs, D. A., and Blank, S. J. 1982. *Sociology and the Human Experience,* 3rd ed. New York: John Wiley & Sons.

Hollingshead, A. G. 1949. *Elmtown's Youth.* New York: Wiley.

Honigmann, J. J. 1954. *Culture and Personality.* New York: Harper & Row.

Hopkins, L. J. 1989. "Wupatki trail boundaries: Steps in the right direction." Mimeograph. Wupatki National Monument Library, Flagstaff, AZ.

Howard, W. E. 1974. "Why wildlife in an urban society?" In *Symposium on Wildlife in an Urbanizing Environment.* Planning and Resources Development Series #28. Amherst: Massachusetts Cooperative Extension Service.

Hughes, J. D. 1975. *Ecology in Ancient Civilizations.* Albuquerque: University of New Mexico Press.

Hutchison, R. 1987. "Ethnicity and urban culture: Whites, Blacks and Hispanics in Chicago's public parks." *Journal of Leisure Research* 19(3):205-222.

Ingram, C. D., and Durst, P. B. 1987. *Nature-oriented Travel to Developing Countries.* Research Triangle Park, NC: Southeastern Center for Forest Economics Research, Forestry Private Enterprise Initiative, FPEI Working Paper No. 28.

Irwin, P. N., Gartner, W. G., and Phelps, C. C. 1990. "Mexican-American/Anglo cultural differences as recreation style determinants." *Leisure Sciences* 12(4):335-348.

Jackson, I. L. 1989. *Conditions and Trends in Caribbean Tourism Influencing the Development of the Southeast Peninsula.* Washington, D.C.: DESFIL/Development Alternatives, Inc.

Jackson, M. H. 1989. *Galápagos: A Natural History Guide.* Calgary: University of Calgary Press.

Japanese National Tourist Organization. 1979. *Tourism in Japan 1978.* Tokyo: Department of Tourism, Ministry of Transport.

Japanese National Tourist Organization. 1981. *Tourism in Japan 1980.* Tokyo: Department of Tourism, Ministry of Transport.

Johnson, D.R., and Aho, J. n.d. "A Suggested Strategy for the Management and Planning of a Sustained Program of Social Information Acquisition at Olympic National Park." Unpublished report. Pacific Northwest Regional Office, National Park Service, Seattle, WA.

Jones, L. 1989. "Project offers *campesinos* alternatives." San José, Costa Rica: *The Tico Times* 33(1024):10 (July 14).

Kahle, J. B. 1983a. "Factors affecting the retention of girls in science courses and careers: Case studies of selected secondary schools." Unpublished paper presented at National Association of Biology Teachers, Washington, D.C.

Kahle, J. B. 1983b. "The disadvantaged majority: Science education of women in science." Association for the Education of Teachers in Science Outstanding Paper.

Kakabadse, Y. 1988. "Ecuador: the promise and problems of wilderness in the third world." In *For the Conservation of Earth:* Proceedings of the Fourth World Wilderness Congress, ed. V. Martin, 180-182. Golden, CO: Fulcrum Press.

Kazantzakis, N. 1960. *The Saviors of God.* New York: Simon & Schuster.

Keefe, S. E. 1984. "Real and ideal extended familism among Mexican American and Anglo Americans: On the meaning of 'close' family ties." *Human Organization* 43(1):65-70.

Keefe, S. E., and Padilla, A. M. 1987. *Chicano Ethnicity.* Albuquerque: University of New Mexico Press.

Keep America Beautiful. 1968. *Who Litters and Why: Results of a Survey of Public Awareness and Concern about the Problem of Litter.* New York: Keep America Beautiful.

Kellert, S. R. 1983. *Children's Attitudes, Knowledge and Behaviors Towards Animals—Phase V.* Fish and Wildlife Service (Dept. of the Interior). Morristown, NJ: Geraldine R. Dodge Foundation.

Kelly, J. R. 1977. "Leisure socialization: Replication and extension." *Journal of Leisure Research* 9(2):121-132.

Kelly, J. R. 1983. *Leisure Identities and Interactions.* London: Allen & Unwin.

Kelly, J. R. 1987. *Freedom To Be: A New Sociology of Leisure.* New York: MacMillan.

Kerlinger, F. N. 1973. *Foundations of Behavioral Research.* New York: Holt, Rinehart & Winston.

Kernan, B., and Ramos, H. H. 1990. *Informe Final de los Talleres y la Conferencia Sobre Conservación y Desarrollo.* Washington, D.C.: DESFIL/Development Alternatives, Inc.

Kissinger, H. 1984. *Report of the National Bipartisan Commission on Central America.* Washington, D.C.: U.S. Government Printing Office.

Knowlton, C. S. 1972. "Culture conflict and natural resources." In *Social Behavior, Natural Resources, and the Environment,* ed. W. R. Burch, N. H. Cheek, Jr., and L. Taylor, 109-145. New York: Harper & Row.

Lastrucci, C. L. 1967. *The Scientific Approach.* Cambridge: Schenkman Publishing Co., Inc.

Lebra, J. S. 1976. *Japanese Patterns of Behavior.* Honolulu: University Press of Hawaii.

Lee, R. G. 1972. "The social definition of outdoor recreation places." In *Social Behavior, Natural Resources and the Environment,* ed. W. R. Burch, Jr., N. H. Cheek, Jr., and L. Taylor. New York: Harper & Row.

Leibow, E. 1976. *Tally's Corner.* Boston: Little, Brown & Co.

Leonard, H. J. 1986. *Recursos Naturales y Desarrollo en América Central: Un Perfil Ambiental Regional.* San José, Costa Rica: Centro Agronomico Tropical de Investigacion y Ensenanza. Informe Tecnico No. 127.

Lewis, C. S. 1969. "On three ways of writing for children." In *Only Connect: Readings on Children's Literature,* ed. S. Egoff, G. T. Slubbs, and L. F. Ashley, 207-220. New York: Oxford University Press.

Lime, D. W., and Lorence, G. A. 1974. *Improving Estimates of Wilderness Use from Mandatory Travel Permits.* USDA Forest Service Research Paper NC-101. St. Paul, MN: North Central Forest and Range Experiment Station.

Linhart, S. 1975. "The use and meaning of leisure in present-day Japan." In *Modern Japan,* ed. W. G. Beasley. Berkeley: University of California Press.

Linn, M. C. 1981. "Male-female differences in formal thought." Washington, D.C: National Science Foundation Paper.

Littlejohn, M. E., and Machlis, G. E. 1990. *A Diversity of Visitors: A Report on Visitors to the National Park System.* Moscow: University of Idaho, Cooperative Park Studies Unit.

Litwak, E. 1960. "Occupational mobility and extended family cohesion." *American Sociology Review* 25:9-21.

Litwak, E. 1961. "Voluntary associations and neighborhood cohesion." *American Sociology Review* 26:258-71.

Lofland, J. 1976. *Doing Social Life: The Qualitative Study of Human Interaction in Natural Settings.* New York: Wiley.

Lucas, D. H. 1974. "The effect that participation in an instruction program at Fernbank Science Center has on upper elementary school students' scientific attitudes." Ph.D. diss. Georgia State University, Atlanta.

MacCannell, D. 1976. *The Tourist: A New Theory of the Leisure Class.* New York: Schocken Books.

Machlis, G. E. 1975. "Families in parks: An analysis of family organization in a leisure setting." Master's thesis, University of Washington, Seattle.

Machlis, G.E. 1989. "Managing parks as human ecosystems." In *Public Places and Spaces, Vol. 10* (HBE series), ed. I. Altman and E. H. Zube. New York: Plenum Publishing Corporation.

Machlis, G. E. 1991. Personal communication, May 27, Moscow, ID.

Machlis, G. E., and Burch, W. R., Jr. 1983. "Relations between strangers: Cycles of structure and meaning in tourist systems." *Sociological Review* 31(4):666-692.

Machlis, G. E., and Field, D. R. 1974. "Getting connected: an approach to children's interpretation." *Trends* 7:19-25.

Machlis, G. E., and Field, D. R. (eds.). 1984. *On Interpretation: Sociology for Interpreters of Natural and Cultural History.* Corvallis: Oregon State University Press.

Machlis, G. E., Field, D. R., and Van Every, M. E. 1982. *Foreign Visitors and Interpretation: A Sociological Look at the Japanese Tourist.* Cooperative Park Studies Unit report, National Park Service, University of Idaho, Moscow, Idaho. CPSU/UI S-82-1.

Machlis, G. E., and Tichnell, D. L. 1985. *The State of the World's Parks: An International Assessment for Resource Management, Policy and Research.* Boulder, CO: Westview Press.

Machlis, G. E., Converse, R. S., and Jensen, E. L. 1981. *Social Conflict at Virginia-Kendall Park Cuyahoga Valley National Recreation Area.* Cooperative Park Studies Unit report, National Park Service, University of Idaho, Moscow, Idaho. CPSU/UI S-81-3.

Machlis, G. E., Costa, D. A., and Salazar, J. C. 1990. *Galápagos Islands Visitor Study.* Moscow: University of Idaho, Cooperative Park Studies Unit.

Machlis, G. E., Field, D. R., and Campbell, F. L. 1981a. "The human ecology of parks." *Leisure Sciences* 4(3):195-212.

Machlis, G. E., McLaughlin, W.J., and Yu-Lian, Liu. 1981b. "An urban park in China: Xuan Wu Hu." *Parks and Recreation* 16:(8):20-29.

MacKinnon, J., MacKinnon, K., Child, G., and Thorsell, J. (eds.). 1986. *Managing Protected Areas in the Tropics.* Gland, Switzerland: International Union for the Conservation of Nature and Natural Resources (IUCN).

Mager, R. F. 1962. *Preparing Instructional Objectives.* Belmont, CA: Fearon Publishers.

Malinowski, B. 1922. *Argonauts of the Western Pacific.* London: Routledge.

Market Opinion Research. 1986. *Participation in Outdoor Recreation among American Adults and the Motivations which Drive Participation.* Report prepared for the President's Commission on Americans Outdoors.

Marks, R. L. 1991. *Three Men of the Beagle.* New York: Alfred A. Knopf.

Martindale, D. 1960. *American Society.* Princeton: D. Van Nostrand.

Marx, L. 1964. *The Machine in the Garden: Technology and the Pastoral Ideal in America.* London: Oxford University Press.

McKendry, J. 1988. *Interpretation: Key to the Park Experience.* National Parks and Conservation Association, Washington, D.C. Vol. 4.

McKenzie, R. D. 1922. "The neighborhood: A study of local life in the city of Columbus, Ohio." *The American Journal of Sociology.* September 1921; November 1921; January 1922; March 1922; May 1922.

McLemore, S. D. 1991. *Racial and Ethnic Relations in America.* Boston: Allyn & Bacon.

McMillen, J. B. 1983. "The social organization of leisure among Mexican-Americans." *Journal of Leisure Research* 15(2):164-173.

McNeely, J. A., Miller, K. R., Reid, W. V., Mittermeier, R. A., and Werner, T. B. 1990. *Conserving the World's Biological Diversity.* Gland, Switzerland: International Union for the Conservation of Nature and Natural Resources, Washington, D.C.: World Resources Institute, Conservation International, World Wildlife Fund-U.S., and the World Bank.

Mead, M. 1964. "Anthropology and the camera." In *Encyclopedia of Photography,* 166-181. New York: Graystone Press.

Mead, M. M. 1928. *Coming of Age in Samoa.* Magnolia, MA: Peter Smith.

Medina, G. 1989. *Campesinos and Conservation: Joining Forces through Environmental Education.* Washington, D.C.: World Wildlife Fund.

Meeker, J. W. 1973. "Red, white and black in the national parks." *North American Review* (Fall):3-7.

Michelson, W. 1976. *Man and his Urban Environment.* Reading, MA: Addison-Wesley.

Mishra, H. R. 1984. "A delicate balance: Tigers, rhinoceros, tourists and park management vs. the needs of the local people in Royal Chitwan National Park, Nepal." In *National Parks, Conservation and Development,* ed. J. A. McNeely, and K. R. Miller. Washington, D.C.: IUCN/Smithsonian Institution Press.

Morales, J. 1987. *Manual para la Interpretación en Espacios Naturales Protegidos.* Anexo 3 del Taller Internacional sobre Interpretación Ambiental en Areas Silvestres Protegidas, December 7-12. Santiago, Chile: Food and Agricultural Organization of the United Nations, Regional Office for Latin America and the Caribbean.

Mudge, S. 1989. *Recommendations of the USAID/FEPROTUR Nature Tourism Working Group.* Quito, Ecuador: U.S. Agency for International Development, Natural Resources.

Mueller, E., and Gurin, G. 1962. *Participation in Outdoor Recreation Behavior: Factors Affecting Demand among American Adults.* Outdoor Recreation Resources Review Commission Study Report 20. Washington, D. C.: U. S. Government Printing Office.

Mumford, L. 1956. "The natural history of urbanization." In *Man's Role in Changing the Face of the Earth,* ed. W. L. Thomas, Jr. Chicago: University of Chicago Press.

Nakane, C. 1970. *Japanese Society.* Berkeley: University of California Press.

Nash, J. E. 1978. "Weekend racing as an eventful experience: Understanding the accomplishment of well being." *Urban Life and Culture* 6.

Nash, R. F. 1988. "Why wilderness?" In *For the Conservation of Earth:* Proceedings of the Fourth World Wilderness Congress, ed. V. Martin, 194-201. Golden, CO: Fulcrum Press.

Nations, J. H., and Leonard, J. H. 1986. "Grounds of conflict in Central America." In *Bordering on Trouble: Resources and Politics in Latin America,* ed. A. Maguire and J. W. Brown, 55-98. Bethesda, MD: Adler & Adler, Inc.

Neumann, R. P., and Machlis, G. E. 1989. "Land use and threats to parks in the neotropics." *Environmental Conservation,* Spring 16(1):13-18.

Noe, F. P., and Snow, R. 1989/90. "Hispanic cultural influence on environmental concern." *Journal of Environmental Education* 21(2):27-34.

Odum, H. W., and Moore, H. 1938. *American Regionalism. A Cultural-Historical Approach to National Integration.* New York: Henry Holt.

Orozco, R. 1989. "The romantic west: The European seekers." Mimeograph. Wupatki National Monument Library, Flagstaff, AZ.

Outdoor Recreation Commission Caravan Surveys, Inc. 1968. *Visits of the United States Public to National Parks.* USDI, National Park Service. Washington, D.C.

Parsons, T., and Bales, R. F. 1955. *Family, Socialization and Interaction Process.* Glencoe: The Free Press.

Pelto, P. J. 1970. *Anthropological Research: The Structure of Inquiry.* New York: Harper & Row.

Peters, C. M., Gentry, A. H., and Mendelsohn, R. O. 1989. "Valuation of an Amazonian rainforest." *Nature* 339(6227):655-656.

Phillip, S. F. 1976. Unpublished term paper. College Station: Texas A & M University.

Polsky, N. 1967. *Hustlers, Beats and Others*. Chicago: Aldine.

Potter, D. R., Sharpe, K. M., Hendee, J. C., and Clark, R. N. 1972. *Questionnaires for Research: An Annotated Bibliography on Design, Construction, and Use*. USDA Forest Service Research Paper PNW-140. Portland, OR: Pacific Northwest Forest and Range Experiment Station.

Rappaport, R. A. 1967. *Pigs for the Ancestors: Ritual in the Ecology of a New Guinea People*. New Haven: Yale University Press.

Redfield, R. 1941. *The Folk Culture of Yucátan*. Chicago: University of Chicago Press.

Redl, F. 1966. *When We Deal with Children*. New York: The Free Press.

Reeves, R. 1984. "Monuments to the horrors of war." Syndicated editorial in *The Idahonian*, Moscow, Idaho, n.d.

Reischauer, E. O. 1978. *The Japanese*. Cambridge: Harvard University Press.

Reiss, I. 1972. *The Family System*. New York: Winterscourt Press.

Robertson, D. A., and Wilson, D. S. 1982. "Toward a 'Natural History' of People in Yosemite National Park." Unpublished manuscript. Davis, CA: University of California.

Rogers, E. M., and Shoemaker, F. F. 1971. *Communication of Innovations: A Cross-Cultural Approach*. New York: The Free Press.

Rosenfeld, S. B. 1980. "Informal learning in zoos: Naturalistic studies of family groups." Ph.D. Diss. University of California, Berkeley.

Runte, A. 1979. *National Parks: The American Experience*. Lincoln: University of Nebraska Press.

Sartre, J. 1957. *Being and Nothingness*. Trans. H. Barnes. Secaucus, NJ: Citadel Press.

Shapiro, L. 1990. "Guns and dolls." *Newsweek*. CXV(22):56-65.

Sharpe, G. 1982. *Interpreting the Environment*. 2nd ed. New York: John Wiley & Sons.

Shelton, N. 1989. "MAB notes." *Park Science* 9(4):14.

Simcox, D. E., and Pfister, R. E. 1990. *Hispanic Values and Behavior Related to Outdoor Recreation and the Forest Environment*. USDA Forest Service Contract Report. Riverside, CA: Pacific Southwest Research Station.

Skolnick, J., Langbort, C., and Day, L. 1982. *How to Encourage Girls in Math and Science*. Englewood Cliffs, NJ: Prentice-Hall, Inc.

Smith, H. 1988. *The Power Game: How Washington Works*. New York: Random House.

Smith, V. L. (ed.) 1977. *Hosts and Guests: The Anthropology of Tourism*. Philadelphia: University of Pennsylvania Press.

Snow, R. 1989. *Biscayne National Park Visitor Survey: Final Report*. National Park Service Cooperative Park Studies Unit Technical Report. Atlanta: Georgia State University.

Spencer, G. 1986. "Projections of the Hispanic population: 1983 to 2080." *Current Population Reports*. Series P-25, No. 796. Washington, D. C.: U. S. Government Printing Office.

Spoehr, A. 1956. "Cultural differences in the interpretation of natural resources." In *Man's Role in Changing the Face of the Earth*. Vol. 1, ed. W. L. Thomas, Jr. Chicago: University of Chicago Press.

Spradley, J. P. 1970. *You Owe Yourself a Drunk: An Ethnography of Urban Nomads*. Boston: Little, Brown.

Spradley, J. P. 1979. *Participant Observation*. New York: Holt, Rinehart & Winston.

Spradley, J. P., and McCurdy, D. W. 1972. *The Cultural Experience: Ethnography in Complex Society*. Chicago: Science Research Associates, Inc.

Sprung, B. 1987. "Beginning science equitably." In *Contributions of the Girls and Science and Technology Fourth International Conference*, eds. J. Z. Daniels and J. B. Kahle. Washington, D.C.: National Science Foundation.

Stankey, G. H. 1973. *Visitor Perception of Wilderness Recreation Carrying Capacity*. USDA Forest Service Research Paper INT-142. Ogden, UT: Intermountain Forest and Range Experiment Station.

Starr, R. 1983. "Not far from wisdom." Editorial in *New York Times*, August 10.

Steadman, D. W., and Zousmer, S. 1988. *Galápagos: Discovery on Darwin's Island*. Washington, D.C.: Smithsonian Institution Press.

Stephan, W. G. 1985. "Intergroup relations." In *The Handbook of Social Psychology* (Vol. II), ed. G. Lindzey and E. Aronson, 599-658. New York: Random House.

Stryker, S., and Gottlieb, A. 1981. "Attribution theory and symbolic interactionism: A comparison." In *New Directions in Attribution Research*. Vol. 3, eds. J. H. Harvey, W. Ickes, and R.F. Kidd. Hillsdale, NJ: Lawrence Erlbaum Assoc., Publishing.

Sussman, M. B., and Burchinal, L. E. 1962. "Kin family network: Unheralded structure in current conceptualization of family functioning." *Marriage and Family Living* 24:231-240.

Thomas, J. W., and Dixon, R. A. 1974. "Cemetery ecology." In *Symposium on Wildlife in an Urbanizing Environment*. Planning and Resources Development Series #20. Amherst, MA: Cooperative Extension Service.

Tienda, M., and Ortiz, V. 1986. "'Hispanicity' and the 1980 census." *Social Science Quarterly* 66(1):3-20.

Tilden, F. (n.d.) *The Fifth Essence*. Washington: National Park Trust Board.

Tilden, F. 1957. *Interpreting our Heritage.* Rev. ed. 1977. Chapel Hill: University of North Carolina Press.

Torres-Rivas, E. 1983. "Central America today: a study in regional dependence." In *Trouble in our Backyard,* ed. M. Diskin. New York: Pantheon.

Travers, P. L. 1969. "Only connect." In *Only connect: Readings on Children's Literature,* ed. S. Egoff, G. T. Slubbs, and L. F. Ashley, 132-206. New York: Oxford University Press.

Travers, R. M. W. 1967. *Research and Theory Related to Audio-visual Information Transmission.* Washington, D.C.: U.S. Department of Health, Education and Welfare.

Turner, J. H. 1978. *The Structure of Sociological Theory.* Homewood, IL: The Dorsey Press.

Turner, V. 1969. *The Ritual Process.* Chicago, IL: Aldine Press.

U. S. Department of Commerce. 1972. *A Study of Japanese Travel Habits and Patterns,* ed. K. Gess. Washington, DC: U.S. Travel Service, Office of Research and Analysis.

U. S. Department of Commerce. 1980. *1979 Population Estimates.* Washington D.C.: Bureau of the Census.

U. S. Department of Interior, National Park Service. 1972. *Part One of the National Park System Plan: History.* Washington, D.C.: U. S. Government Printing Office.

U. S. Geological Survey. 1987. *National Wilderness Preservation System.* Reston, VA: USDI, U. S. Geological Survey.

U. S. Travel Service. 1978. *A Regional Analysis of International Travel to the U.S.* Washington, D.C.: U.S. Department of Commerce.

UNESCO. 1987a. "UNESCO-UNEP international congress on environmental education and training." *Connect* 12(3):1-8. Paris: United Nations Educational, Scientific and Cultural Organization.

UNESCO. 1987b. "The international environmental education program." *Connect* 12(4):1. Paris: United Nations Educational, Scientific and Cultural Organization.

UNESCO. 1991. "From awareness to action via nonformal environmental education." *Connect* 16(1):1-3. Paris: United Nations Educational, Scientific and Cultural Organization.

Valero, G. 1989. "Wukoki: An expression of tranquility." Mimeograph. Wupatki National Monument Library, Flagstaff, AZ.

Vayda, A. P., and Rappaport, R. A. 1968. "Ecology, cultural and noncultural." In *Origins of Human Ecology* (Benchmark papers in ecology: 12), ed. G. L. Young, 124-150. New York: Hutchinson Ross Publishing Company.

Vogel, E. G. 1963. *Japan's New Middle Class.* Berkeley: University of California Press.

Wagar, J. A. 1972a. "Evaluating interpretation and interpretive media" (Paper presented at the Association of Interpretive Naturalists Meeting, Callaway Gardens, Pine Mountain, Georgia, April 7, 1972).

Wagar, J. A. 1972b. *The Recording Quizboard: A Device for Evaluating Interpretive Services.* USDA Forest Service Research Paper PNW-139. Portland, OR: Pacific Northwest Forest and Range Experiment Station.

Warner, W. L. 1963. *Yankee City.* New Haven: Yale University Press.

Washburne, R. F. 1971. "Visitor response to interpretive facilities at five visitor centers." Master's thesis, University of Washington, Seattle.

Washburne, R. F. 1978. "Black under-participation in wildland recreation: Alternative explanations." *Leisure Sciences* 1(2):175-189.

Webb, E. J., Campbell, D. T., Schwartz, R. D., and Sechrest, L. 1966. *Unobtrusive Measures: Nonreactive Research in the Social Sciences.* Chicago: Rand McNally.

Wedel, J. 1981. "I didn't think it would be so wild and so preserved: Tourist experiences in Yellowstone National Park." Unpublished manuscript. Berkeley, California.

Weitzman, L. J. 1979. *Sex Role Socialization.* Palo Alto, CA: Mayfield Publishing Company.

Wellman, J. D. 1987. *Wildland Recreation Policy.* New York: Wiley & Sons.

Werner, D. 1980. *Donde No Hay Doctor.* Palo Alto, CA: Hesperian Foundation.

Werner, D., and Bower, B. 1982. *Helping Health Workers Learn: A Book of Methods, Aids and Ideas for Instructors at the Village Level.* Palo Alto, CA: Hesperian Foundation.

West, P. C. 1989. "Urban region parks and Black minorities: Subculture, marginality, and interracial relations in park use in the Detroit Metropolitan Area." *Leisure Science* 11(1):11-28.

Wetrogan, S. I. 1988. "Projections of the population of states by age, sex, and race: 1988 to 2010." *Current Population Reports,* Series P-25, No. 1017. Washington, D. C.: U. S. Government Printing Office.

Whyte, W. F. 1943. *Street Corner Society.* Chicago: University of Chicago Press.

Wicker, A. W. 1969. "Attitudes versus actions: The relationship of verbal and overt behavioral responses to attitude objects." *Journal of Social Issues* 35(4):41-78.

Wilson, M. A., and Laarman, J. G. 1987. *Nature Tourism and Enterprise Development in Ecuador.* Research Triangle Park, NC: Southeastern Center for Forest Economics Research, Forestry Private Enterprise Initiative, FPEI Working Paper No. 27.

Winkfield, K. M. 1989. "Child monsters: Observing family tourism at Wupatki." Mimeograph. Wupatki National Monument Library, Flagstaff, AZ.

Wood, D. S., and Wood, D. W. 1987. *How to Plan a Conservation Education Program*. Washington, D.C.: International Institute for Environment and Development/U.S. Fish and Wildlife Service, Office of International Affairs.

World Resources Institute. 1990. *World Resources 1990-91*. New York: Oxford University Press.

Wright, G. M., Dixon, J. S., and Thompson, B. H. 1933. *Fauna of the National Parks of the United States: A Preliminary Survey of Faunal Relations in National Parks*. Washington, D. C.: U. S. Government Printing Office. USDI National Park Service Fauna Series, No. 1, 142 pages.

Wright, Q. 1942. *A Study of War*. Chicago, IL: University of Chicago Press.

Wright, R. G. 1984. "The challenges for interpretation in the new Alaskan parks." *Journal of Interpretation* 9(1):39-46.

Young, G. L. (ed.) 1983. *Origins of Human Ecology* (Benchmark papers in ecology; 12). New York: Hutchinson Ross Publishing Company.

Zaner, R. 1970. *The Way of Phenomenology*. New York: Pegasus.

Zelinsky, W. 1973. *The Cultural Geography of the United States*. Englewood Cliffs, NJ: Prentice-Hall.

Index